About this Book

Health social science is an area of research and practice that has evolved rapidly since the late 1980s. As this volume shows, it has grown out of a desire to forge partnerships across the social science and health fields in order to advance the relevance of social science to health and to increase equity in health and health care. Health social science is essentially transdisciplinary in its perspective, seeking to synthesize diverse fields of knowledge in pursuit of understanding and solving complex health problems.

This volume presents ten case studies which exemplify some of the best practice in health social science in developing countries. The action research studies are drawn from Africa, Latin America, Asia and the Pacific. Each addresses the critical question of how social/behavioural science approaches can make a difference in improving significant health problems. These problems range across such diverse issues as AIDS, people's reliance on traditional healers, their use of both indigenous and modern types of medicine, STDs, smoking, heart disease, and psychological stress. The cases were selected by an international panel of judges drawn from the International Forum for Social Science and Health.

The initial and concluding chapters, written by the editors, provide an overview of the evolving role of health social science research in addressing human health problems. They examine some of the most promising health social perspectives illustrated by the case studies – in particular, those around the knowledge–behaviour gap, transdisciplinary research, and community participation. The editors also reflect on future challenges and potential groundbreaking innovations in health social science research.

This book will be a valuable resource for policymakers, planners and foundations supporting international health development, as well as scholars and public health practitioners.

Applying Health Social Science: Best Practice in the Developing World

edited by Nick Higginbotham, Roberto Briceño-León and Nancy A. Johnson

Zed Books

LONDON • NEW YORK

in association with

International Forum for Social Sciences in Health

Applying Health Social Science: Best Practice in the Developing World was first published by Zed Books Ltd, 7 Cynthia Street, London N1 9JF, UK and Room 400, 175 Fifth Avenue, New York, NY 10010, USA in 2001

in association with The International Forum for Social Sciences in Health, PO Box 47795, Caracas 1040-A, Venezuela

Distributed in the USA exclusively by Palgrave, a division of St Martin's Press, LLC, 175 Fifth Avenue, New York, NY 10010, USA

Cover designed by Andrew Corbett
Set in Monotype Ehrhardt and Franklin Gothic by Ewan Smith
Printed and bound in Malaysia

A catalogue record for this book is available from the British Library

Library of Congress Cataloging-in-Publication Data: available

ISBN 1 84277 050 0 cased
ISBN 1 84277 051 9 limp

Contents

Acknowledgements

This project, which represents the outcome of our global search to identify and present 'best cases in applying social sciences to issues of human health', was inspired by the members and supporters of the International Forum for Social Sciences and Health (IFSSH). We are deeply grateful to all.

Without the generous encouragement and grant support from key donor organizations, the project would have never reached fruition. Prominent among those sharing both intellectual and financial resources were Pat Rosenfield, Carnegie Corporation of New York, in partnership with Jose Barzelatto, the Ford Foundation, and their associates, Marjorie Muecke and Rosalee Karefa-Smart. Similarly, the Rockefeller Foundation (Scott Halstead, Seth Berkeley) and Canada's International Development Research Centre (Annette Stark, Bertha Mo) provided valuable assistance.

Under the inspiring leadership of Santhat Sermsri, the inaugural Secretary General of the IFSSH, this project was initially conceived and funds were allocated within the organization's global budget. We are grateful for Professor Sermsri's energetic promotion of this project and continuing support. IFSSH steering committee members during that time also provided invaluable assistance: Mary-Jo DelVecchio Good, Dennis G. Willms, Yvo Nuyens, Joseph Wang'ombe, Paul Nkwi, Ellen Hardy, Mario Bronfman, Peter Kundstadter, Akile Gursoy, Peter Makara and Montasser Kamal.

Particular appreciation is also extended to the organizing committees that took part in the search for candidate research studies and selection of finalists: Social Science and Medicine Africa Network (Joseph Wang'ombe, Anne Pertet), Latin America Network (Ellen Hardy, Mario Bronfman) and the Asia Pacific Network (Pilar Ramos-Jimenez and Karla Karinen).

These cases were first discussed at the Social Science and Medicine Conference held in Peebles, Scotland in 1996 and we appreciated the cooperation extended by the conference organizers, especially Peter McEwan, and the liaison role assumed by Kris Heggenhougen. A number of discussants offered helpful comments on the best case presentations at the Peebles workshop. We are thankful to: Mario Bronfman, Manisha

Gupte, Mary Haour-Knipe, Ellen Hardy, Kris Heggenhougen, Judith Justice, Melchizedek Leshabari, and Pilar Ramos-Jimenez. We wish to thank Olga Avila for her research assistance with portions of the manuscript and acknowledge Sonia Freeman and Linda Connor for their valuable suggestions strengthening the introduction and conclusion chapters. Lastly, we are indebted to Joanne and Chuck Edmondson for providing the editors office facilities in Alpine, California during the final preparation of the book. Indeed, our warmest appreciation to everyone committed to the improvement of human health through applying the social sciences.

Preface

Despite the widespread recognition that many of today's health problems have significant social, behavioural and economic dimensions, the role of social scientists in studying and solving these problems and contributing to health policies is surprisingly still a subject of debate among health professionals and policy-makers. The International Forum for Social Sciences in Health (IFSSH) was initially established to address this situation. The IFSSH appealed to its early supporters – the Rockefeller Foundation, the Ford Foundation and the International Development Research Centre, as well as the Carnegie Corporation – because of the shared recognition on the part of the donors and the early organizers of the IFSSH that promoting new approaches to the study and solution of health problems required more than funding individual research projects. In order to improve health policies and health programmes by recognizing and utilizing social science research, it was necessary to bring together a critical mass of scholars and practitioners who could share ideas and experiences while enhancing collaborative action across disciplines, institutions, countries and continents.

The IFSSH has evolved into a dense network of institutions and individuals that move across space and time. Across space, the IFSSH and its participants have reinforced each other by moving beyond the core group of original organizers to bring in many other like-minded individuals and networks. The trust and reciprocity that exist across the regional activities have led to sharing of resources and ideas so that the networks have developed into self-sustaining entities. With such outreach and sustained activities, the networks have formed strategic alliances to strengthen activities at the national level as well as policies at the international level. The IFSSH and its individual and network members are also well placed to use these strategic alliances to move forward the agenda of promoting health social sciences.

As many of the chapters in this volume show, continuity is also an important element in sustaining the work of the IFSSH. Training programmes have been developed that enable new participants to join in and replace any who have moved out, or to extend the membership to bring in the next generation of scholars and practitioners. Continuity, through extending the work of the IFSSH across time and space, is critically important to ensuring the accumulation and consolidation of knowledge, so that theories and best practices emerge from a solid base of scholarship. The publication of the best case studies in the field of social sciences and health is a major contribution to building that knowledge base.

Reviews of networks conducted by the *Harvard Business Review* as well as the MacArthur Foundation reinforce the remarkable accomplishments of the IFSSH. In a 1991 article in the *Harvard Business Review* on how networks reshape organizations for results, Ram Charan highlighted what constitutes a successful network: 'networks really begin to matter when they begin to affect patterns of relationships and change behavior – change driven by the frequency, intensity and honesty of the dialogue among managers on specific priorities'. Drawing on specific corporate case studies, Charan examined how these networks empowered their participants by building trust, changing the perspective for evaluating problems and in-creasing access to up-to-date information. He highlighted the critical role of information, 'in a network, especially a global network that extends across borders, information must be visible and simultaneous'. Reinforcing the importance of communication and dynamism, Robert Kahn, in his assessment of the MacArthur Foundation strategy to promote programme development through networks, noted that: 'Durability is not a static characteristic. It requires a thoughtful and continuous process of renewal.' Bringing in new people, asking new questions and considering the network as a means and also an end are all strategies for achieving success. Kahn suggests two main criteria for an assessment of networks: 'One is the quality and influence of their scientific findings, the other is the extent to which their example of intellectual collaboration and interdisciplinary work leads other research organizations and supporting agencies toward more flexible and innovative policies.' The IFSSH has successfully achieved a high level of communication and collaboration across many different boundaries. It is affecting policy in-country, regionally and globally, through its activities with relevant health organizations as well as the institutions in which the researchers are engaged. The IFSSH has amply illustrated that networking is not only a means, but also a method by which goals can be achieved, and thus an outcome in itself.

Through this timely publication, the IFSSH and its participants are demonstrating the theoretical as well as practical relevance of health social sciences. The IFSSH is building a new field of knowledge by illustrating how health social sciences and transdisciplinary approaches to health prob-lems can be applied successfully in a wide range of situations. The results show the considerable value of networking across networks, as well as across disciplines, institutions and countries. Through the case studies presented in this volume, the work of the IFSSH significantly contributes to meeting the challenge put forward by Edward Wilson in his controversial book *Consilience: The Unity of Knowledge*. Wilson makes the case for the integration of knowledge as a necessity for achieving human security in the twenty-first century; he focuses on biology as the integrating discipline. In his book, he emphasizes that the social sciences have failed in an effort to help unify knowledge, and he argues that the disciplines of anthropology, sociology and economics can contribute to improving the human condition only by basing their work on biology. By focusing on the social science contributions to improving health, the authors in this volume turn around this argument. They demonstrate the results of a multi-layered approach, drawing on the social sciences, but open to knowledge from other fields as well as, in many cases, the community at risk and the relevant practitioners and policy-makers. This publication is thus a landmark in the effort to develop a new field of research.

The International Forum for Social Sciences in Health provides a rare example of constructive globalization across intellectual and geographic divides. I believe the work of the IFSSH, as exemplified by the chapters in this volume, will have a lasting impact on research and practice aimed at improving human well-being and development.

Patricia Rosenfield, Ph.D

References

Charan, R. (1991) 'How networks reshape organizations – for results', *Harvard Business Review* 69: 104–15.

Kahn, R. I. (1993) 'An experiment in scientific organization', Occasional Paper, Chicago, IL: MacArthur Foundation.

Wilson, E. O. (1998) *Consilience: The Unity of Knowledge*, New York: Knopf.

Abbreviations

ABRASCO	Brazilian Collective Health Association
AED	Academy for Educational Development
ALAMES	Latin American Association for Social Medicine
APNET	Asia-Pacific Network (IFSSH)
CHHB	Coalfields Healthy Heartbeat project
COHRED	Council on Health Research for Development
DALY	Disability Adjusted Life Year
EMCA	Eastern Mediterranean and Central Asian network
FGD	Focus Group Discussion
HBM	Health Belief Model
IFSSH	International Forum for Social Sciences in Health
IGD	Interactional Group Discussion
INCLEN	International Clinical Epidemiology Network
INRUD	Intenational Network for Rational Use of Drugs
KAP	knowledge, attitude and practice (survey)
LANET	Latin America Network
MSH	Management Sciences for Health
NACP	Zimbabwean National AIDS Control Program
PAHO	Pan American Health Organization
PRA	participatory rural appraisal
RAP	rapid assessment procedure
RHA	reproductive health and sexuality
SANA	Sustainable Approaches to Nutrition in Africa
SASBIL	Association of Social Sciences in Health (Turkey)
SOMA-Net	Social Science and Medicine Africa Network
STD	sexually transmitted disease
TDR	Tropical Disease Research programme (WHO)
USAID	United States Agency for International Development
WHO	World Health Organization

Part I

Applying Social Science to Improve Human Health

1

Health Social Science: Transdisciplinary Partnerships for Improving Human Health

Nick Higginbotham, Roberto Briceño-León and
Nancy A. Johnson

Health social science is a dynamic and evolving domain of research and practice. It sprang, in the late 1980s, from the desire of individuals and organizations working across the spectrum of social science and health fields to forge partnerships that would 'advance the relevance of social sciences to health and increase equity in health and health care' (IFSSH 1994: 1). Health social science bridges the gap between health care practitioners, whose primary interest is healing individual bodies, and population health practitioners, who strive to understand and influence positively the interrelationships between the embodied self, the social body and the body politic. This new domain of interconnecting fields of knowledge has captured the attention of researchers working within and beyond universities, as well as policy-makers, health planners and programme managers from regions of the North and South.

Significantly, the development of health social science as a domain of professional practice has become the focus of a global network – the International Forum for Social Sciences in Health (IFSSH) – comprising regional networks in Africa (Social Science and Medicine Africa Network – SOMA-Net), Asia-Pacific (Asia-Pacific Network – APNET), Latin America (LANET), the Eastern Mediterranean and Central Asia region (EMCA), and the Arab region (Arab Forum for Social Sciences and Health). This textbook presents 'best case' examples of the application of health social science, chosen from the three original IFSSH regional networks (SOMA-Net, APNET and LANET).

While embracing such diverse areas of application as tropical diseases, HIV/AIDS, heart disease and therapeutic decision-making, health social science has as its core a 'transdisciplinary' perspective. Transdisciplinary thinking is a process of synthesizing diverse fields of knowledge in the quest for creative understandings of, and solutions for, complex health problems (Higginbotham et al. 2001). Thus health social scientists apply social and behavioural science theories and methods, in active partnership with complementary knowledge from biomedical and health sciences, to gain a comprehensive understanding of health problems such as the epidemic of coronary heart disease in a rural coalmining community in Australia (see Chapter 3). In addition, transdisciplinary thinking about a specific concern may require insights from fields as diverse as biology, ecology, physics and climatology to complement the perspective of health social science. The philosophy of this new domain is collaboration between different but equally valid perspectives with the purpose of improving human health. Data emerging from a synthesis of disciplinary views, as well as from government agencies, NGOs and community stakeholder views, are used to develop change strategies that produce benefits in both clinical indicators and perceived quality of life; are sustainable in the context of the local environment; and are equitable across the society. Importantly, health social science fosters community participation in defining and achieving health needs and has promoted a rethinking of the relationship between knowledge and practice.

A Global Organization for Health Social Science: The International Forum for Social Sciences in Health (IFSSH)

By the 1980s, donor agencies and academic groups addressing health research and research training needs in developing countries began to combine social and health science expertise as a means of achieving programme goals. Prominent among these were the World Health Organization/Tropical Disease Research/Social and Economic Research Programme (WHO-TDR), Carnegie's Strengthening Human Resources in Developing Countries programme, the Applied Diarrheal Disease Research Project (ADDR) of the Harvard Institute of International Development, the Ford Foundation's Child Survival/Fair Start for Children programme, and the International Network for the Rational Use of Drugs (INRUD) (see Trostle 1992). During the 1980s, health social science graduate training was added to the Rockefeller Foundation's initiative to build clinical epidemiology research capacity in Asia, Latin America and Africa through the creation of the International Clinical Epidemiology Network (INCLEN) (Higginbotham 1992, 1994). As it evolved, the INCLEN model aimed to 'infuse' a transdisciplinary perspective into international health by equipping social scientists to speak a common language with clinical epidemiologists, and sensitizing clinicians to the ways in which social sciences contribute to research and policy.

Through efforts to design the new INCLEN social science curriculum two compelling and generalizable needs surfaced. The first was to identify successful applications of social science methods and concepts, broadly defined, to local health priorities, along with the individuals who had expertise in making these translations. Second, once this knowledge is distilled and passed on to a new cohort of social scientists working on health issues, there is a need to ensure that new graduates have a sustainable career. Such a career includes academic security, continuing research grants, consultation with content experts, further education, involvement in major research projects from an array of donors, and access to policy-makers and planners (Higginbotham 1994: 133).

A small group of social scientists active in international health programmes met in 1988 first to imagine and then to formalize an organization that could address these two needs (see IFSSH 1994).[1] They envisioned a structure activated by regional networking and integrated through global coordination, operating to secure health social science as a professional and scientific community. Through planning meetings in Kenya and New York in 1991, the International Forum for Social Sciences in Health was formally organized during an INCLEN scientific conference in Bali, Indonesia in January 1992. Donor support during these formative years was provided through grants from the Carnegie Corporation, the Rockefeller Foundation, the Ford Foundation and the IDRC.

The IFSSH was born out of the realization that health issues could be solved only through 'strong collaboration among social and health scientists, international scientific bodies, academia, health workers, policy planners, government and non-government organizations and women and men' (IFSSH 1997, preface). The rationale for the IFSSH's formation was that:

> The diversity of social science disciplines, in collaboration with biomedical and health scientists, provide potential strength that enables the social sciences to play a major role in the pursuit of innovative means to remedy the unequal distribution of resources devoted to health and to enhance the health status of all the world's populations. (IFSSH 1994: 1)

Currently, the IFSSH is an international voluntary organization made up of five regional fora in Africa, Asia Pacific, Latin America, the Arab countries and the Eastern Mediterranean and Central Asia. Efforts are under way to establish similar networks in Europe and North America. While each regional forum functions as an autonomous body governed by its own set of statutes and by-laws, all share IFSSH objectives to:

- build a network of social and health scientists that will support and encourage these colleagues to work together;
- advance social and health science perspectives, concepts, theories and methods to broaden the understanding of health;

- bridge theoretical and applied pursuits in the social and health sciences;
- attract and sustain the involvement of social scientists in the study and solution of health-related problems; and
- encourage health professionals to consider the social and cultural determinants of health.

Many of the activities undertaken by APNET, SOMA-Net and LANET to promote the teaching and application of health social science within their regions are described in the introductions to Parts 2, 3 and 4 of this book. Biennial meetings, training workshops, best case competitions, newsletters, websites, inventories of donor funding interests, membership directories and, more recently, publications are common activities and projects across the regional networks (e.g. Barta and Briceño-León 2000; Briceño-León 1999; Briceño-León et al. 2000; Bronfman and Castro 1999; Ramos-Jimenez et al. 1996; Silva and Ramos-Jimenez 1996; SOMA-Net 1997).

Since the IFSSH best case competition that gave rise to this book, two new regional networks – the Arab Forum for Social Sciences and Health and the EMCA Forum for Social Sciences and Health – have been formed. The founding meeting of the Arab Forum was held in Brummana, Lebanon in June 1996. At the meeting, which gathered more than one hundred professionals and practitioners from nine Arab countries, an interim Executive Committee and Secretary were elected and charged with drafting a set of by-laws and securing funding for the nascent network. Subsequent regional conferences were held in Amman, Jordan in September 1997 and in Tunis, Tunisia in November 1999. A key challenge for the future is to build effective groups within each Arab state. This has recently been achieved in Turkey, where the EMCA regional forum has established a national association of social science in health. The Association of Social Sciences in Health (Turkey), or SASBIL, currently has 150 members and is growing. In April 2000, SASBIL organized the second EMCA regional meeting in Instanbul. Efforts continue to strengthen the EMCA network's links with Europe and its presence in Central Asia and the Newly Founded States where a 'new space' is perceived to be opening up in terms of the development of health social science.

The IFSSH plays a key role in facilitating regional initiatives and promoting interregional seminars such as the Workshop on Capacity Enhancement for the Social Sciences in Health, held in Huntsville, Ontario, Canada in October 1995 and the Workshop on Determinants of NCDs in Urban Areas in Developing Countries: From Evidence Base to Action, jointly organized by the IFSSH, the WHO and the Centers for Disease Control in August 2000. It also pursues links with complementary international organizations such as the Council on Health Research for

Development, the Global Forum for Health Research and the World Health Organization 'to create an intellectual space within which to contribute to the definition and construction of the conceptual field of social science and health, as well as advocate for a stronger social science participation in health promotion programmes' (IFSSH 2000: 3).

Advancing Research in Health Social Science: Best Cases

One of the challenges facing the IFSSH has been the need to develop the conceptual and methodological bases for applying social sciences to health research and using social science insights to inform health interventions. One means of addressing this problem is to develop curriculum material using case studies of the successful application of social sciences to health problems. This book fulfils this strategy by disseminating case studies from a range of health fields and circumstances to aid understanding of health social science models (IFSSH 1995: 2). In 1996, the IFSSH organized a 'best case study' competition in the three regional networks then comprising the global forum – Africa, Latin America and Asia-Pacific. Case studies were required to address the critical question of how social/behavioural science approaches are able to make a difference in improving a significant problem of human health. The winning authors presented their research projects at a workshop held in conjunction with the international Social Science and Medicine Conference in Peebles, Scotland. Eighty submissions were received from the three regions; seven were selected for presentation and appear in this text along with three additional cases selected after the competition.

Overview of the Book

Part 1 of the book is the introductory chapter. Part 2 presents four case studies describing health research and intervention activities in diverse social settings in the Asia-Pacific Region. Pilar Ramos-Jimenez introduces this section by highlighting the felt need of Asia-Pacific Network (APNET) members for examples of collaborations demonstrating how transdisciplinary social sciences theories and methods can be applied locally to areas of health policy formulation, capacity-building, research, and intervention designs. Basing her argument on national reports delivered during a series of APNET conferences, Ramos-Jimenez concludes that health social science has developed unevenly across the region (Ramos-Jimenez and Condor 1998). Moreover, regionally, there is little agreement about the core curriculum in this domain, few social science concepts and methods are integrated into health sciences courses, and, when they are, it is often medical doctors rather than health social scientists who teach these materials.

In Chapter 2 Hector Wing-hong Tsang presents the first case in the Asia-Pacific section. His study, carried out in Hong Kong, offers an indigenous (i.e. Cantonese) work-related social skills training model for persons with schizophrenia. Hector Tsang shows how social science theory and methods were used to formulate the indigenous model of work skills training. In particular, he notes that the model draws on cognitive-behavioural learning theory, social learning theory and psycho-educational theory. A combination of social science methods is employed to verify the validity and relevance of the model and to evaluate the success of the training programme.

Chapter 3, by Nick Higginbotham, Sonia Freeman, Gaynor Heading and Ann Saul, explores cultural constructions of risk regarding heart disease in the Coalfields of New South Wales, Australia. This chapter describes the development, implementation and outcome of a large-scale community activation programme to prevent heart disease in the Coalfields. Lessons learned from the authors' ten years of involvement with the people of the Coalfields are presented. In particular, the authors critically examine the divergent expectations of the research team and the community relating to assumptions about initiating change, risk perception and participation. Complexity theory is advanced as a framework for understanding the patterns of community response to health threats as well as the intervention's successes.

Johana E. Prawitasari Hadiyono, in Chapter 4, describes the emergence of a transdisciplinary approach to promote rational drug use over the course of three intervention studies carried out in Gunungkidul District, Central Java, Indonesia. She reflects on some of the growing pains that can be experienced during such collaborative team efforts and stresses the importance of clarifying taken-for-granted disciplinary use of language as well as openly discussing role expectations. Importantly, Prawitasari Hadiyono extends the data-gathering role of focused group discussions into the arena of attitude and behaviour change, revealing that systematic self-observation can produce long-lasting change towards improved medication use.

In Chapter 5, Gary Groth-Marnat, Simon Leslie, Mark Renneker, Sunia Vuniyayawa and Maerewai Molileu recount how the residents of a small Fijian village successfully gave up smoking. Key elements underpinning the success of the project were that the decision to give up was initiated by the community itself, formalized with a public pledge and a ceremony in which a taboo was placed on smoking, and reinforced by national media attention. The cohesive and self-contained nature of the community and the establishment of a long-term relationship with the medical team are also identified as important factors. An important insight from the Fijian case is that a community's or individual's readiness for change may, in part, rest on the historical confluence of situational, social and cognitive influences. So too might the individual and social energy available for change rest on such a confluence.

Part 3 of the book highlights three case studies selected by the Social Science and Medicine Africa Network (SOMA-Net). Drawing on his long experience as an African academic, Layi Erinosho discusses the development of health social science across the continent. He describes the success of SOMA-Net in organizing regional and international conferences for promoting health social science, the movement towards localized rather than international training, and the goal of promoting an independent interdisciplinary centre within the university, which would help integrate social and medical science training and research. Erinosho points out that, despite their seeming diversity, the three case studies presented in this section have in common their investigation of culture-specific approaches to health research, the interplay between traditional and biomedical community health approaches, and the effectiveness of the ethnographic method in illuminating underlying social processes in illness and health behaviour.

The first African case study (Chapter 6) describes a community-action intervention to improve medical services in Kinshasa, Congo. The authors, René Devisch, Lapika Dimomfu, Jaak Le Roy and Peter Crossman, outline a multidisciplinary action-research initiative to improve the use of the medical, folk and faith healing services in two poverty-stricken suburbs of Kinshasa. They show how a combination of ethnographic and survey methods was used to gain a better understanding of health-seeking practices and the indigenous explanations of disease aetiology that, in part, inform these practices. Drawing on the renewed importance of kin groups and neighbourhood networks in contemporary Kinshasa, the action component of the project sought to create lay therapy management groups that would direct patients and their families in their health-seeking strategies and coordinate the use of the three health service systems.

Chapter 7 deals with the question of how to represent adequately the profound impact of HIV/AIDS upon the people of rural Uganda. The life situation of Maama Mali, a female alcohol-seller in the Rakai district of Uganda, is used by Nelson Sewankambo, Patricia Spittal and Dennis Willms to demonstrate the use of genograms to complement narratives and epidemiological data in uncovering and representing how AIDS has affected households, extended family and community. Sewankambo and his co-authors also highlight the process whereby genograms can facilitate discussion and generate problem-solving in the community.

Chapter 8, the final case study from Africa, is by Dennis Willms, Nancy

Johnson, Alfred Chingono and Maureen Wellington. These researchers present a training strategy for traditional healers in Zimbabwe aimed at preventing the transmission of HIV/AIDS in the community. The chapter introduces the notion of 'culturally compelling' health interventions – that is, interventions that are 'not only culturally appropriate in language, idiom and expression, but persuasive in their ability to help people recognize their vulnerability, alter the nature of their assumptive world, and become compelled not only to think, but also to feel and act differently'. How such an HIV/AIDS educational intervention was developed in collaboration with Zimbabwean traditional healers is described. The authors also demonstrate the importance of ethnographic research in elucidating how HIV and AIDS are understood by healers and patients as well as in identifying the social, political and economic barriers to the acceptance of health educational information.

Part 4 comprises three Latin American case studies. Roberto Briceño-León, secretary-general of the IFSSH, offers in his introduction an insightful history of health social science in Latin America, noting that it is only recently that this domain has become institutionalized. Briceño-León describes how social science in health developed in the context of medication shortages and limited access to technology. It arose in an environment in which physicians and public health specialists maintained a traditional orientation towards the broader determinants of health, including social, environmental and lifestyle factors. Political movements, inspired by Marxist thought, also shaped the field's regional development: the focus on individual health and preventive medicine in the 1960s was replaced with concern for improving collective health through comprehensive social change. The traditional goals of public health, such as sanitation and housing, were transformed to pursue macro-social change in areas such as justice, equity and exploitation of workers. Finally, Briceño-León observes recent trends in Latin America whereby collective health action takes the form of micro-scale activities by grassroots groups aimed at incremental social change to remedy health problems. It is in this context that the IFSSH developed in this region as an inclusive, ideologically pluralistic organization capable of accommodating a range of paradigms and social theories for improving health.

In Chapter 9 Mónica Gogna and Silvina Ramos present their investigation of how gender stereotypes underlie risk-taking that is associated with sexually transmitted diseases (STDs) in Argentina. A multi-method qualitative approach was applied involving free list and pile sort techniques in the context of focus group and one-to-one interviews. Gogna and Ramos seek to elucidate lay notions about the aetiology, symptoms and modes of transmission of STDs held by men and women from a low-income neighbourhood in Greater Buenos Aires. Drawing on feminist theory and the social constructivist approach to sexuality, the authors also explore the influence of gender and sexuality stereotypes, norms and values on people's ability to protect themselves and others from STDs. They argue that effective health interventions must aim not only to communicate certain key messages, but also to foster a critical awareness of the circumstances influencing one's life through reflection on internalized images and norm and value systems often taken for granted.

Chapter 10, by Iván Dario Vélez, Susana Jaramillo, Sonia del Pilar Agudelo, Gloria Palma, Jorget Gallego and Bruno Travi, describes an interdisciplinary effort to develop a control programme for visceral leishmaniasis among the Zenú Indians of the Caribbean coast of Colombia. Social scientist team members were responsible for illuminating and detailing the health knowledge and practices of the Indian community with respect to the illness and for facilitating the entry of the clinical and biological scientists into the community.

Roberto Briceño-León, in the book's final case study, recounts his involvement with a community-based housing programme for rural peasants in Venezuela designed to control Chagas' disease, a fatal condition caused by infection with the *Trypanosoma cruzi* parasite. The first phase of this two-part research intervention carried out by the Laboratorio Ciencias Sociales (LACSO) involved a survey that helped clarify the association between housing construction conducive to infestation by the Chagas vector and a number of social variables. The latter included home ownership, occupation-income, plans to remain in the locality, locus of control, and expectation of control of the disease. Based on the survey findings, a housing programme was implemented that encouraged the construction of traditional wattle and daub homes, viewed as culturally and economically most accessible to peasant families. The programme also aimed to remove financial constraints on making housing improvements and to foster a sense of self-efficacy and individual responsibility by goal-setting and granting credits for construction materials.

In Part 5, the editors conclude the book by distilling the main lessons learned from applying health social science across the regions. Themes and principles emerging from the cases include: the central role of situational realities in determining health action; re-evaluation of local knowledge in framing interventions; the potential for culturally compelling programmes to bridge the knowledge–behaviour gap in health protection; the continuing value of encouraging collective action towards communal health goals; and the use of transdisciplinary principles to harness collective knowledge towards problem analysis and resolution.

Finally, the editors reflect on potentially groundbreaking innovations in health social science research and methods. Prominent among these are the extension of complexity theory to analyse health problems as open, complex systems and translational research – a strategy for designing culturally compelling health programmes. Moreover, in the new era of 'on-line communities', cyber-medicine and cyber-ethnography have emerged to reflect the fundamental transformations taking place in the relationships between health care consumers, health knowledge, health practitioners and health researchers.

Note

1. When the INCLEN social science programme began in 1987, Nick Higginbotham sought advice from Pat Rosenfield about health social scientists in Asia, Africa and Latin America whom she had met through her work with WHO-TDR and the Carnegie Corporation and who might be interested in helping with the emerging INCLEN initiative. During this conversation, Pat and Nick realized that there would be considerable value in creating a means for bringing together the scattered expertise in health social science, enabling people to share their experiences and support one another, perhaps on the same scale as the health science networks such as INCLEN. This discussion prompted the planning of the 1990 meeting of 20 social scientists working in international health, which took place prior to INCLEN VIII in Puebla, Mexico. This event precipitated the organization formation process leading to the formal establishment of the IFSSH in 1992. Interestingly, a parallel meeting next door to our gathering became known as the 'Puebla Group' and resulted in the formation of the Commission on Health Research for Development. The recommendations from the Commission's report (1990) led subsequently to the creation of the Council on Health Research for Development (COHRED) and the Global Forum for Health Research.

References

Barta, R. B. and R. Briceño-León (2000) *Domenças Endêmicas: Abordagens Sociais, Culturais e Comportamentais*, Brazil: Oswaldo Cruz Foundation.

Briceño-León, R. (1999) *Las Ciencias Sociales y la Salud en America Latina: Un Balance*, Caracas: Fundación Polar.

Briceño-León, R., C. Minayo and C. E. A. Coimbra, Jr. (2000) *Salud y Equidad: Una Mirada desde las Ciencias Sociales*, Brazil: Oswaldo Cruz Foundation.

Bronfman, M. and R. Castro (1999) *Salud, Cambio Social y Politica*, Del Valle, Mexico: Edamex.

Commission on Health Research for Development (1990) *Health Research. Essential Link to Equity in Development*, New York: Oxford University Press.

Higginbotham, N. (1992) 'Developing partnerships for health and social science research: the International Clinical Epidemiology Network (INCLEN) social science component', *Social Science and Medicine* 35(11): 1325–7.

— (1994) 'Capacity building for health social science: the International Clinical Epidemiology Network (INCLEN) Social Science Program and the International Forum for Social Science in Health (IFSSH)', *Acta Tropica* 7: 123–37.

Higginbotham, N., G. Albrecht and L. Connor (2001) *Health Social Science: A Trans-disciplinary and Complexity Perspective*, Melbourne: Oxford University Press.

IFSSH (1994) 'Linking a global core agenda with regional activities for the application of social sciences in health', Working Paper No. 1, Bangkok: IFSSH.

— (1995) *Mission: The International Forum for Social Sciences*, Nakornpathom: IFSSH.

— (1997) *Proceedings of the Fourth Steering Committee Meeting of the International Forum for Social Sciences in Health (IFSSH)*, Peebles, Scotland, 1 September 1996.

— (2000) *Proceedings of the Sixth Steering Committee Meeting of the International Forum for Social Sciences in Health (IFSSH)*, Istanbul, Turkey, 19–20 April 2000.

Ramos-Jimenez, P., J. Aluning and J. Berja, Jr. (eds) (1996) *The Asia and Pacific Regional Network on Gender, Sexuality and Reproductive Health and Fora on the Teaching of Health Social Science Conference: Proceedings*. Task Force on Social Science and Reproductive Health, Social Development Research Center, De La Salle University, Manila, Philippines.

Ramos-Jimenez, P. and C. M. V. Condor (eds) (1998) *The Teaching of Health Social Science: Cases from the Asia-Pacific Region*, Asia-Pacific Network (APNET) of the International Forum for Social Sciences in Health and Task Force on Social Science and Reproductive Health Social Development Research Center, De La Salle University, Manila, Philippines.

Silva, K. T. and P. Ramos-Jimenez (1996) *Towards a Healthy Society: Case Studies in Health Social Science Partnerships in Asia-Pacific Region*, Asia-Pacific Network of the International Forum for Social Sciences in Health and the Social Development Research Center, De La Salle University, Manila, Philippines.

SOMA-Net (1997) 'African health in the 21st century: social science in health approaches', *Report of the Social Science and Medicine Africa Network (SOMA-Net) Third International Conference*, Harare, Zimbabwe, 20–24 July 1997.

Trostle, J. (1992) 'Building research capacity for health social sciences in developing countries – special issue', *Social Science & Medicine* 35(11): 1321–420.

Part II

Asia and the Pacific

Introduction

Pilar Ramos-Jimenez

Over half of the world's population resides in Asia-Pacific. The region, which consists of five major sub-regions (South Asia, East Asia, Indo-China, Southeast Asia and the Pacific Oceania), exhibits the best and worst human health conditions. Differential access to health care and services and the varying social, political and economic arrangements in diverse societies and cultures contribute to inequalities in health status. At the same time, the region is a fertile ground for innovative development programmes and strategies in health and other sectors.

The Asia-Pacific region hosts a network of social scientists, biomedical scientists, health practitioners and activists engaged in health research, training and intervention. Founded in 1994, the Asia-Pacific Network (APNET) is affiliated to the International Forum for Social Sciences in Health (IFSSH). With a thousand members, APNET's mission is to encourage the development, promotion and application of health social science in the improvement of human health through interdisciplinary and transdisciplinary approaches. Much of APNET's energy is focused on the implementation of its core agenda of promoting partnership endeavours, particularly in the areas of networking, capacity-building, institutional strengthening, research/action, and policy and resource allocation. APNET publishes a newsletter, updates its directory, and produces occasional publications. It also brings its members together at a biennial conference (the first was held in 1992) as well as at special conferences to discuss theoretical aspects and critical issues in health social science.

A topic often raised for discussion in these meetings is how inter-disciplinary and transdisciplinary perspectives can be operationalized at various levels of health work. The IFSSH competition to select the best cases of collaborative research and intervention projects demonstrates how social scientists are able to utilize their theories and methods in addressing human health problems. APNET continues to encourage its members who are engaged in collaborative studies to participate in the IFSSH best case competitions and to disseminate their work to the widest possible audience. They also continue to be asked to present these experiences at the biennial regional conference as well as at other global gatherings. Despite APNET's efforts, the development of health social science has been uneven in the region. Few countries have recognized health social science as a field of study. At an APNET- and Ford Foundation-sponsored conference in 1996, social scientists and practitioners from eleven countries (Ramos-Jimenez et al. 1996) reviewed the teaching of health social science. The application of social science theories and tools in health curricula was found to vary in the sub-regions and among countries within each sub-region. A few countries (for example, Thailand, Philippines and Australia) offer health social science as a degree programme or as a special field of study. Their curricular offerings, however, are not the same. In many countries, social science theories and methods are yet to be accepted or integrated into the biomedical and other health fields. Despite the use of social science concepts and tools in some biomedical science courses, such as preventive medicine and community health, medical doctors rather than health social scientists often teach these courses. The common issues raised by the 1996 conference participants focused on the need to: (a) define health social science as a field of study; (b) develop a health social science curriculum; (c) create a policy that promotes health social science; (d) reduce the rigid boundaries among disciplines (especially between the social science and biomedical fields) and institutions; (e) increase the number of trainers or teachers in health social science; and (f) develop local and regional health social science training materials.

While social science concepts and tools may be appreciated, their application in the study of health problems is not clear to many conference participants. Further, a health social science curriculum is not readily available as reference for those who intend to utilize or integrate it into their pedagogy. Existing, rigid disciplinary boundaries in social and biomedical sciences within universities or other institutions often hamper cross-fertilization of theories and methods that would facilitate the development of interdisciplinary and transdisciplinary approaches to health problems. The absence or inadequate number of trained faculty is another constraint faced by university administrators wanting to integrate health social science perspectives into their curricula. In addition, materials pertinent to the health realities in a given region are badly needed to facilitate training and promotion of health social science.

Networking, promotion of health social science within and across countries, training of more health social scientists, development of relevant training materials and curricula, and exchange of professors and publications were recommended as strategies to overcome these difficulties. In particular, APNET intends to help build the capability of young health social scientists through training seminars/workshops in research and through the teaching of health social science. The regional network envisages exchange visits by APNET members, including junior scholars, to observe institutions and agencies with 'best practices' in health endeavours. Attempts will also be made to identify support for scholarships to enable young biomedical and social scientists to undertake special training in health social science (Silva and Ramos-Jimenez 1999).

It is clear that biomedical and social scientists, health practitioners and activists are inclined to view interdisciplinary and transdisciplinary perspectives as sound approaches in health research and intervention. Lacking are demonstrations of how such perspectives actually work in the real world. In 1996 and 1997, APNET published two documents that focused on strategies and issues of partnerships in health and social science, derived from presentations at the 1994 biennial conference in Manila (Silva and Ramos-Jimenez 1996; PSSC–APNET 1997). There is continual clamour, however, for more case studies or models showing how interdisciplinary and transdisciplinary approaches operate at the national and local levels, particularly in the areas of health policy formulation, capacity-building, research and intervention.

The publication of best cases of collaborative research, emphasizing the contribution of social science theories and tools in addressing various human health problems, is a major response to this demand. The four Asia-Pacific cases highlight the experiences of social scientists who were engaged in health research and intervention activities over a length of time in varied social settings in three sub-regions. Dr Hector Wing-hong Tsang describes how he developed an 'indigenous work-related social skills training model for persons with schizophrenia in Hong Kong', attuned to his government's policy to integrate people with disability into their community. Dr Nick Higginbotham, APNET's dedicated interim secretary from 1994 to 1996, illustrates how he and his colleagues (Sonia Freeman, Gaynor Heading and Ann Saul) collaborated with various sectors of the community to address heart disease, a major ailment in the New South Wales Coalfields, Australia. Dr Johana E. Prawitasari Hadiyono, a hardworking member of APNET's Steering Committee from 1994 to 1998, demonstrates how she was able to develop a transdisciplinary approach to promote the rational use of drugs in the public health system in Yogyakarta, Indonesia. Dr Gary Groth-Marnat and his co-authors (Simon Leslie, Mark Renneker, Sunia Vuniyayawa and Maerewai Molileuu) describe how they assisted a traditional Fijian village in its effort to stop smoking and prevent relapse.

In drawing lessons from the work of our outstanding colleagues who have patiently reflected and documented their valuable experiences, it is to be hoped that many of us who are currently engaged in collaborative ventures in various aspects of health will reflect on and write about our own efforts. In this way, we will build on what has been started in this book and will contribute to the growing body of literature in health social science in the Asia-Pacific region.

References

PSSC–APNET (1997) *Meeting the Health Challenges of the 21st Century: Partnerships in Social Science and Health Science. Asia and Pacific Second Social Science and Medicine Conference (APSSAM) May 23–27, 1994*, Manila, Philippines.

Ramos-Jimenez, P., J. Aluning and J. Berja, Jr. (eds) (1996) *The Asia and Pacific Regional Network on Gender, Sexuality and Reproductive Health and Fora on the Teaching of Health Social Science Conference: Proceedings*, Task Force on Social Science and Reproductive Health, Social Development Research Center, De La Salle University, Manila.

Silva, K. T. and P. Ramos-Jimenez (1996) *Towards a Healthy Society: Case Studies in Health Social Science Partnerships in Asia-Pacific Region*, Asia-Pacific Network of the International Forum for Social Sciences in Health and the Social Development Research Center, De La Salle University, Manila, Philippines.

— (1999) 'The Asia-Pacific Network (APNET) of the International Forum for Social Sciences in Health (IFSSH): a proposal for support to develop health social science in the next millennium', unpublished.

2

An Indigenous Work-related Social Skills Training Model for Persons with Schizophrenia in Hong Kong

Hector Wing-hong Tsang

Schizophrenia is a complex illness that cannot be adequately understood by recourse to the traditional disease model. Although research suggests that schizophrenia may have biological roots such as genetic inheritance and neurological dysfunction, it is also closely related to psychological and social factors. The *Diagnostic and Statistical Manual of Mental Disorders* (American Psychiatric Association 1994) states that schizophrenia involves problems in one or more major areas of functioning (such as interpersonal relations, work or self-care). Treatment of schizophrenia based only on the medical model is therefore not adequate. From a rehabilitation point of view, schizophrenia can be best understood by using bio–psycho–social (Engle 1977) social and transdisciplinary (Albrecht et al. 1998) models that attempt to deal with its complexity. Within such frameworks, interventions derived from social science have much potential in the treatment and rehabilitation of persons with schizophrenia. A person with schizophrenia usually experiences deficits in the social aspects of life, which prevent him or her from leading a full life. One of the most significant difficulties is finding and keeping a job. Research suggests that a steady job or valued occupation is important in maintaining the mental health of any individual. In Hong Kong being gainfully employed is given special emphasis; contributing to the household income is a major source of self-esteem and of respect from family members and outsiders. The research reported in this chapter attempted to transcend the dominance of the medical model in treating persons with schizophrenia in Hong Kong. The project applied insights and treatment techniques derived from social sciences to increase social competence and hence the vocational success of those suffering from schizophrenia.

Literature Review

Government statistics in Hong Kong show that approximately 26,400 persons, or 8.8 per cent of those with disabilities, suffer from mental disorders. Of the population with mental illness, the largest group needing long-term hospitalization and community care are people diagnosed as schizophrenic. That such people have significant deficits in social skills and social performance is well documented (Anthony and Liberman 1986; Bellack et al. 1990; Bryant et al. 1976; Christoff and Kelly 1985; Goldstein and Manderscheid 1982; Kerr and Neale 1993; Sims 1986; Wallace 1986). A recent study by Tsang (1994) reported similar findings for this group of individuals in Hong Kong. The application of social skills training in the field of psychiatric rehabilitation therefore needs to be addressed by both social scientists and health care professionals.

Numerous frameworks for conceptualizing social skills in general have been proposed by social scientists (Argyle 1988; Hargie et al. 1981; Liberman et al. 1986; McFall 1982). Similarly, social skills training programmes have been designed and implemented for the psychiatric population. In Hong Kong, numerous attempts have also been made (Ngai 1992; Tsang and Tsang 1988; Tsang 1992).

In recent years, it has been pointed out that social skills and social skills training are closely related to specific social situations (Douglas and Mueser 1990; Kelly 1982; Liberman et al. 1986; Wallace et al. 1980). Social skills acquired in one situation are not easily transferred to another situation. The problem of transferability of general social skills training has been widely demonstrated (Gomes-Schwartz 1979; Leblanc and Matson 1995; Wong et al. 1993). Consequently, there has been a trend towards tailoring training to meet the demands of specific situations or instrumental roles, family relationships, work settings, friendships or peer support.

It is 'common wisdom' among mental health workers that people suffering from schizophrenia have serious employment problems, which include getting and keeping a job. This situation is especially prominent in Hong Kong – a highly economically developed city. A cross-cultural comparative study undertaken by the World Health Organization reported that patients with schizophrenia living in urban areas tend to develop the more severe, chronic pattern of social and occupational impairment compared with those living in rural areas (Jablensky 1987). It has been hypothesized that this may be due to stronger rejection by the community and less social support as a result of change in family size and family and social structure during the process of industrialization, in addition to the failure to find meaningful and valued employment.

Hong Kong is a place where one's worth is judged to a large extent by one's income. Economic recession, however, has resulted in a further deterioration in employment opportunities for people with schizophrenia. Their abilities are not adequate to cope with higher demands and tougher competition for jobs.

Impairment in occupational functioning is likely to be a result of inadequacy in social performance (Argyle 1988). An early study by Cheadle and Morgan (1972) showed that better social relationships are associated with a return to work after hospital discharge of people with a psychotic disorder. Similarly, Watts (1978) reported that a positive response to supervision from staff in the rehabilitation setting is also a good predictor of return to work for people with schizophrenia. It is thus highly desirable from a rehabilitation point of view to give more attention to applying social skills training in work-related situations. Previous personal experience with those suffering from schizophrenia (Tsang and Tsang 1988; Tsang 1992) shows that social skills training in general is not specific enough to help them cope with problematic social situations at work. A specific conceptual model for work-related social skills and studies of work-related social skills training for psychiatric rehabilitation are lacking. In view of the above, it is timely that research be designed to explore the area of work-related social skills and develop a training programme specific to environments most likely to employ workers with the educational and socio-economic status of the majority of patients with schizophrenia in Hong Kong public hospitals. Thus, the research initiative sought to address the following problems:

1. Lack of a model for work-related social skills specific to the Hong Kong context that can be applied to help rehabilitate people suffering from schizophrenia.
2. Lack of a validated assessment instrument for assessing work-related social skills of people suffering from schizophrenia.
3. Lack of an inventory of skill components that can be used to create an assessment instrument and training package for rehabilitation purposes.
4. Lack of an effective training package for enhancing the job-securing and job-keeping capacities of people suffering from schizophrenia in Hong Kong.

The current study adopted elements of existing theoretical frameworks developed by social scientists in the area of work-related social skills, but the content of the training package was developed by undertaking research on the needs and priorities of persons with schizophrenia in the specific circumstances of Hong Kong. The investigation took place in three stages. The objectives for each stage were:

Stage I

1. To propose a theoretical framework for analysing work-related social skills.
2. To conduct a survey to verify validity and relevance of the framework for guiding rehabilitation of people suffering from schizophrenia in Hong Kong.
3. To generate an inventory of skill components that can be used to create an assessment instrument and training package.

Stage II

1. To create an assessment instrument based on the results from Stage I.
2. To evaluate the reliability and validity of the assessment instrument.

Stage III

1. To design a training package based on results from Stage I.
2. To evaluate the package's effectiveness in improving the social competence necessary for people diagnosed with schizophrenia to secure and retain a job with the help of the assessment instrument developed in Stage II.

The Proposed Indigenous Model

In formulating the indigenous model of work-related social skills (Figure 2.1), reference was made to McFall's (1982) two-tiered model of social skills and Liberman's interpersonal problem-solving model (Liberman et al. 1986; Liberman et al. 1989). The proposed model is, in fact, an integration and elaboration of these models in the workplace. McFall's two-tiered model of social skills differentiates between social skills and social competence. In his model, social skills are seen as sequential organismic steps through which incoming stimuli are transformed into responses or task performance that are then judged as competent or incompetent. Liberman's approach, on the other hand, interprets social skills in the context of the interpersonal problem-solving process that determines the social competence of an individual. Three sets of social skills – receiving skills, processing skills and sending skills – are considered the most important. The limitation of both models is that neither attempts to delineate specific social skills required within relevant concrete social situations. The proposed indigenous model therefore integrates the essence of these two models within the context of the Hong Kong workplace.

Work-related social skills are conceptualized as a three-tier structure in which the three tiers have a hierarchical relationship, with the bottom tier providing a foundation upon which the other two tiers are based. From a learning point of view, a person should first master concepts and skills in

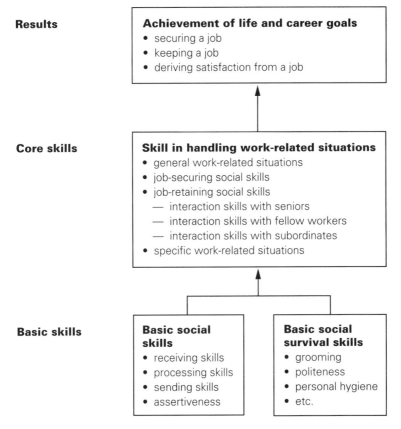

FIGURE 2.1 A three-tier model for work–related social skills

the fundamentals stage before he or she proceeds to learn the more advanced one. The model is presented schematically in Figure 2.1.

The first tier is comprised of basic social skills and basic social survival skills. Basic social skills focus on interpersonal communication and include skills related to the receiving, processing and sending of information as defined by Liberman et al. (1986). Basic social survival skills consist of such skills as grooming, politeness and personal appearance, which are necessary for social competence.

The second tier is comprised of two clusters of core skills. Core skills are defined as those needed in handling both general and specific work-related situations. The first cluster includes those skills needed for coping with any job irrespective of its specific nature. General work-related skills can be divided into job-securing social skills and job-retaining social skills.

The latter set of skills may further be divided according to the three groups of people with whom an employee must interact: supervisors, colleagues and subordinates. The second cluster of core skills consists of skills vital for coping with situations specific to a particular kind of job. For instance, a security guard in a building must possess skills necessary for dealing with complaints from the tenants; a sales person in a fashion shop has to know how to sell the store's products and how to cater to the needs of the customers.

Finally, the third tier of the model encompasses the goals to which the basic and core skills point – in other words, the benefits that a person can obtain if he or she possesses these skills. These benefits embrace getting a job, settling into a job, maintaining a job, and deriving a sense of achievement and satisfaction from the job, which are also goals of vocational rehabilitation for people with schizophrenia.

Stage I: Testing the Validity of the Indigenous Model

Since the above model was constructed on the basis of a literature review and clinical observation, it was by no means certain whether it could survive an empirical test. A survey was conducted to assess qualitatively its validity among three groups of individuals: professional workers ($N=102$), including social workers, occupational therapists, medical officers and others; ordinary workers not suffering from schizophrenia ($N=90$); and people suffering from schizophrenia ($N=128$). The questionnaire consisted of six open-ended questions that asked the respondents their opinions in relation to a person with schizophrenia. These questions pertained to: (1) abilities required to get a job; (2) abilities needed to keep a job; (3) difficulties encountered when seeking a job; (4) difficulties encountered in retaining a job; (5) social skills required to get a job; and (6) social skills required to keep a job.

Also included were 41 items related to different constructs of work-related social skills. The items were generated from the proposed conceptual framework, the literature, and the clinical experience of related professionals, such as occupational therapists and social workers. In this portion of the survey, the respondent was asked to rate the importance of each item for a person with schizophrenia to secure and retain a job according to a seven-point scale, with 1 indicating totally unimportant and 7 indicating extremely important.

Both qualitative and quantitative analysis of the data supported an indigenous model that follows a hierarchical structure and consists of constructs such as basic social skills, basic social survival skills and job-securing social skills. Also, a list of representative elements in each construct of the model was generated (for instance, interacting with others politely, participating appropriately in a job interview, and resolving minor conflict with a colleague).

Stage II: Measurement of Work-related Social Skills

In the second stage of the investigation, a two-part instrument was developed to measure the work-related social skills of persons with schizophrenia. The first part is a self-administered checklist that assesses patients' subjective perception of their competence in social skills related to job securing and job retaining. The second part is a simple role-play exercise that assesses patients' social performance in simulated job-related situations.

The self-administered checklist consists of ten items. The items were derived from the results of the survey questionnaire and pertain to situations that may be encountered by people with schizophrenia in the workplace and when they are looking for a job.

Clients rate each of the ten items according to the degree of difficulty they experience in handling the situations. The clients judge their difficulty level based on their present performance or competence. A six-point scale is used where 1 = continuous difficulty, 2 = very frequent difficulty, 3 = frequent difficulty, 4 = occasional difficulty, 5 = usually manageable and 6 = no difficulty. The higher the score, therefore, the more competent the person perceives him- or herself to be.

The role-play exercise involves two simulated situations: participation in a job interview and requesting urgent leave from a supervisor. These two situations, which are representative of job-securing and job-retaining social skills, were selected based on the results of the survey questionnaires. The client performs in the role-play situations with a well-briefed person (either an occupational therapist or social worker in this project) who acts as the interviewer in the first role-play and the supervisor in the second scenario. The confederate need not be a qualified mental health professional. However, it is preferable that he or she has some experience working with psychiatric patients. The performance of the client is recorded with a video-camera and rated by an independent rater who has been trained for this task. Behaviours rated include basic social survival skills (e.g., politeness), basic social skills related to voice quality (e.g., volume), non-verbal components (e.g., facial expressions), and verbal components (e.g., turn-taking), and situation-specific items (e.g., performance in the job interview and requesting urgent leave. The rater uses a five-point rating scale in which 4 = normal performance and 0 = poor performance with either excesses or deficiencies in the desirable behaviours. In order to ensure that the scoring process is objective and fair, the rater follows a set of rating guidelines for each of the items.

Test reliability and validity of the assessment instrument Two groups of respondents were recruited for this part of the study. The first group consisted of 80 people with schizophrenia recruited from rehabilitation service programmes provided by non-governmental organizations to patients discharged from psychiatric hospitals. The second group comprised ordinary workers recruited either from participants of activity classes organized by the Trade Unions of Commerce and Industry or individuals randomly approached on the street in industrial zones to take part in interviews. Both groups were tested with the newly developed measure for work-related social skills.

The internal consistency reliability of the self-administered checklist assessing perceived competency in job skills was .80 ($p<.01$). The correlation coefficient between the test and re-test scores was .78 ($p<.01$). Also, the difference in the total scores between people with schizophrenia and ordinary workers was statistically significant ($t=2.51$, $df=138$, $p<.05$). The internal consistency reliability of the role-play test was .96 ($p<.01$). The correlation coefficient of the total scores between the two independent raters who were blind as to the group status of the participant was .80 ($p<.01$). Also, the difference between the total scores between people with schizophrenia and ordinary workers is statistically significant ($t=2.58$, $df=58$, $p<.01$). These results indicate that the measure had acceptable reliability and differentiated between known groups (criterion validity).

Stage III: Testing the Effectiveness of the Indigenous Work-related Social Skills Training Programme

Developing the work-related social skills training programme Social skills training has its historical roots in behaviour therapy and social psychology (Douglas and Mueser 1990; Wilkinson and Canter 1982). Initial developments grew from assertiveness training developed by Wolpe (1958) and the application of social learning theory developed by Bandura (1969). Social skills training is concerned with learning new behaviours. The content of social skills training is derived from the experimental work of Argyle (1975, 1988). In a recent review, seven categories of intervention procedures involved in social skills training were identified: operant intervention, cooperative learning, contingent social reinforcement, modelling, social learning intervention peer-mediated intervention and cognitive-behavioural intervention (Elliott and Gresham 1993).

In designing the work-related social skills training programme, the

TABLE 2.1 Content of the training programme

Session	Content
1	Introduction Revision of basic social skills • non-verbal and verbal skills
2	Basic social survival skills • grooming, personal hygiene, politeness, etc.
3	Job-securing social skills (1) • approaching potential employers • preparing for a job interview
4	Job-securing social skills (2) • participating in a job interview • skills practice

5	Job-retaining social skills (1)
	• interacting with senior workers
	  • assertive skills
	  • requesting urgent leave

6	Job-retaining social skills (2)
	• interacting with senior workers
	  • assertive skills
	  • declining unreasonable requests

7	Job-retaining social skills (3) • interacting with fellow workers • cooperative skills
8	Job-retaining social skills (4) • interacting with fellow workers • resolving conflicts
9	Skills in handling specific work-related situations
10	Problem-solving skills and summary • identifying problem situation • generating and comparing alternatives • selecting the best alternatives, etc. • summary

elements applied to social skills training in general were also adopted. The exact layout and content of the training programme, however, differs from the generic approach to social skills training. In fact, the programme is consistent with the configuration of the indigenous model shown in Figure 2.1. Also, the layout and presentation of the materials follow the hierarchical structure of the model constructs. The first-level skills, consisting of basic social skills and basic social survival skills, are practised prior to the core skills, which include job-securing and job-retaining social skills. The training programme consists of ten sessions, each lasting for one and a half to two hours. This schedule is achievable within the clinical workload of most rehabilitation professionals and social workers in Hong Kong.

The format of individual training sessions follows the general format of typical social skills training and involves a combination of techniques or procedures described by pioneers in social skills training (Curran 1979; Shepherd 1983; Spence 1985; Wallace et al. 1980; Wilkinson and Canter 1982). Each session includes: warm-up activities, instruction, demonstration, role-play, feedback and homework. The content of the training sessions is presented in Table 2.1.

Testing the Effectiveness of the Indigenous Work-related Social Skills Training Programme

Ninety-seven participants were recruited from halfway houses, sheltered workshops or rehabilitation services of non-governmental organizations. Participants were unemployed men and women between the ages of 18 and 50 whose previous occupation was production, clerical or service-related work. Participants' education level ranged from Primary 5 (age 11) to Form 5 (age 17). All had been diagnosed by a registered medical practitioner in Hong Kong as suffering from schizophrenia and had been hospitalized for not less than one year. None suffered from mental retardation and all were willing to participate in a work-related social skills training programme. Participants were randomly assigned to one of the three groups: treatment group with follow-up support ($N=30$), treatment group without follow-up support measures ($N=26$), and control group ($N=41$). Those in the treatment group with follow-up support received a course of training in work-related social skills. In addition, there were follow-up contacts (group or individual) with the participants for a period of three months. The treatment group without follow-up contact participated in the course of work-related social skills training but without any follow-up support after the training programme was completed. Finally, the control group participants received standard treatment, without any form of work-related social skills training or follow-up contact.

Three sets of assessment instruments were used to evaluate the effectiveness of the training programme. The first one was the two-part assessment instrument developed in Stage II of the study. The second was a simple checklist for determining the motivation of the participants in joining the work-related social skills training group. Finally, a follow-up questionnaire that collected information about vocational outcome and adjustment was distributed three months after the training programme was completed.

A baseline assessment was done for all groups using the motivation checklist and the two-part assessment instrument. Subsequently, participants in the two experimental groups participated in the training programme. About one week after the training was completed, all of the participants were reassessed using the two-part assessment instrument (post-treatment assessment). Participants in Group 1 received follow-up support for a period of three months. Three months post-treatment, all the participants were assessed using a follow-up questionnaire. This questionnaire was designed to assess the outcome of the participants in relation to their employment status after completion of the training programme. The questionnaire consisted of questions about the number of job interviews attended, number of jobs taken, reasons for job loss, degree of job satisfaction, and relationships with colleagues. A comparison of test scores between groups prior to the treatment showed no significant difference. Several significant intervention outcomes were found:

1. The self-perceived social competence in work-related situations, measured using the self-administered checklist, was higher in the two treatment groups compared with the control group after receiving the work-related social skills training programme [One-way ANOVA, $F(2,87)=14.79$, $p<.01$].

2. Similarly, work-related social skills of the two treatment groups, assessed by the role-play test, were higher than the control group after receiving the training programme [One-way ANOVA, $F(2,69)=26.86$, $p<.01$].

3. The treatment group with follow-up support was more motivated to seek open employment than the treatment group without follow-up support. Altogether, a total of 40 interviews were attended by the 30 participants with follow-up support whereas only six job interviews were attended by the 26 participants without follow-up.

4. The treatment group without follow-up support was itself more motivated than the control group in seeking open employment in the competitive job market. While job interviews were obtained by the 26 participants without follow-up, only one job interview was obtained among the 41 control participants.

5. The treatment group with follow-up support was more successful in job finding than the treatment group without follow-up support. Fourteen out of the 30 individuals receiving treatment plus follow-up support were employed at the three-month follow-up assessment, whereas only six out of the 26 participants who received the treatment but no follow-up support were employed at this assessment.

6. The treatment group without follow-up support was more successful in job finding than the control group. One of the 41 individuals in the control group was employed upon follow-up assessment.

7. The participants in the treatment group with follow-up were in general satisfied with their job and able to develop harmonious relationships with their supervisors and colleagues, as shown by the follow-up questionnaire.

Implications

The results of this investigation have far-reaching implications for the day-to-day clinical practice of rehabilitation professionals and social workers, training of related professional workers, social welfare and health policy, and psycho-social rehabilitation methods used in mainland China.

Indeed, our results suggest that work-related social skills training should become an integral part of rehabilitation programmes, in psychiatric hospitals, psychiatric day facilities, sheltered workshops or halfway houses so that clients' chances of being gainfully employed are enhanced. The manner in which this training is incorporated into the rehabilitation process, however, needs special consideration. As previous studies have also determined, acquisition of work-related social skills follows a hierarchical structure in which basic skills are more fundamental than the core skills. This finding has significant implications for formulating strategies in training people suffering from schizophrenia in socially skilled behaviour. Clients should first be trained in basic social skills (Tsang 1992), after which advanced training focusing on work-related social skills should be implemented.

Although this study confirms that work-related social skills training is effective in helping people with schizophrenia in vocational settlement and adjustment, few people suffering from schizophrenia and participating in rehabilitation programmes in various settings in Hong Kong are currently able to benefit from this. While the significance of social skills training is becoming more and more obvious to practitioners in the field of psycho-social rehabilitation, policy-makers in the government are not aware of, and hence do not put much emphasis on, this new trend in the development of services for people with mental illness. For the past few years, front-line workers in the field of psychiatric rehabilitation have been implementing social skills training programmes without additional budget or personnel. Many others, however, lack opportunities for in-service training in this area. The lack of policy support from government officials is a major obstacle to the further development of social skills training in the vocational rehabilitation context (Tsang 1996).

The study's findings, however, are in line with the overall policy objective of the Hong Kong government to integrate people with a disability into the community. Government officials should, therefore, incorporate this aspect of psycho-social rehabilitation into health policy so that additional resources, in terms of training funds and personnel, may be allocated to centres providing psychiatric rehabilitation services.

Following the reversion of political sovereignty over Hong Kong to China in 1997, professionals of different backgrounds are giving consideration to the 'China dimension' – that is, how professional knowledge and expertise developed in Western countries can be applied in the China context. Psychiatric rehabilitation is no exception.

Pearson and Phillips (1994) provide a lucid description of the development of psychiatric rehabilitation in mainland China. From the mid-1950s to the late 1970s, teaching and research in the field of social sciences were prohibited in China for political reasons. During this period, the practice of psychiatry focused on biological explanations and the related medical model. The psycho-social aspects of psychiatric rehabilitation, including social skills training, based on advances in the social sciences, were given no attention. This, along with differences in employment practices between Hong Kong and China, led to the underdevelopment of the skills training approach to work and social life. In the community system that existed prior to modernization in the 1980s, people were allocated jobs for life by the government. There was no need for people, including those suffering from mental illness, to equip themselves with job-hunting skills in order to survive in the job market. Skills training of the type developed in this project would have been of no direct relevance to mainland China at that time.

However, since the mid-1980s, China has undergone rapid modernization in science, technology and, to some extent, the market economy. Within this current political atmosphere, China is more receptive to the application of social sciences. Also, the practice of the 'contract-responsibility system' in the employment context has made a significant difference in employment practices. Increasingly, people have to look for jobs by themselves. As a result, work-related social skills training has become relevant for people suffering from mental illness. If people with schizophrenia in the urban regions of mainland China are trained by a programme such as the one developed in this project, their chance of being gainfully employed will be enhanced.

The Effect of the Economic Context on the Outcome of the Study

Caution must be exercised in interpreting the findings with respect to the success rate of the participants in the two experimental groups in securing a job. Success may also have depended on the economic conditions that prevailed in Hong Kong in 1994 when this study was conducted. During this year, there was about a 5 per cent growth in the economy of Hong Kong and the unemployment rate was below 3 per cent. Many business organizations had to recruit additional employees. Such factors may help to explain why so many of the participants, especially from the treatment group with follow-up support, were able to find a job. If the study had been repeated in 1996 when the unemployment rate was higher, success in securing a job might have been lower. This emphasizes the socio-economic nature of the rehabilitation process, where there is a continuous and reciprocal interaction between individuals and the social and economic environment in which they live.

Strengths and Limitations of the Application of Social Sciences in Formulating Treatment Strategies

Although medical science has dominated the practice of psychiatry, it has recently become more widely accepted that the medical model is inadequate in addressing the social and occupational impairments of people with mental illness. This trend had led to the application of social sciences in formulating treatment strategies for the psychiatric patient. In this study, cognitive-behavioural learning theory, social learning theory and psycho-educational theory were adopted in formulating an indigenous model and related training package. The application of social sciences to health problems not only allows for the realization of a holistic approach to the treatment of patients with mental illness, but promotes a multidisciplinary approach in the rehabilitation of people with mental illness. In the first stage of the study the opinions of physicians, social workers, occupational therapists and care-workers in the sheltered workshops and halfway houses were incorporated in developing and validating the indigenous model. The evaluation of the effectiveness of the training package in Stage III required further cooperative efforts between different disciplines.

Social sciences-based interventions nevertheless have their own limitations. If the participant is experiencing florid psychotic signs and symptoms, the training package is by no means therapeutic to him or her. In such a situation, the patient's mental state must be stabilized by using psychotropic drugs and other proven physical treatments based on biomedical sciences as well as by intensive psycho-social support before training can proceed. In other words, medical sciences and social sciences individually are insufficient in the process of psychiatric rehabilitation. Instead, they have to be integrated to form a holistic basis for treating those suffering from schizophrenia.

Appendix 2.1: Self-administered Checklist

Item number	Items
1	Make appointment for a job interview over phone
2	Participate appropriately in a job interview
3	Dress appropriately to attend a job interview
4	Request urgent leave from supervisor
5	Resolve a conflict with supervisor
6	Resolve a conflict with a colleague
7	Not be involved in destructive gossip
8	Cooperate with colleagues to perform a group task
9	Refuse request from supervisor to work overtime when you are very tired
10	Help to instruct or demonstrate a task to a new colleage

Rating scale	
1	Always difficult
2	Often difficult
3	Sometimes difficult
4	Occasionally difficult
5	Seldom difficult
6	Not difficult at all

References

Albrecht, G., S. Freeman and N. Higginbotham (1998) 'Complexity and human health: the case for a transdisciplinary paradigm', *Culture, Medicine and Psychiatry* 22: 55–92.

American Psychiatric Association (1994) *Diagnostic and Statistical Manual of Mental Disorders: DSM-IV*, 4th edn, Washington, DC: American Psychiatric Association.

Anthony, W. A. and R. P. Liberman (1986) 'The practice of psychiatric rehabilitation', *Schizophrenia Bulletin* 12: 365–83.

Argyle, M. (1975) *Bodily Communication*, London: Methuen.

— (1988) *The Psychology of Interpersonal Behavior*, New York: Penguin.

Bandura, A. (1969) *Principles of Behavioral Modification*, New York: Holt, Rinehart and Winston.

Bellack, A. S., R. L. Morrison, K. T. Mueser, J. H. Wade and S. L. Sayers (1990) 'Role play for assessing the social competence of psychiatric patients', *Psychological Assessment: A Journal of Consulting and Clinical Psychology* 2(3): 248–55.

Bryant, B., P. Trower, K. Yardley, H. Urbieta and F. J. J. Letemendia (1976) 'A survey of social inadequacy among psychiatric out-patients', *Psychological Medicine* 6: 101–12.

Cheadle, A. J. and R. Morgan (1972) 'The measurement of work performance of psychiatric patients', *British Journal of Psychiatry* 120: 437–41.

Christtoff, K. A. and J. A. Kelly (1985) 'A behavioral approach to social skills training with psychiatric patients', in L. L'Abate and M. A. Milan (eds), *Handbook of Social Skills Training and Research*, New York: Wiley, pp. 361–87.

Curran, J. P. (1979) 'Social skills: methodological issues and future directions', in A. Bellack and M. Hersen (eds), *Research and Practice in Social Skills Training*, New York: Plenum Press, pp. 319–54.

Douglas, M. S. and K. T. Mueser (1990) 'Teaching conflict resolution skills to the chronically mentally ill: social skills training groups for briefly hospitalized patients', *Behavior Modification* 14: 519–47.

Elliott, S. N. and F. M. Gresham (1993) 'Social skills interventions for children', *Behavior Modification* 17: 287–313.

Engel, G. L. (1977) 'The need for a new medical model: a challenge for biomedicine', *Science* 196(4286): 129–36.

Goldstein, I. and R. Manderscheid (1982) 'The chronically mentally ill: a descriptive analysis from the uniform client data instrument', *Community Support Service Journal* 2: 4–9.

Gomes-Schwartz, B. (1979) 'The modification of schizophrenic behavior', *Behavior Modification* 3(4): 439–68.

Hargie, O., C. Saunders and D. Dickson (1981) *Social Skills in Interpersonal Communication*, London: Croom Helm.

Jablensky, A. (1987) 'Multi-cultural studies and the nature of schizophrenia: a review', *Journal of the Royal Society of Medicine* 80: 162–7.

Kelly, J. A. (1982) *Social Skills Training: A Practical Guide for Interventions*, New York: Springer Publishing Company.

Kerr, S. L. and J. M. Neale (1993) 'Emotion perception in schizophrenia: specific deficit or further evidence of generalized poor performance?', *Journal of Abnormal Psychology* 2: 312–18.

Leblanc, L. A. and J. L. Matson (1995) 'A social skills training program for preschoolers with developmental delays. Generalization and social validity', *Behavior Modification* 19(2): 234–46.

Liberman, R. P., W. J. DeRisi and H. K. Mueser (1989) *Social Skills Training for Psychiatric Patients*, New York: Pergamon Press.

Liberman, R. P., K. T. Mueser, C. J. Wallace, E. Jacobs and H. K. Massel (1986) 'Training skills in the psychiatrically disabled: learning coping and competence', *Schizophrenia Bulletin* 12: 631–47.

McFall, R. M. (1982) 'A review and reformation of the concept of social skills', *Behavioral Assessment* 4: 1–33.

Ngai, S. Y. (1992) 'Social skills training with ex-mental patients', *Asia Pacific Journal of Social Work* 2(1): 86–102.

Pearson, V. and M. R. Phillips (1994) 'The social context of psychiatric rehabilitation in China', *British Journal of Psychiatry* 165 (Supplement 24): 11–18.

Shepherd, G. (1983) 'Introduction', in S. Spence and G. Shepherd (eds), *Development in Social Skills*, London: Academic Press.

Sims, A. (1986) 'Social aspects of schizophrenia: overview' in A. Kerr and P. Snerith (eds), *Contemporary Issues in Schizophrenia*, London: Gaskell, pp. 327–31.

Spence, S. H. (1985) *Social Skills Training with Children and Adolescents: A Counsellor's Manual*, Windsor: NFER.

Tsang, W. H. (1992) 'Social performance, work success and social skills training for schizophrenics in Hong Kong', unpublished MPhil dissertation, City University of Hong Kong.

—— (1994) 'Social performance of schizophrenics in Hong Kong', *Journal of the Hong Kong Association of Occupational Therapists* 7: 18–25.

Tsang, W. H. and V. Pearson (1996) 'A conceptual framework on work-related social skills for psychiatric rehabilitation', *Journal of Rehabilitation* July/August/September: 61–7.

Tsang, S. and W. H. Tsang (1988) 'Social skills training group for psychiatric out-patients', *Journal of the Hong Kong Psychiatric Association* 7: 34–8.

Wallace, C. J. (1986) 'Functional assessment', *Schizophrenia Bulletin* 12: 604–30.

Wallace, C. J., C. J. Nelson, R. P. Liberman, L. D. Aitchison, J. P. Elder and U. Ferris (1980) 'A review and critique of social skills training with schizophrenic patients', *Schizophrenia Bulletin* 6: 42–63.

Watts, F. N. (1978) 'A study of work behavior in a psychiatric rehabilitation unit', *British Journal of Social and Clinical Psychology* 17: 85–92.

Wilkinson, J. and S. Canter (1982) *Social Skills Training Manual: Assessment, Program Design and Management of Training*, New York: John Wiley and Sons.

Wolpe, J. (1958) *Psychotherapy by Reciprocal Inhibition*, Stanford, CA: Stanford University Press.

Wong, S. E., J. A. Marinez-Diaz, H. K. Massel et al. (1993) 'Conversational skills training with schizophrenic inpatients: a study of generalization across settings and con-versants', *Behavior Therapy* 24: 285–304.

3

Cultural Constructions of Risk: Heart Disease in the New South Wales Coalfields, Australia

Nick Higginbotham, Sonia Freeman, Gaynor Heading and Ann Saul

Coronary heart disease is a leading cause of death in Australia and a major cause of illness (Australian Institute of Health and Welfare 1996). The Hunter region of New South Wales (NSW) is an area of high risk relative to other parts of Australia, and within this region the Coalfields district has the highest rates of death from heart disease (Dobson et al. 1988). The high rates of heart disease in the Coalfields identified in the 1970s (Leeder et al. 1983) led to the formation of the Coalfields Healthy Heartbeat (CHHB) community action programme in 1990. The CHHB programme, aimed at heart disease prevention, was based on the philosophy of 'community activation' – a health promotion strategy reported to be beneficial for reducing heart disease (LeFebvre et al. 1987; Puska 1984; Winett et al. 1989) and associated with empowerment, participatory democracy and self-sustainment (Davis and George 1993: 378).

This chapter describes the development, implementation and outcome of the Coalfields action programme. The complex community responses to the intervention are explained in terms of cultural constructions of risk (anger about risks from environmental hazards imposed by industrialists as opposed to individual risk-taking) and the historical orientation towards communal rather than individual responsibility for health (establishment of community-'owned' emergency services and hospitals versus concern with 'lifestyle'). The chapter uses complexity theory as a framework for understanding the patterns of community response to health threats and highlights lessons learned from the authors' ten years of involvement with the people of the Coalfields.

History of the Coalfields: Setting and Demographics

At the turn of the century, the discovery of the Greta coal seam transformed the pastoral Hunter Valley area into a predominantly industrial landscape centred on underground coal mining. Townships sprang up next to the pits and rail heads and the area became identified as 'the Coalfields'. Historical, social and political developments were inextricably linked with the mining industry and took place in a climate of struggle and resistance, which continues to shape present-day community reactions and the socio-political make-up of the area (Metcalfe 1988).

There is a large percentage of people of Anglo-Celtic background in the Coalfields. Many of these are descended from miners who migrated from northern England and Wales in the early part of the twentieth century. Traditionally, the main forms of employment were in mining and manufacturing (ABS 1988). Today, the Coalfields area is characterized by a predominance of manual occupations, low educational attainment and high unemployment levels (see Dobson et al. 1991). Unemployment has been exacerbated by the closure of many of the coal mines.

Although population increased during the first half of the twentieth century, over the past twenty years there has been a population decline in some areas due to natural ageing and to changes in the mining industry. In some locations, however, growth in the wine industry and tourism has led to considerable development and new housing.

Surveillance of Myocardial Infarction Defines the Problem

In 1979, researchers at the University of Newcastle began surveillance of heart attack episodes in the Hunter Valley and reported attack rates for men averaging 25 per cent higher than almost any other World Health Organization surveillance centre (Leeder et al. 1983; Wheeler et al. 1981). From the early 1980s, a group at the University of Newcastle became a collaborating centre for the WHO's MONICA Project to Monitor the Trends and Determinants of Cardiovascular Disease. Between 1984 and 1994, the MONICA project maintained a register of all cases of acute myocardial infarction (MI) and suspected MI. Data were collected through a network of research nurses making regular visits to hospitals in the Lower Hunter region (Dobson et al. 1988).

The MONICA Project confirmed earlier studies showing that, compared to other parts of Australia, the Hunter region had consistently high mortality rates from heart attacks. The rate of death from coronary disease was especially high in the Coalfields, which contains about one-tenth of the region's population. Furthermore, rates of non-fatal heart attack were more than 50 per cent higher in the Coalfields in 1993 than in the rest of the Hunter region (calculated from data presented in Steele and McElduff 1995). Similarly, the standardized mortality rates for all causes of death are significantly higher in the Coalfields compared to the rest of the region

(Page et al. 1990) and the state of New South Wales (Glover and Woolacott 1992).

Community Development Intervention: The Coalfields Health Heartbeat

The high rates of heart disease in the Coalfields led university re-searchers in community medicine, in partnership with the MONICA Project, to apply for a five-year Commonwealth government research grant to initiate a community development strategy. In 1990, a coalition of Coalfields stakeholders was brought together to form a heart disease preven-tion programme, which became known as the Coalfields Healthy Heartbeat (CHHB).

Models for the CHHB programme were large-scale community-wide programmes to prevent heart disease, which assumed that broadly based interventions would result in lasting and cost-effective individual and community change (see Egger et al. 1983; Lefebvre et al. 1987; Maccoby and Altman 1988; Puska 1984). For example, results from the Stanford Five Cities Project suggested that residents in intervention communities had increased knowledge of cardiovascular risk factors and had achieved decreases in systolic and diastolic blood pressure, resting pulse rate and smoking rate (Maccoby and Altman 1988). The Coalfields intervention would gauge the effectiveness and generalizability of a community develop-ment approach in the Australian context and test whether effective strategies could be devised to reduce risk factors in working-class communities that had not experienced declines in heart disease mortality similar to those in the educated affluent communities (Dobson et al. 1985).

Initial plans were for the CHHB to evolve as a self-sustaining com-munity action group responsible for heart health. Action by this group would ideally lower the prevalence of behavioural risk factors (e.g., dietary fat intake, cigarette smoking, low levels of exercise), which, in the long run, would lead to reduced mortality. The group would also promote environmental supports for healthy heart behaviour in key community settings such as schools, workplaces, social clubs and food outlets and would also reduce risk imposition such as dominance of fatty foods on restaurant menus and easy access to cigarettes by children. The action group's activities would be observed and evaluated by graduate students and results fed back to the group to assist decision-making (Higginbotham and Titheridge 1993).

Specific objectives of the CHHB were reduction of the prevalence of cardiovascular mortality and related risk factors to at least the equivalent of regional rates; creation of a self-sustaining organization, locally controlled and responsive to changing felt needs; broad participation in, and demand for, heart health promotion activities by all stakeholders; efficient coordination of cardiovascular prevention elements; and innovative interventions at multiple levels (institutional, environmental and policy, as well as social group and individual) tailored to local needs and conditions. A set of general strategies and operating principles were devised to achieve these objectives.

Initial Stages in Community Development

Assumptions Researchers initiating the community development strategy were motivated by the belief that social inequalities underlie health status differences and planned the programme based on several assumptions. It was envisaged that the heart disease prevention initiative should aim to bring about social justice by empowering local people to make necessary changes (Heading 1996: 24). It was assumed that community members would become actively involved in lifestyle change activities, and that there would be widespread support. Residents' sense of programme ownership would sustain their participation in the long run and lead to strong dissemination of change strategies through social groups and inclusion of heart health in their day-to-day activities (Higginbotham and Titheridge 1993). These assumptions influenced the initial setting up of the programme and had wide-ranging ramifications.

The start-up stage In 1990, the university researchers and programme coordinator organized two widely publicized public meetings: the first to announce the initiative and identify local leaders to form a core; the second to list and gain consensus on targets of change and strategies to achieve change. Researchers expected to organize community leaders and groups wanting to form the coalition into sub-group clusters, so that any conflicts would be contained and not lead to a collapse of the whole group.

Reaction Reaction to the two meetings was positive, although attendance was less than expected.[1] No spontaneous coalition of local leaders or interested community people emerged but a long list of issues and strategies was endorsed and a steering committee was formed with two council members, including the mayor, local health workers, university representatives, and several local people.

Researchers were aware of the need for 'ethnographic input' in community development projects and had consulted an anthropologist who had researched socio-political aspects of the mining industry in the Coalfields. Despite this attempt at social preparation, lack of local knowledge resulted in tensions between a pre-existing heart health support group, mostly comprising lay people who had sponsored awareness-raising activities, and the CHHB 'newcomers'. The CHHB team had been wrongly informed that the earlier group had disbanded when the community health nurse working with them had left. Instead, this group gained new impetus from the publicity about heart disease and became a competitor. Several months were spent trying to reconcile and then merge the two groups. With hindsight, this problem occurred because researchers were unaware of the various local agendas and how the university initiative cross-cut those interests.

The reorientation stage The desire of the lay people on the steering committee was for a leader to mobilize the masses, to help de-institutionalize health. Their vision of how the project would proceed involved awareness-raising activities and promotions initiated by them and carried out by a community worker. In contrast, the health and service providers and university researchers favoured a long-term democratic process that would lead to community ownership and structural change.

The lay people also saw their role as 'link agents', keeping informed other community organizations to which they belonged and thereby committing these other groups to the task. Team-building was made difficult by different expectations and assumptions of each group during this reorientation period.

Expectations during reorientation The researchers' main expectation during this phase was that the key community representatives would readily supply support persons/activities/opportunities in accordance with their understanding of popular involvement in community development. However, the relationship between the health professionals and university people and the lay people on the steering committee was complicated by a suspicion of outsiders and the historic 'workers and bosses' class structure of the region (see Daniel 1994; Heading 1996: 219; Metcalfe 1988). While they were willing to help in particular ways, the expectations of the professional people that community representatives would spontaneously create opportunities for accessing community groups and for on-going fundraising were disappointed. The death of the lay leader early in this period was a significant factor in this communication breakdown as there was no natural leader to take his place (Heading 1996: 222–3; Higginbotham and Titheridge 1993).

The researchers also assumed that funding to institutionalize the intervention locally would be forthcoming through the state government's Hunter Area Assistance Scheme. Expectations of this were overstated, perhaps as an inducement for the university to commit resources. The researchers' faith in the funding process and its associated politics proved to be naive. The fact that funding took several years to achieve was a significant inhibitor and diversion within the project during this phase.

It was also assumed that a local person would be employed as the programme coordinator. One of the major benefits of being a 'local' is being able to tap into local knowledge and social networks. Being of the place, she or he would be aware of the prevailing culture, the politics and the unwritten rules, and have access to community networks. However, the initial part-time programme coordinator was a university appointee who was not from the area. As a result, she expended a great deal of energy in earning credibility and undergoing the 'rites of entry'.

The programme coordinator's difficulties in working with the steering committee included power plays by people with their own political agendas and the unavailability of steering committee members for practical activities because of their professional or business commitments. The lack of funding meant that much of the coordinator's time was spent raising money (see Heading 1996: 220–1).

The programme coordinator succeeded in initiating a range of activities and making presentations to a variety of organizations, but was continually frustrated at the difficulty in mobilizing local people and organizing fundraising activities. For instance, local people appeared reluctant to buy raffle tickets from the 'outsider' coordinator but were seen to buy them if they stopped to chat with a local person who was selling tickets (Heading 1996: 211).

Reflecting on the Limitations of the CHHB Intervention

An important first step in planning community-based health interventions is to distinguish between 'felt needs', which are socially and culturally relevant needs expressed by members of a community; 'basic needs', which are criteria for interventions determined by project planners on the basis of epidemiological surveys and economic imperatives; and 'effective demand', the willingness of groups to contribute resources to a project.[2] The uncritical merging of 'felt needs' and 'basic needs' with 'effective demand' may produce a negative impact on both the immediate success and the long-term viability of health promotion programmes.

Assumptions about community participation Less than optimal involvement by the community in the CHHB may be related to differing expectations by the researchers and members of the community about the form of community participation in the intervention. Community participation may be defined in several ways involving varying degrees of shared control by researchers and the target group. 'Community activation' involving participatory action research offers community members the most opportunity to plan, control and evaluate a health intervention. At the other end of the scale, some interventions envisage 'community participation' mainly in terms of the contribution of money or labour to an externally initiated project, with minimal or zero community input into planning and controlling the intervention (Muller 1983: 190–1; Oakley 1989; Rifkin 1986). This kind of community participation may fail to engender a sense of ownership if community members perceive that participation really means complying with the demands of the project managers. The assumption that community participation would be in the form of voluntary labour for awareness and fundraising with a consequent lack of ownership may account for much of the 'frustration' experienced by the CHHB project coordinator (see Heading 1996).

Intervention methods The methods employed by the CHHB drew heavily on social marketing techniques. One of the basic premises of social marketing is that it 'seeks to influence behaviours not to benefit the marketeer but to benefit the target audience and the general society' (Andreason n.d.: 6). This is problematic because it is not always the case that behavioural changes that benefit the general society also benefit individuals in society.[3] Andreason distinguishes between the 'product-', 'selling-' and 'customer-' oriented approaches to social marketing. The 'product' orientation concentrates on marketing products and services; while the 'selling' orientation views marketing as a means of persuading 'reluctant customers' of the virtues of the organization's offerings (Andreason n.d.: 8).

These approaches are utilized in large-scale community-based health promotion programmes such as those on which the CHHB is modelled. For example, the Stanford Three Community Study in the USA combined a media blitz about the dangers of cardiovascular heart disease with interpersonal behavioural strategies to affect the behaviour of the entire community (Winett et al. 1989: 132).

Alternatively, the 'customer-oriented' approach to social marketing seems more appropriate for interventions that take account of the 'felt needs' of the target group. The philosophy behind this approach is to 'begin with what the target audience needs and wants not what the organization needs and wants' (Andreason n.d.: 9).

In the Coalfields intervention, a contradiction occurred because the CHHB, although it espoused the principles of community development and endeavoured to follow the customer-oriented social marketing philosophy, had preconceived notions about what the community needed (i.e., to reduce CHD) and how this would be achieved (i.e., primarily through behavioural change), which led to an intervention based mainly on 'product' or 'selling' methods.

Tensions between lay and professional participants Winett et al.
(1989: 146) note that for the long-term success of community health
projects, the emphasis needs to be changed from 'do-to' or 'do-for' strategies
to 'do-with' interventions in which the project managers and the community
cooperate to ensure the success of a jointly agreed upon programme. The
intervention should incorporate a framework for structural, procedural and
organizational change that permits the community to adapt interventions
to meet its specific needs.

In theory, empowering a community in this way makes it more likely
that a sense of 'ownership' will develop, thereby increasing the prospect of
long-term success. However, in practice, researchers are likely to be faced
with 'dialectical tensions' between maintaining control over the intervention
and empowering the community to assume control. For the community,
there may be dialectical tensions between the desire for autonomy and
their dependence on professional researchers' expertise (Winett et al. 1989:
145–7).

Working through dialectical tensions between lay and professional participants on the steering committee was crucial to the continued viability
of the CHHB project. Particular problems to be overcome included a
feeling of 'them' and 'us' between university and lay members and resent-
ment by steering committee members who had been part of the earlier lay
heart support group about a perceived lack of acknowledgement of their
achievements (Heading 1996: 219–20).

For whom does heart disease really matter? Three years after the
CHHB was set up researchers concluded that: '[D]espite considerable
efforts by those involved, people have not flocked to involve themselves
in the lifestyle change programmes promoted by the Coalfields Healthy
Heartbeat; perhaps it was presumptuous of us to think that they would'
(Higginbotham and Titheridge 1993). Before the heart health activities
began in earnest, however, a needs survey (N=435) canvassed residents'
views of health issues and a baseline survey (N=800) assessed knowledge,
attitudes and behaviours in relation to heart disease. The 1990 needs survey
revealed that local people were not overly concerned with heart disease
(Higginbotham et al. 1993). Indeed, because of its prevalence in the Coalfields, we could say that heart disease is regarded as 'normal'.

The lack of interest in changing behaviour to reduce heart disease was
a major cause of frustration to researchers, who continued to see it as a
problem needing remediation. Interest in the topic had to be continually
stimulated through 'awareness-raising activities' based on the assumption
that once people knew about the problem they would act to change the
situation. This proved to be a misplaced assumption. A sociological survey

by Heading revealed that it was not simply a lack of knowledge about heart disease that led to some segments of the community resisting heart health promotion messages; sub-sections of the community had their own understandings and orientation to health risk that conflicted with the views of health promoters (Heading 1996).

One Community? After reviewing several heart health community programmes in the USA, Winett et al. (1989: 125–42) concluded that 'community activation' offers the greatest opportunity for successful long-term community participation. But is a community a homogeneous entity, or do we need to address the fact that various individuals and groups in a community may have different interests, goals and attitudes? In relation to the Coalfields Healthy Heartbeat project, research by the project sociologist suggests we classify local residents into three groups:

1. The 'resisters' have an awareness of the relationship between lifestyle and risk factors but find this insufficient reason to change their practices. Their 'now' quality of life; the social and cultural norms within their family, work, sport and social communities; and their distrust of the health messengers all reinforce their resistance.
2. For the 'pragmatists', the cost and convenience of readily available foods together with the pleasure derived from consuming them make it easier not to make lifestyle changes.
3. 'Acceptors' take on new health ideologies (espoused by health promoters), but this may be for reasons other than disease-specific fears, such as a desire to look good physically and cope better or an interest in body maintenance (Heading 1996).

Heading's survey revealed that those who were most resistant to heart health messages were more likely to have lower educational levels, lower incomes, and be male. Nevertheless, this group had *more* heart-related food knowledge than those who accepted the validity of heart health messages (1996: 286).

These findings sounded a warning that simplistic social marketing interventions based on the assumption that knowledge about heart health would lead to behaviour change were inappropriate for reaching all groups in the community. Instead, the project team targeted those members of the community considered to be most amenable to heart-health messages. The rationale was that tailoring the message to make it relevant to the various groups may have more impact on the uptake of healthy behaviours than a specific disease message delivered to the general population. And indeed, the greatest success has been achieved by the CHHB working with sub-groups in the community (Higginbotham and Titheridge 1993).

Finding a Way Forward

Sub-group strategies The needs survey identified two community themes that could be used. A focus on 'opportunities for children' was relevant for interventions within school communities. Among the older generation, 'losing one's health' was important for people who have had personal experience with heart disease.

Schools The Kurri Kurri School healthy heart project is an example of a Coalfields initiative targeting 'opportunities for children' (Plotnikoff et al. 1996: 21–5). This project was initiated by a parents' association at Kurri Kurri Public School because of concern about students' health and fitness. It was conducted with Grade 6 (age 11) classes and consisted of classroom heart health education lessons, daily physical education and attention to the physical environment of the school (for example, equipment and shade). The programme was a collaboration between parents, teachers, the school principal, researchers, staff from the University of Newcastle and health professionals from the Coalfields district.

Researchers evaluated the programme through pre- and post-measures of heart health knowledge, attitudes, self-reported behaviour and health-related fitness. The results showed a positive trend in outcomes compared to a control school. Experimental students experienced positive improvements in heart health knowledge, success in following a low-fat diet, intention of getting adequate exercise (girls), and not trying or discontinuing smoking (boys).

The programme was developed to include substantial teacher training in heart health as well as enhanced school, parental and community involvement. Healthy heart school lessons for all grades (ages 5–12) required the children to complete activities at home that involved their parents, such as completing a diet diary or skinning a chicken. Fifteen out of 18 government primary schools in the school district adopted the expanded programme in 1994. This led to the development of the Coalfields Health Promoting Schools Project, in which schools share resources, ideas and strategies to promote heart health throughout the district.

The project has also supported the schools to initiate structural changes – for example, provision of healthy food choices from the school canteen, or development of a health-related mission statement. Since 1995, the project has further expanded to include the area's private and church-sponsored schools, while the three local high schools are pursuing a smoking cessation and prevention initiative.

Heart Support – Australia The establishment in 1992 of a local branch of Heart Support – Australia (HSA), a self-help organization providing information and support for heart patients and their families through a voluntary counselling service, has been the catalyst for greater grassroots involvement. The group is involved in counselling and training Coalfields people with CHD to enable them to provide support to other families in the area coping with the disease.

HSA also contributed to a cardiac rehabilitation trial being undertaken at the university teaching hospital, and has established a coordinated cardiac rehabilitation service. The rehabilitation service, which has close to one hundred regular participants, provides information on diet, medication and exercise as well as a group exercise activity for people who have had a heart attack or undergone heart surgery.

Incorporating the CHHB into the Community

The CHHB now consists of a steering committee of service providers from industry, local council, education and health sectors and a growing team of volunteers who provide administrative and worker support. It shares office space, and is mutually supportive with, Heart Support – Australia. The office area accommodates a walk-in community resource facility. Activities include institutional development, environmental and policy action; mobilizing community resources; and developing the individual (skills, choices, confidence). As Table 3.1 shows, the project has successfully incorporated many heart health initiatives in the community and has proved to be a valuable networking resource for many Coalfields residents.

What was the real mission of the intervention? Looking back, researchers working on the CHHB have asked themselves: what was the real mission of the intervention? To prevent excessive deaths or build local capacity to control health resources? We need to consider two barriers that we may have inadvertently erected. By creating this 'condition', which diagnoses the Coalfields as worse than the rest of the region and the state, have we disempowered the community? Have we disempowered them by highlighting their incapacity to be 'healthy', and consequently created the need for experts and superiors to show them the way? If so, we have set up the old dynamics of master–worker, and generated the traditional response of the underdog and the victim: to celebrate and indulge in the behaviours that are in disrepute.

While we worked to prevent excessive deaths within *our* framework of medical and social responsibility, and demanded changes to eating, smoking and exercise patterns, did we clash with the world view of those whom we wanted to empower by divorcing these behaviours from the social and cultural roots from which they draw their meaning?

TABLE 3.1 Coalfields Healthy Heartbeat intervention strategies: level of participation and years initiated

Awareness-raising and public relations (since 1986)

Media releases
Public displays
Heart health promotions (e.g. Heart Week)
Guest speaking at clubs, schools, worksites
FM radio broadcasts (on-going)

Heart health rehabilitation (since 1992)

Heart support – Australia, branch office (40 regular members)
Rehabilitation exercise programme (150 users)
Telephone counsellors trained (> 45 counsellors)

Promoting healthy lifestyles

Cooking classes (since 1993; 200 users)
Low–fat cooking class
Healthy cooking for families
Healthy cooking demonstration
Supermarket tours (nutrition education)

Weight control (1994; 20 users)
Regular classes
Classes targeted at the obese

Gentle exercise (1993; >200 users)
Tai Chi classes
Regular classes with child care provided
Walking for pleasure – walking trails book published

Anti-smoking programmes (1994)
QUIT
Adolescent QUIT

Institutional and environmental development

Walk-in Heart Health Resource Centre (opened 1993)

Schools (launched 1992)
Healthy Heart Schools Network (15 primary and 2 high schools)
Health promoting schools (alcohol awareness, sun protection, Quit Smoking programmes at 3 high schools).

Restaurants, clubs and retailers (1993)
'Healthy Eats' restaurant programme (10 clubs and restaurants)
Fast food outlet accreditation (6 shops)
Reduction in access of minors to cigarettes campaign

Industry programs (1991)
Aluminium smelter
Garment manufacturing

Mobilizing institutional resources

University research and educational resources (1990)
Regional Assistance Scheme funding (since 1994)
CHHB on-going funding by NSW Health Department (1996)

Mobilizing community resources (1990)

Local management committee
Rehabilitation research
Healthy Communities Programme
Community consultation meetings (yearly)
Incorporating heart health into community events:
Fun Run, motorcycle race, agricultural college events, Tidy Towns Programme, High School Health Expo

Our task has been to dismantle these barriers. Our course has been to blur the delineation, challenge the community to determine the areas and levels of action, and to respond to their requests. Therefore, we now work with schools, local council, community support services, workplaces and health-service providers in a resource and advocacy role.

Evaluating the 'Success' of CHHB

Epidemiological evaluation of risk factors After more than ten years of Coalfields community effort to improve the picture of heart disease, where do things stand now? To evaluate whether the CHHB programme made any change in the health of the Coalfields population, the trends of risk factor levels and the rates of coronary events in the Coalfields were compared with other local government areas (LGAs) in the Hunter region for the period 1983–94. A framework for the CHHB programme was provided by the MONICA Project.[4]

Figure 3.1 shows that although the rates of major coronary events in the Coalfields area have declined over the study period they are still consistently higher than the rest of the region. Figure 3.2 shows that the percentage of people with more than one risk factor (smoking, physical inactivity, high blood pressure, high cholesterol levels and excess alcohol consumption) declined slowly in the Hunter region between 1982 and 1994, while the Coalfields percentage declined rapidly until 1988 and has since risen to higher levels than before.

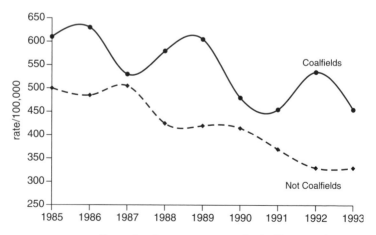

FIGURE 3.1 Rates of major coronary events in the Hunter region for 35–69-year-olds, 1985–93

While this may appear discouraging, the positive result is that, although the number of Coalfields men and women who have heart attacks has not fallen, the number who die from heart attacks has greatly fallen over the past ten years. The Coalfields leads the Hunter region in the percentage of patients who survive a heart attack. The records show that more Coalfields people go directly to the hospital when they have an attack, which shows greater community awareness of the problem and how to handle it. All persons involved in helping someone with a heart attack, including family, workmates and neighbours, as well as ambulance, nursing and medical staff, share credit for this dramatic improvement in survival.

What about changes in 'risk' behaviours that are linked to possible future heart disease? The picture here is less clear. The surveys showed improvements for men in diastolic blood pressure over the ten-year period. Also, Coalfields men were not gaining weight significantly, unlike men in the rest of the Hunter region. However, the high levels of smoking found ten years ago have not gone down (38 per cent are smokers), nor have there been gains in regular physical activity or a lowering of cholesterol among men.

Coalfields women are leading the Hunter region in taking up physical exercise. On the other hand, more women are smoking now than in 1983 (28 per cent are now smokers). The trend throughout the Hunter region in gaining weight is shared by Coalfields women, but they do not enjoy the improvement seen in the rest of the Hunter region in average cholesterol levels.

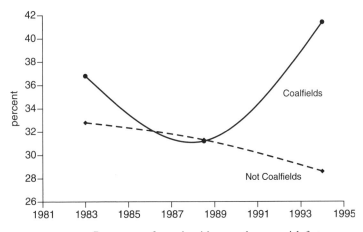

FIGURE 3.2 Percentage of people with more than one risk factor, 1981–95

Given the amount of energy expended in the past ten years, how can we explain the continuing high risk factor levels in the Coalfields? Is the explanation to be found in the particular socio-cultural characteristics of this area?

Socio-cultural evaluation of CHD in the Coalfields Over a five-year period (1990–95) we considered various socio-cultural factors that might have an impact on patterns of coronary heart disease in the Coalfields.

Heredity It has been hypothesized that because many people in the Coalfields are descended from relatively small areas of Wales and northern England there may be an unusually high prevalence of recessive genes associated with heart disease risk (Malcolm 1993: 103). This hypothesis requires further research.

Socio-economic indicators The Coalfields area has proportionally more people with lower levels of education and lower socio-economic status than many other parts of Australia with a predominance of manual occupations (ABS 1988). Epidemiological surveys have found that those in manual occupations have relatively higher levels of heart disease. Dobson et al. (1991) tested the hypothesis that the CHD rates in the Hunter region could be explained by considering the area's occupational structure. The researchers found that mortality rates for ischaemic heart disease for different occupational groups were consistent with established differences associated with socio-economic status. However, rates were higher for most occupational groups in the Hunter region than for the *same* groups in NSW as a whole, so it was concluded that the region's occupational structure 'cannot alone explain the high death rate' (Dobson et al. 1991: 172).

Social and cultural incongruity of health promotion messages Another hypothesis is that reductions in heart disease gained overall in Australia have not benefited the Coalfields because traditional heart health promotion messages lack social and cultural meaning in the local community. Specifically, the standard health promotion communications that have credibility among well-educated professionals and the urban middle class are culturally inappropriate outside those contexts. There are three strands to this argument:

- *Heart disease is not a priority community concern* The first argument is that heart disease, and health in general, pales in comparison with other more immediate concerns of working-class communities such as work problems, housing and opportunities for one's children. Hence heart health messages are ignored as irrelevant to current needs. The New-castle team carried out a needs survey listing 17 community/social problems. The survey was mailed to a random selection of Coalfields adults, and a sample of adults from an upper-middle-class area of Newcastle. Only 35 per cent of Coalfields and 27 per cent of Newcastle respondents endorsed heart attack as a 'high worry' topic. Issues of major concern in the Coalfields were drugs, crime and road safety (over 78 per cent endorsement) (Higginbotham et al. 1993).

• *Health promotion campaigns have low impact* As a result of heart health communications having low priority, and being presented in ways that make little sense locally, we would expect them to have a low impact on people's awareness. This hypothesis receives support from other data collected in the needs survey. In a comparison of awareness of previous health promotion activities, Coalfields men and women were significantly less likely to have heard about or paid attention to 'Eat Less Fat', 'Eat Fruit and Vegetables at Every Meal', and 'Quit for Life' campaigns than the comparison group in the nearby city. Coalfields women were less likely than city women to have heard of 'Walk for Pleasure' and 'Healthy Cooking' classes. While a majority of Coalfields residents approved of the dietary campaigns, over two-thirds of them had not heard about or had paid little attention to the smoking cessation pro-gramme (Higginbotham et al. 1993).

• *Heart disease and health ideology* One's health ideology, with its origins in cultural beliefs, embodied experience and gender relations, forms the lens through which health promotion messages are filtered, responded to or rejected. Heading's (1996) study examined Coalfields residents' food and health beliefs, the reasons behind current eating patterns and health behaviour and interest in heart disease prevention. Her research analysed the way in which health communications about diet are understood and acted on by groups of community members in the Coalfields in the light of their own value systems as resisters, acceptors or pragmatists.

Social history of discrimination against miners Andrew Metcalfe's (1988) ethnography and social history of the Coalfields, *For Freedom and Dignity*, recounts the stress and strain endured by miners and their families. Metcalfe's theory is that socio-political, environmental and cultural factors were influential in the formation of modes of thought and behaviour that are typified as the 'larrikin' and 'respectable' responses (1988: 76). The larrikin and respectable categories are 'ideal types', drawn from cultural models that miners created to make sense of their lives. The larrikin response celebrates behaviours that are criticized by outsiders, such as gambling, drinking and fighting, and contributes to a sense of communal solidarity. Values that are seen as being imposed from outside, such as religion, education and law, are treated with suspicion. Health education messages fall into this category. Interacting with the larrikin world view is a 'respectable' response: those who identify themselves as 'sober hard-working men', and women concerned about their families, acknowledge that miners' 'larrikin' lifestyles are undesirable and express a willingness to change. The respectable response acts to undermine the larrikin lifestyle in directions that are consonant with outside prescriptions, including the idea of reducing individual risk factors to maximize health chances (Metcalfe 1990).

Metcalfe (1990) provides an historical account of miners' diminished social standing outside their own social circle. He argues that acceptance or rejection of heart health messages has been influenced by the belief that health promoters were reproducing past injustices. By implying that the susceptibility of Coalfields people to heart disease was the result of their inability to control their appetites, well-meaning health promoters implied that Coalfields people were irresponsible 'fatties'.

Explaining the Results: Risk Factors Versus Risk Imposition

In an effort to draw together the various socio-cultural and biological elements of influence affecting CHD in the Coalfields, Albrecht et al. (1998) synthesized the data outlined above into a coherent narrative, using principles of complexity theory as a conceptual framework. We examined how the adoption of practices such as smoking, eating a diet high in saturated fat, and drinking alcohol to excess can be traced to particular ways of understanding the world. In turn, these 'world views' are associated with historical events that have contributed to the formation of ideas relating to both risk factors for CHD and risk imposition from environmental health hazards. Furthermore, the Coalfields narrative draws attention to the need to understand differing meanings attached to 'risk' and, in particular, why the goal of reducing 'risk factors', while of crucial importance for epidemiologists and health professionals, was not an attractive proposition for the residents of the Coalfields. Instead, the notion of 'risk imposition' underpinned community mobilization to improve health and health services.

Risk factors   The basic rationale underlying surveillance of CHD is a set of socially constructed beliefs concerning 'risk'. Skolbekken (1995: 297) argues that these socially constructed beliefs about risk have been 'reified': that is, 'established as natural phenomena which can only be identified by means of scientific tools, and not as products of human conduct'. Advances in scientific thinking, the development of probability statistics, and computer technology provide the tools for legitimating scientific understandings of risk and risk factors. Health promotion provides the ideological framework that justifies interventions to reduce CHD risk factors and the application of medical technologies to improve the health of populations in relation to CHD.

These developments are underpinned by a change in attitudes to life and death on the part of the scientific community. The acceptance of risk, in the form of a fatalistic attitude, is being replaced by an ideology that stresses the goal of individual mastery over life and death. A basic tenet is that the 'locus of control' for health has changed from factors outside human agency (nature and the supernatural) to factors inside our control (lifestyle change) (Skolbekken 1995: 297–8).

Ogden (1995) outlines how the concept of risk in psychosocial theory was transformed during the twentieth century by changing ideas relating to the construction of the self: as a response to passive external events, in terms of interaction between the individual and the environment, and, most recently, through the interaction of the self with the self. In health promotion terms, this translates into an increasing emphasis by health professionals on personal responsibility for the maintenance of health, in particular responsibility for following a 'healthy lifestyle' (Davison et al. 1992: 675).

While health professionals are attracted to these recent trends in psychosocial theory, lay people continue to employ earlier discourses surrounding risk (e.g. Heading 1996). For example, Davison et al. show that fatalistic attitudes towards risk and health are still common in South Wales, and probably within the lay community at large. However, their research supported the view that most people were 'neither out and out fatalists nor did they believe that a healthy lifestyle would guarantee complete immunity' (1992: 677).

Widespread credence was given to the notion that a healthy lifestyle could contribute to good health, but there was also recognition of a wide range of other influences. These included 'personal differences' (heredity, upbringing, inherent traits); 'social environment' (relative wealth and access to resources, risks and dangers associated with occupation, loneliness); and 'physical environment' (climate, natural dangers, environmental contamination). Luck, chance and fate were viewed as processes that governed the other influencing forces listed above. Therefore, beliefs about these processes were crucial in the formation of health-related attitudes and practices (Davison et al. 1992: 677–9).

Notions about health highlighted in the Davison et al. study of coal mining areas in Wales are relevant to understandings of health in the

Australian Coalfields. Our research revealed that ideas about risk are certainly not limited to lifestyle factors; they include imposed risk from the social and physical environment (such as social discrimination and pollution from industry) (Albrecht et al. 1998). Moreover, the larrikin world view embraces an active denigration of conventional preoccupations with putative 'risk factors'. Male identity and attachment to male groupings is, in part, established through confronting risk. 'Crash or crash through', an idiom associated with rugby league football, epitomizes the sense of single-minded determination to break through the line of one's opponents, or perish trying. Confrontation with risk is a defining characteristic of group membership, not, as health promoters admonish, something to be avoided. More importantly, taking the risk (e.g. rushing forward to tackle an opponent) means doing your expected duty to your team mates, not letting them down, affirming your connection with the corporate body.

Risk imposition and the anti-dross group Epidemiologists and bio-statisticians look at risk in terms of relative risk, attributable risk and population attributable risk; estimates of risk derived from case-control studies and cohort studies. Clinical research on risk relates exposure to outcome factors, which excludes consideration of contextual issues. This is appropriate for determining population statistics, but concepts of risk based on population statistics do not translate effectively to the individual level. Inconsistencies between epidemiological data and the reality of people's lives lead to lay explanatory theories based on everyday observations (Davison 1993).

How do the everyday circumstances of people's lives contribute to the construction of cultural meanings that affect lay concepts of risk? An illuminating way of understanding community attitudes to health risks in the Coalfields is to look at differing forms of community mobilization. The Albrecht et al. (1998) Coalfields narrative examined the mobilization of resources to fight CHD (the Coalfields Healthy Heartbeat) and contrasted it with a group formed to resist the development of an aluminium dross smelter close to homes and schools. The CHHB is locally managed but embodies an outward orientation, seeking support, ideas, information and working relationships with a variety of educational, medical, research and community organizations. In our observation, this orientation was identified with the 'respectable response', and efforts to engage other community segments in the Coalfields Healthy Heartbeat fell short of expectations.

In contrast, the anti-dross group's orientation is compatible with the 'larrikin response'. This group arose spontaneously from the community in 1994 and rallied members by referring to past struggles by workers against injustices imposed by 'outsiders' (Albrecht et al. 1998). While the rationale underpinning the CHHB is the prevention of CHD by reducing risk factors, the primary concern of the anti-dross group is risk imposition from environmental dangers to health.

The moral dimension To what extent are risk perceptions determined by moral values held by lay and professional people? The notion of 'responsibility' for risk contains an inherent value judgement that needs to be examined. In relation to risk factors, the concept of responsibility is linked to 'prevention' and is generally based on the assumption that individuals, not environments, suffer illness and disease. These ideas may be used to justify developing interventions aimed at bodies, not at environments or institutions.

Fineman and Bennett (1995: 2) note that attributing ill health primarily to lifestyle choices implies individual irresponsibility, while attributing ill health solely to environmental or institutional agents denies individual responsibility. However, it is rare for disease to be caused solely by either lifestyle or environmental agents. Rather, we need to address the complexity of human health on all levels, looking at biological disorders in terms of the synergistic effects of specific historical, environmental and contextual factors relating to the aetiology, prevention, amelioration and treatment of ill health (Fineman and Bennett 1995: 2). The next section details the complexities surrounding community responsibility for the treatment of CHD in the Coalfields.

Explaining the Decline in Mortality: Community Responsibility for Health

As detailed earlier, a paradox facing researchers is why deaths from CHD have declined in the Coalfields over the past ten years, while morbidity (i.e. non-fatal heart attacks) and risk factor trends have not shown significant change. Our examination of CHD in the Coalfields using complexity theory alerted us to the notion that complex social systems are characterized by the evolution of patterned forms of order. The clash of socio-political, economic and historical forces, both locally and in society generally, provided the basis for an explanation of why, during the past ten years, a significant number of Coalfields residents failed to reduce their exposure to risk factors that could have reduced the incidence of heart disease (Albrecht et al. 1998).[5] Those same powerful socio-political, economic and historical forces also provide a plausible hypothesis for why the number of people who actually die from heart attacks has gone down during the past ten years.

Historically, mining communities in the Coalfields have taken responsibility for their own health in terms of the provision of health care facilities and support for the sick and injured. The extremely dangerous conditions in mines constituted one of the prime motivations. In 1900, for example, the Mineworkers' Accident Fund was set up to pay a small allowance to victims of mining accidents. In the early days, miners contributed half of the scheme's funds, with the remaining costs being shared by the government and mine owners (Metcalfe 1988: 231). More recently, miners' lodges in the Hunter Valley have levied their workers to provide donations to the Hunter Rescue Helicopter Service, which transports seriously ill patients to the major teaching hospital in the area. Threats to replace this service with a private commercial operation from outside the region resulted in the Miners' Federation signing up helicopter operators as union members so that industrial action could be taken if necessary to protect the service.

Ongoing medical care was also a shared concern in the Coalfields. In the early part of this century, miners' lodges introduced a 'medical scheme' that employed salaried doctors to treat mining families free of charge (Metcalfe 1988: 117). Mining lodges, miners and mining communities in the Newcastle and Hunter Valley area were also responsible for pooling their resources to establish local hospitals.[6]

Clearly there is a cultural heritage of local community responsibility for providing treatment for the ill and injured: of 'looking after your own'. This is very different from ceding control of decision-making concerning health matters to 'outsiders'. Having contributed to the establishment and ongoing 'ownership' of medical services, Coalfields families feel that it is their right to use these services when necessary.

Health-promotion activities have alerted Coalfields residents to the fact that lives may be saved by prompt medical treatment of heart attack and there is no dissonance between acting on this advice and maintenance of local beliefs, social cohesion and autonomy. The same communitarian spirit, ethos of participatory democracy and male solidarity that underpinned the evolution of the larrikin response, and prompted some to reject the heart health promotion messages of outsiders, has also underpinned the creation of 'grassroots' health services that are used by all when necessary, including heart attack victims.

Theorizing the Coalfields Findings: Using Complexity Theory

Complexity theory adds to our understanding of CHD prevention and treatment using the concepts of 'entropy', 'attractors' and 'dissipative structures' (see Albrecht et al. 1998 and Higginbotham et al. 2001 for an in-depth discussion of these theoretical concepts). The Coalfields community and its rate of heart disease is conceived as an open system patterned by multiple influences, ranging from the bio-chemical through the psychological and cultural to the wider global economic and historical. Entropy is a measure of 'the degree of disorder of a system' (Pais 1991: 81). While all systems tend to move towards disorder, complexity theory draws on the understanding of chaos mathematics to envisage self-organizing systems that combat this and create 'attractors' around which cultural and individual energies are organized and dissipative structures that export entropy to other levels of the system. Dissipative stuctures, such as the larrikin and respectable world views, can evade an increase in entropy by consuming resources to maintain social, biological and cultural patterns, but this is at the price of exporting some disorder into its environment (in this case the biological environment of the bodies of community members).

Self-regulating groups in the Coalfields social system (such as the groups identified with the larrikin response) export the social entropy caused by perceived condemnation of their lifestyle by ignoring efforts to reduce heart disease risk factors. But in doing so they create biological entropy in the form of disordered cardiovascular systems (Albrecht et al. 1998).

Complexity theory also postulates 'attractors', which are 'states to which the system eventually settles' (Lewin 1993: 20). We believe that the idea of an attractor generating order applies to the complex dynamic system that is human society. We define a 'social attractor' as a stable set of shared beliefs and practices, historically situated, which binds a group together (Albrecht et al. 1998). Complex systems form patterns around attractors and follow predictable paths of development.[7] Non-linear systems can possess more than one attractor so that 'their actual state depends on their history as well as their environment' (Firth 1991:1567). While attractors form more or less stable states, they are not fixed but rather enduring patterns that can be influenced but only in subtle, non-linear ways, hence the difficulty of designing effective interventions.

Much of the energy in the Coalfields is organized around the notion of 'risk imposition' and community responsibility for providing and utilizing health services. The same level of social energy is not available for efforts based on the risk factor logic conveyed by the standard public health ideology. The Coalfields Healthy Heartbeat project was able to release only a modest quantum of energy to reduce CHD risk factors. Activities were largely restricted to the victims of heart attacks and their families, health professionals and school leaders. Indeed, the difficulties of getting the project established and promoting community 'ownership' exhausted the energy of researchers and a small group of local professionals.

Complexity theory claims that spontaneous order and organization can come from flux and change in natural systems. We hypothesize that the health-related community organizations in the Coalfields are 'culturally compelling' social attractors influenced by changing views of risk.

Culturally compelling attractors Willms and Sewankambo (1994) provide a useful explanation of the term 'culturally compelling' in relation to health interventions. The terms 'culturally sensitive' and 'culturally appropriate' are often used to describe particular types of interventions. Yet such interventions do not necessarily result in behaviour change because, even when messages are conveyed in terms that are compatible with a particular group's socio-cultural experience, they may still not feel vulnerable or at risk. 'Culturally compelling' programmes are co-developed in partnership with members of the community and are designed to generate compelling evidence that will stimulate people not only to alter their beliefs but also to alter their behaviours.

Initial data about risk factors in the Coalfields were 'culturally compelling' for researchers and a small number of community leaders, and the Coalfields Healthy Heartbeat was formed. But after ten years, MONICA data show no significant change in CHD morbidity or risk factor trends. The scientific discourse surrounding 'risk factors' attracted scientists, the media, health workers, a few 'respectables' and people who have had heart disease and been socialized into the fundamental logic of biomedicine and health promotion. Yet this discourse was not culturally compelling for the majority of Coalfields residents (Heading 1996). Remarkably, in a parallel sphere of action, a significant number have agitated to reduce perceived health risks from a proposed aluminium dross smelter and to maintain health services in their area (Albrecht et al. 1998: 28–38).

Perhaps part of the attraction of this mobilization is the opportunity to protest against outside intervention in the chosen lifestyle of Coalfields residents. The socio-political outlook of residents has led to resistance to the idea that individuals should comply with the dictates of outsiders, whether they be industrialists, governments or public health officials. Coalfields residents value self-reliance, participatory democracy and a communitarian ethos symbolized by the slogan 'united we stand, divided we fall'.

Traditionally, Coalfields mobilization was around causes, not individuals. The 'body-politic' and the 'body-social', rather than the 'embodied self', were the pre-eminent targets (Scheper-Hughes and Lock 1987). A history of having to struggle to achieve satisfactory health services was spurred on by the fear of sudden catastrophic events, such as mining disasters and sudden illnesses, which could incapacitate whole families economically.[8] At such times, the community rallied to assist victims. For Coalfields residents, security comes from mobilizing to provide medical services and to protest against outside threats to health by imposed authority; and freedom comes from being able to avail themselves of health services when they choose.

What Have We Learned from the Case of the Coalfields?

The CHHB evolved over a five-year period and is now releasing as much energy as possible, given funding and manpower constraints, to provide services and resources for those with a 'respectable' orientation and those with heart disease. But we have been challenged by our lack of success in making changes that include *all* segments of the community and by the fact that such changes that have occurred have not necessarily been within our framework of individual responsibility for altering 'risk' factors. Many in the Coalfields community resist and resent the value system represented by attempts by outsiders to change their behaviour, while they show great willingness to assist those in trouble (for instance, heart attack victims) and to defend community resources. Within their historical and cultural framework this makes sense and should not be dismissed as merely an uneducated reluctance to make the kinds of lifestyle changes that are advocated within a middle-class 'individualist' model of health improvement. The spontaneous community response to threats by outside forces to build a polluting smelter in their neighbourhood, or to deprive the community of hard-won health facilities that are seen as vital to deal with the real dangers of mining work, show that there is great concern with health and considerable willingness to mobilize to improve it. It is just that the energy is available for community improvement rather than individual self-advancement or body maintenance.

Researchers need to examine how such culturally compelling attractors affect beliefs and actions on health-related issues. A major contribution of the health social science approach is the perspective that awareness-raising about health-related issues is a two-way process between members of the scientific and lay communities.

We have learned that the rhetoric of community development does not create effective 'ownership' of a project if the aims have been defined from outside and are in conflict with the values of a section of the community. Additionally, we underestimated the length of time needed to achieve local control and management and some of the barriers to doing so. We should reassess the time frame in which to expect major changes in the incidence of risk factors or mortality: should it be 15 or 20 years rather than six?

The use of Complexity Theory provides a framework to integrate highly disparate sources of information. The Coalfields study highlights the value of employing both qualitative and quantitative data to cast light on each other and to illuminate the complexity of people's understanding of health risk and health action. Without this, not only would some of the empirical findings not be intelligible, but our conclusions would scarcely do justice to the reality of the lives of the participants.

Notes

1. At the first meeting there were 17 Coalfields residents and eight university members; the second meeting attracted 15 Coalfields residents and six university members (Heading 1996: 206).

2. Bradshaw (1972) discusses the difference between 'normative need', 'felt need', 'expressed need' and 'comparative need' in relation to the provision of social services.

3. Strategies aimed at bringing about a general reduction in a particular risk factor may result in many people changing their lives for no personal benefit (for example, they would not have had a heart attack anyway). Rose has called this situation the 'prevention paradox' (Davison et al. 1991: 15).

4. Risk factor levels were monitored over the ten-year period 1983 to 1994 for the Hunter region by three community-based risk factor prevalence studies conducted in 1983, 1988/9 and 1994. The study population for the CHHB programme evaluation consists of a stratified sample of people aged 35–64 years living in the local government areas of Newcastle, Lake Macquarie, Cessnock, Maitland and Port Stephens and selected from the Commonwealth electoral roll for the 1983 and 1988/89 surveys, and the New South Wales electoral roll for the 1994 survey. The sampling fraction was greater for the older age strata. People chosen for the sample were invited to attend study centres to complete a self-administered questionnaire and to have physical measurements and blood samples taken. The response rate for 1983 was 66 per cent, for 1988/89 was 64 per cent, and for 1994 was 63 per cent. The risk factors examined to evaluate the CHHB programme included smoking, physical inactivity, high blood pressure, high cholesterol levels and excess alcohol consumption. Information on cardiac events was obtained by following up all residents in the study population whose experience satisfied the criteria of non-fatal definite myocardial infarction (MI), non-fatal probable MI, fatal possible MI or coronary death with insufficient information for further classification (Dobson et al. 1990). Research nurses interviewed patients while they were still in hospital to obtain information on symptoms, medical history and other variables. Cardiac enzyme results were extracted from hospital notes and electrocardiographs (ECG) were copied for subsequent classification. Details of fatal cases were obtained from death certificates, from post-mortem records, and from doctors, relatives, and other informants.

5. Using complexity theory principles we explained how the pull of rival social attractors was instrumental in the formation of the larrikin response, part of which is a disinclination to act on the advice of outsiders regarding heart health messages. Those who accepted the validity of the larrikin response resisted messages about the need to stop smoking, eat less fat, and so on, because of the perceived threat to their valued lifestyle. Until a heart attack was experienced, complying with the advice of health promoters and other outsiders did not have as powerful an attraction as maintaining ties within the immediate social group (Albrecht et al. 1998).

6. Balance sheets of the Richmond Main Lodge at Kurri Kurri for the years 1934, 1950 and 1959, for example, show that the lodge raised regular levies for Kurri Kurri District Hospital and for funeral, medical and sick leave funds (Metcalfe 1988: 117).

7. Complexity theorists such as Goodwin (1995: 169–73) and Kauffman (1993) apply

the concept of 'dynamical attractors' to explain pattern emergence in natural systems (such as organs, organisms, species and ecosystems). Authors such as Lewin (1993: 21) and Dyke (1988: 358) have also applied the concept of an attractor to cultural evolution and the structure of cities.

8. On 14 November 1996, as this chaper was being prepared, the worst mining disaster in seventeen years occurred near Newcastle when four men working at the coal face unknowingly breached an abandoned mine tunnel filled with water and were tragically drowned. Four others were injured and flown by the Hunter rescue helicopter to the Newcastle teaching hospital.

References

ABS (Australian Bureau of Statistics) (1988) *ABS Census of Population and Housing, 30 June, 1986 – Profile of Legal Government Areas – Usual Resident Counts; New South Wales* (Cat. no. 2470.0) Canberra: Australian Bureau of Statistics.

Albrecht, G., S. Freeman and N. Higginbotham (1998) 'Complexity and human health: the case for a transdisciplinary paradigm', *Culture, Medicine and Psychiatry* 22: 59–92.

Andreason, A. R. (n.d.) 'Social marketing: its potential contribution in the public sector', *Healthcom*, Washington, DC: Academy for Educational Development, pp. 5–32.

Australian Institute of Health and Welfare (1996) *Australia's Health: The Fifth Biennial Report of the Australian Institute of Health*, Canberra: Australian Government Publishing Service.

Bradshaw, J. (1972) 'A taxonomy of social need', in G. McLachlan (ed.), *Problems and Progress in Medical Care; Essays on Current Research*, 7th Series, London and New York: Oxford University Press for the Nuffield Provincial Hospitals Trust.

Daniel, A. (1994) 'Medicine, state and people: a failure of trust?', in C. Waddell and A. Petersen (eds), *Just Health: Inequality in Illness, Care and Prevention*, Melbourne: Churchill Livingstone.

Davis, A. and J. George (1993) *States of Health*, Sydney: Australian Harper Educational.

Davison, C. (1993) 'Health and culture in the South Wales Valley', in S. Parsons (ed.), *Changing Primary Health Care: A Collection of Papers from the Teamcare Valleys Conference*, Cardiff: University of Wales, pp. 44–51.

Davison, C., G. Davey Smith and S. Frankel (1991) 'Lay epidemiology and the prevention paradox: the implications of coronary candidacy for health education', *Sociology of Health and Illness* 13(1): 1–19.

Davison, C., S. Frankel and G. Smith (1992) 'The limits of lifestyle: re-assessing "fatalism" in the popular culture of illness prevention', *Social Science and Medicine* 34(6): 675–85.

Dobson, A., R. W. Gibberd, S. R. Leeder and D. L. O'Connell (1985) 'Occupational differences in ischaemic heart disease mortality and risk factors in Australia', *American Journal of Epidemiology* 122: 283–90.

Dobson, A., S. Halpin and H. Alexander (1991) 'Does the occupational structure of the Hunter Region explain the high rates of ischaemic heart disease among its men?', *Australian Journal of Public Health* 15(3): 172–6.

Dobson, A. J., R. W. Gibberd, S. R. Leeder et al. (1988) 'Ischemic heart disease in the Hunter Region of New South Wales, Australia, 1979–1985', *American Journal of Epidemiology* 128(1): 106–15.

Dobson, A. J., A. Russell, H. Alexander et al. (1990) *Hunter Region Heart Disease Prevention Programme. Cessnock/Hunter Comparisons: Death Rates, Heart Attack Rates, Risk Factor Levels Data Book*, University of Newcastle, New South Wales: Hunter Region Heart Disease Prevention Programme.

Dyke, C. (1988) 'Cities as dissipative structures', in B. H. Weber et al. (eds), *Entropy, Information and Evolution: New Perspectives on Physical and Biological Evolution*, Cambridge, MA: MIT Press.

Egger, G., W. Fitzgerald, G. Frape, A. Monaem, P. Robenstein, C. Tyler and B. McKay (1983) 'Results of large scale media anti-smoking campaign in Australia: North Coast "Quit for Life" program', *British Medical Journal* 287: 1125–8.

Fineman, R. and L. Bennett (1995) 'Guilt, blame and shame: responsibility in health and sickness', *Social Science and Medicine* 40(1): 1–3.

Firth, W. J. (1991) 'Chaos – predicting the unpredictable', *British Medical Journal* 303: 1565.

Glover, J. and T. Woolacott (1992) *A Social Atlas of Australia*, Vol. 2 (Cat. no. 4385.0), Canberra: Australian Bureau of Statistics.

Goodwin, B. (1995) *How the Leopard Changed Its Spots: The Evolution of Complexity*, London: Phoenix Giants.

Heading, G. (1996) 'Missing bodies: exclusionary health discourses and participatory heart disease programs', unpublished doctoral thesis, Faculty of Medicine and Health Sciences, University of Newcastle, New South Wales.

Higginbotham, N., G. Heading, J. Pont et al. (1993) 'Community worry about heart disease: a needs survey in the Coalfields and Newcastle area of the Hunter Region', *Australian Journal of Public Health* 17(4): 314–21.

Higginbotham, N. and C. Titheridge (1993) 'Coalfields Healthy Heartbeat Program: a case study in community development', unpublished paper presented at the Public Health Association Meeting, University of New South Wales, Sydney, 30 September 1993.

Higginbotham, N., G. Albrecht and L. Connor (2001) *Health Social Science: A Transdisciplinary and Complexity Perspective*, Melbourne: Oxford University Press.

Kauffman, S. A. (1993) *The Origins of Order: Self-Organization and Selection in Evolution*, New York: Oxford University Press.

Leeder, S., A. J. Dobson, R. W. Gibberd and D. M. Lloyd (1983) 'Attack and case fatality rates for acute myocardial infarction in the Hunter region of New South Wales, Australia, in 1979', *American Journal of Epidemiology* 118: 42–51.

Lefebvre, R., T. M. Lasater, R. A. Carleton and G. Peterson (1987) 'Theory and delivery of health programming in the community: the Pawtucket Heart Health Program', *Preventive Medicine* 16: 80–95.

Lewin, R. (1993) *Complexity: Life on the Edge of Chaos*, London: Phoenix.

Maccoby, N., Altman, D. (1988) 'Disease prevention in communities: the Stanford Heart Disease Program', in R. Price et al. (eds), *14 Ounces of Prevention: A Casebook for Practitioners*, Washington, DC: American Psychological Association.

Malcolm, J. A. (1993) 'Social factors in outcomes after acute myocardial infarction', unpublished doctoral thesis, Faculty of Medicine and Health Sciences, University of Newcastle, New South Wales.

Metcalfe, A. (1988) *For Freedom and Dignity: Historical Agency and Class in the Coalfields of NSW*, Sydney: Allen and Unwin.

—— (1990) 'Living in a clinic: Heartbeat Wales, Heartbeat New South Wales', *Planet: The Welsh Internationalist*.

Muller, F. (1983) 'Contrasts in community participation: case studies from Peru', in D. Morley et al. (eds), *Practising Health for All*, Oxford: Oxford University Press.

Oakley, P. (1989) *Community Involvement in Health Development: An Examination of the Critical Issues*, Geneva: World Health Organization.

Ogden, J. (1995) 'Psychosocial theory in the creation of the risky self', *Social Science and Medicine* 40(3): 409–15.

Page, T., P. Lam and R. W. Gibberd (1990) *Mortality in the Hunter Region of New South Wales, 1984–1988*, Newcastle, NSW: Hunter Health Statistics Unit, September.

Pais, A. (1991) 'Niels Bohr's Times', in *Physics, Philosophy and Polity*, Oxford: Clarendon Press.

Plotnikoff, R., P. Williams and N. Higginbotham (1996) 'An evaluation of the Kurri Kurri Public Schools Healthy Heartbeat Project', *The ACHPER Healthy Lifestyles Journal* 43(2): 21–5.

Puska, P. (1984) 'Community-based prevention of cardiovascular disease: the North Karelia Project', in J. D. Matarazzo et al. (eds), *Behavioural Health: A Handbook for Health Enhancement and Disease Prevention*, New York: John Wiley, pp. 1140–7.

Rifkin, S. B. (1986) 'Lessons from community participation in health programmes', *Policy and Planning* 1(3): 240–9.

Scheper-Hughes, N. and M. Lock (1987) 'The mindful body: a prolegomenon to future work in medical anthropology', *Medical Anthropology Quarterly* 1(1): 6–41.

Skolbekken, J. (1995) 'The risk epidemic in medical journals', *Social Science and Medicine* 40(3): 291–305.

Steele, P. and P. McElduff (1995) *Hunter Region Heart Disease Prevention Program: Newcastle MONICA Date Book – Coronary Events 1984–1994*, Newcastle, NSW: Centre for Clinical Epidemiology and Biostatistics, University of Newcastle.

Wheeler, D. J., S. J. Flynn and S. R. Leeder (1981) 'The Hunter Valley heart attack study: some methodological problems in community surveillance for acute myocardial infarction', *Community Health Studies* 5(1): 32–6.

Willms, D. and N. Sewankambo (1994) 'An intervention discourse: emerging questions, evolving research designs, and epistemological relevances encountered in the dialogue between epidemiology and anthropology', unpublished paper presented at the XII Annual INCLEN Meeting, Chiangmai, Thailand, 28 January 1994.

Winett, R., A. C. King and D. G. Altman (1989) *Health Psychology and Public Health*, New York: Pergamon Press.

4

The Development of a Transdisciplinary Approach to Promote the Rational Use of Drugs: The Indonesian Experience

Johana E. Prawitasari Hadiyono

The inappropriate use of medicines is a common problem in developing countries. The idea of a multi-country effort to address the issue was initially discussed in Germany in July 1989 at a meeting of clinical pharmacologists from Asian and African countries and representatives of Management Sciences for Health (MSH), a US-based non-profit health consulting company, the Drug Policy Group of Harvard Medical School, and the Department of International Health Care Research of Karolinska Institute, Sweden. The International Network for Rational Use of Drugs (INRUD) was established later in the same year with the goal of promoting the rational use of pharmaceuticals (Ross-Degnan et al. 1992). Strategies formulated to achieve this goal are: (1) adopting an interdisciplinary focus, linking clinical and social sciences; (2) engaging in activities originating from country-based core groups of individuals from ministries of health, universities, non-governmental organizations and private sector institutions who are committed to sharing relevant experiences and technical co-operation; (3) emphasizing the importance of understanding behavioural aspects of drug utilization and prescribing; (4) promoting the development of well-designed research studies leading to reproducible interventions to improve drug use; and (5) developing useful tools for research, including standard methodologies, simplified sampling and data collection strategies, and user-accessible computer software (INRUD News 1991a). At present, six African countries (Ghana, Nigeria, Sudan, Tanzania, Uganda and Zimbabwe) and five Asian countries (Bangladesh, Indonesia, Nepal, Philippines and Thailand) are member countries of the network, which holds global and regional meetings.[1]

The rational use of drugs was defined in 1985 by WHO experts as those instances when: 'patients receive medicine according to their clinical needs, in doses that meet their own individual requirements, for an adequate period of time, and at the lowest cost to them and the community' (WHO 1987 in Santoso 1995a). Irrational prescribing occurs, as Santoso (1995a) notes, when no drug therapy is indicated or 'with [drugs of] unproven efficacy or uncertain safety status; with wrong dosages, administration and duration; and the failure to prescribe a well-known safe, effective and more affordable drug'. Irrational prescribing as indicated by Santoso (1995a) is common in Indonesia. According to a study done by the Ministry of Health of the Republic of Indonesia (1988), in collaboration with MSH and Yayasan Indonesia Sejahtera, various forms of inappropriate use of drugs were observed, including polypharmacy and over-use of antibiotics and injections (primarily antibiotics injected without proper diagnosis). It was found that over 60 per cent of patients received at least one injection, and that the use of injections did not vary with diagnosis.

Indonesia core group members of INRUD include medical doctors, pharmacists and myself, a clinical psychologist. Since 1990, we have collaborated on two major research projects to improve the appropriate use of drugs in public health facilities. One study involved a controlled trial of small group face-to-face educational interventions versus formal seminars in improving the rational use of drugs in acute diarrhoea (Santoso et al. 1996).[2] The second was a controlled trial using a behavioural intervention, specifically Interactional Group Discussion (IGD), to reduce the use of injections in public health facilities (Prawitasari Hadiyono et al. 1996).[3]

A third activity undertaken by INRUD core group members was to assist the District Health Administration to operationalize drug use indicators in its health delivery system (Bimo et al. 1994). The activities took place in Gunungkidul District, about 45 kilometres from Yogyakarta, where polypharmacy as well as the over-use of injections and antibiotics were common problems (Bimo et al. 1994). These activities began in June 1993 and continued until August 1995.

As a clinical psychologist, I saw joining INRUD as an opportunity to employ behavioural assessment and intervention methods to promote the rational use of drugs, especially to enhance the understanding of prescribing and drug use behaviour. One of the greatest challenges was learning how to collaborate successfully with health scientists, especially medical doctors, as equal partners. Psychologists working in medical schools are involved in a broad range of clinical, teaching and research activities, often under the leadership of their medical colleagues. As a member of the Faculty of Psychology, Gadjah Mada University (GMU), I enjoy greater autonomy and have more bargaining power in deciding the nature of my collaborative research activities than my social science colleagues, who are Medical School faculty members. To collaborate on an equal footing demands self-confidence, secure knowledge and a willingness to learn and communicate across discipline boundaries on the part of all team members. This collaboration leads to a multidisciplinary approach in the beginning, an interdisciplinary approach in the process and, ideally, a transdisciplinary approach in the long run, as suggested by Rosenfield (1992) and Albrecht et al. (1998).

Building Collaboration: Towards a Transdisciplinary Approach

Different disciplines may use the same term in different contexts or with a different intended meaning. For example, health scientists often include, as qualitative methods, any methods designed to measure non-tangible physical matters. Behavioural measurement, although it uses scoring systems and numerical values, is considered by health scientists to be a qualitative rather than quantitative method. For behavioural and social scientists, qualitative methods are techniques of investigation that produce textual rather than numerical data. Attitudes, beliefs and behaviours that are scored in terms of strength or intensity by questionnaires or observation forms, while seen as quantitative methods by behavioural scientists, are nevertheless still referred to as qualitative methods by health scientists. This difference in point of view needs to be clarified early in the collaboration or significant misunderstanding can result.

Another issue that arises early in the collaboration is negotiation of ground rules. An important ground rule is sharing a commitment to the objective of each activity. If there are conflicting interests, the collaboration will be jeopardized and basic trust among the group members will be destroyed, ending the collaboration before it begins. Respect and fairness are the guiding principles behind another ground rule. Responsibility must be shared from the outset and be based on the expertise of each team member. Health scientists may not know initially what to expect from social scientists in terms of their potential contribution to the project, viewing their participation as 'token' – required by the funding terms of some international agencies' research programmes. This devaluation of the social scientists' contribution can lead to confusion and frustration for the social scientists about their role as team members. Open communication among the team members must be established in the beginning to identify the rights and responsibilities of each member. Open and shared management of the budget is highly advisable.

Willingness to learn and to communicate across disciplinary boundaries is also crucial to successful collaboration. To learn means to open one's mind to new and seemingly strange ideas. Remaining grounded within one's own discipline, however, is important. The collaboration, it is to be hoped, will change the attitude of team members towards their colleagues' endeavours. Health scientists with a critical view of non-medical perspectives on the problem may acquire a more open attitude. The psychologist or the social scientist may become more concrete in the way she or he presents ideas, rather than use technical jargon or abstract terms. If team members are willing to learn from one another, communication flows and a 'common language' emerges. This view accords with the findings of a study by Jetten et al. (1996) in which they demonstrate the importance of in-group norms and the power of the group to define the self and guide behaviour. The collaboration begins in earnest once the team members can understand each other's language and establish basic trust. Understanding each other's messages, openness to others' ideas, supporting each other's work, and, at times, supporting one another in personal matters are norms that ensure the group's productivity. Likewise, Suryawati (1997) notes that an equal commitment, an equal openness and a willingness to respect other opinions are needed in order for the transdisciplinary research team to be successful. She adds, however, that the contribution of each team member does not have to be equal, but will depend upon project needs that have been agreed from the start. One member does not have to feel discouraged when her or his contribution to the project is less central.

The process of building a solid collaboration takes time. Before joining the INRUD country core group, I was invited by the health scientist team leader to present a paper on the psychological aspects of obesity at a seminar. The intent of the invitation, although I did not know it at the time, was to assess whether I would be a compatible team member. A collaboration is analogous to a marriage. Although the practice might sound strange to non-Indonesians, Javanese tradition allows the prospective bridegroom in a pre-arranged marriage and his family to observe the bride at a gathering arranged by other family members in order to decide whether she would make a suitable wife and daughter-in-law. A few months after the seminar I was invited to join INRUD. Like a 'Javanese bride', I accepted, naively perhaps, knowing little about the health scientists who had asked me to join their team, nor exactly what I was expected to contribute. My judgement was that joining INRUD was a challenging opportunity to expand the application of psychological assessment and intervention to the field of drug use. Joining this group would also provide an opportunity to collaborate internationally. These two considerations formed the basis of my commitment to join the group. One lesson learned from this experience is that prospective social scientist 'brides' need to consider whether they will be ensured an opportunity to enrich their own professional growth before they decide to engage in a 'marriage' with the health scientists. Like marriage partners, members of a collaborative research team have to be compatible with one another.

During the inauguration of INRUD in 1990 in Yogyakarta, I suggested involving patients to promote the rational use of drugs and using small group discussions as both an assessment and intervention tool. Focus Group Discussions (FGDs) could be used to assess prescribers' and consumers' beliefs and practices regarding drug use in the community. A second series of FGDs, later renamed Interactional Group Discussions (IGDs), would function as an intervention by bringing together patients and prescribers to discuss findings from the prior FGDs. By participating in the same group discussion, prescribers and patients could learn from sharing points of view. The facilitators, who would be clinicians and behavioural scientists, could educate members of the group in the appropriate use of medicine. This idea met with resistance from the clinicians, to whom it represented a different way of approaching the problem. The source of clinicians' resistance derived mostly from the fact that patients were considered ignorant about appropriate drug use. It was also considered unethical as well as impractical to bring together patients and prescribers in the same group, since prescribers have a higher status in the community than do patients. Clinicians were afraid that the patients would be intimidated by the differential power relationship and not say anything. I acknowledged their objections but worked hard to convince them of the merits of the idea. By the same token, this kind of collaboration, in which social scientists participate not only in delineating the problem but also in developing solutions, was new to me – as it may be to other social scientists working within a multidisciplinary framework. Many social scientists view their role as detached observers and critics of health practices without offering solutions. As a clinical psychologist, I was attracted by the action-oriented approach of INRUD and the opportunity it afforded for integrating social science perspectives into finding solutions to health problems rather than criticizing the limitations of the biomedical model.

The first collaborative project undertaken was an evaluation of the effectiveness of two different educational intervention methods – namely, the large group seminar and small group face-to-face discussion in the treatment of acute diarrhoea in children (Santoso et al. 1996). The proposal was developed before I joined the team. Thus it had been decided by the team leader that my initial task would be to write the FGD guides and lead the collection and analysis of qualitative data on beliefs and perceptions related to the treatment of acute diarrhoea in children. Although all team members were present during the data collection, my psychology colleagues and I took responsibility for conducting 18 FGDs with mothers, paramedics and medical doctors in six health districts. Data from the FGDs were used to develop intervention materials. This differentiation of tasks and separation of responsibility at the start of the project betrayed a multidisciplinary team approach in which each team member worked consecutively or concurrently from a specific disciplinary perspective to address a common problem (Rosenfield 1992). In designing and implementing the intervention, the research team addressed the problem from an interdisciplinary framework. The intervention strategies employed large group seminars conducted in a lecture format and face-to-face discussions. The initial intervention strategy, a single face-to-face intervention, was modified to accommodate my suggestion that small group discussions would be more efficient because they would allow the team to cover each health centre in a single visit. Together, the team planned how two supervisors from two district health offices would carry out the small group discussions. The team then trained the two supervisors, who became the group facilitators and assessed and revised the training format. It was at this point that the team began to function in a transdisciplinary manner. Team members moved from working jointly but from a disciplinary-specific basis to working jointly using a shared conceptual framework that drew together disciplinary-specific theories, concepts and approaches to address the problem (Rosenfield 1992: 1351). This movement accords with what Albrecht et al. (1998: 60) describe in the second approach to developing a transdisciplinary research team: 'Disciplinary boundaries are blurred as researchers work cooperatively to bring together into some unified framework the diverse elements of a total explanation, including the objective and subjective, the reductionistic and holistic and so on … Under a shared conceptual framework, discipline boundaries disappear altogether or are "transcended" and a new or "transdisciplinary" way of explaining a problem is created.'

A Transdisciplinary Approach to Changing Prescriber Behaviour

The second project undertaken by the group was conducted entirely within a transdisciplinary framework (Prawitasari Hadiyono et al. 1996). The team expanded to include two new physician team members – one from the university and the other the medical officer (MO) in the District Health Office (DHO). The idea I presented during the inauguration of INRUD in 1990 was formally followed up in 1992 in this study aimed at reducing the over-use of injections in public health facilities. Although most health research projects are led by a health scientist, I became the principal investigator and received the full support of the health scientists on the team as well as health scientists in the District Health Administration (DHA) office. The project was first offered to a district health office in Central Java, where the injection rate with no specific diagnosis was high. (The delivery of the injection itself was seen by both patients and providers – who are mostly paramedics – as a cure for the patients' complaints. Patients were injected with vitamins.) When it failed to generate enthusiasm from the MO there, the study was offered to Gunungkidul District, where the injection rate was also high. The team worked in a highly interactive way, sharing the tasks of writing the proposal, developing the intervention procedure, collecting and analysing the data and writing the manuscript for publication. During the writing period, the INRUD support groups in Boston, Geneva and Newcastle actively reviewed and provided valuable input on the manuscript.

Santoso (1995b) observes that, 'overuse of injections often stems from misconceptions of their value and efficacy by both the prescriber and the patient'. To pilot-test their effectiveness in modifying patient and prescriber behaviour with respect to injection drug use, IGDs were conducted with prescribers from Yogyakarta and volunteer patients. IGD participants were medical doctors, paramedics and patients, who were mostly mothers. Their composition, in which membership is heterogeneous, differentiates them from FGDs, in which membership is homogenous. The objective of FGDs is obtaining information, whereas that of IGDs is imparting information. Two trial IGDs were conducted at the Faculty of Psychology, GMU. The first IGD trial experienced some difficulties. The facilitators were perceived as attacking the personal practice of participants with respect to injection use. The prescribers, in particular, became defensive. Ideally the discussion has to be pleasant so that no one in the group loses face. The IGD was, however, informative for the patients who gained knowledge of the circumstances in which injections are necessary, such as emergency care or the treatment of major infection. The first trial provided an opportunity for the team to work together in revising the discussion procedure. The strategy was changed in the second IGD trial to diffuse the defensiveness of the medical doctors and encourage them to participate in teaching the paramedics and patients about the proper use of injections.

In the main study, IGDs proved effective in reducing the use of injections. The hypothesized mechanism of behaviour change involved reality testing assumptions about patient beliefs, imparting scientific information about efficacy of injections, and establishing peer norms around correct injection use behaviour (Prawitasari Hadiyono et al. 1996). Six prescribers and six patients (mostly mothers and a small number of fathers) participated in each IGD. Prescribers were physician managers of health centres, paramedics and other medical doctors. A psychologist and a clinician/pharmacologist facilitated the discussions that took place in a restaurant in Wonosari, Gunungkidul (see Prawitasari Hadiyono et al. 1996 for details). Findings from previous unpublished FGD research identified gaps between prescribers' and consumers' perceptions regarding the use of injections in health centres. Prescribers claimed that it was patients who asked for injections. In contrast, patients said that it was the prescribers who recommended giving injections. To test the reality of the situation, at the beginning of the discussion the facilitators asked how many of the patients either preferred receiving injections or requested them. This information then became the focus of discussion. Group members were also guided to discuss the proper use of injections and the possible risks of misuse. At the end of the IGDs prescribers agreed to reduce the misuse of injections and patients agreed to inform their family and neighbours about their experience in the group and not to ask for injections unnecessarily. This agreement supported the development of peer norms about correct use of injections.

To assess the effectiveness of IGDs, prescribing surveys were conducted in 24 health centres in the study area three months before and three months after the IGDs. These health centres were randomly assigned to intervention and control groups. Prescribers from twelve health centres participated in IGDs and those from the other twelve health centres served as control groups. Twelve prescribers in each health centre recruited twelve patients. The patients were exchanged between IGD groups so that the prescribers would not be in the same group as their patients. The prescribing survey was done retrospectively at the end of the observation period by using health centre records. Each prescribing survey, at minimum, consisted of the last 100 cases of the month from each health centre.

Figure 4.1 shows a significant decrease in the use of injections in the intervention groups compared with the control groups. Following the IGDs, there was a rapid and stable reduction in the use of injections from

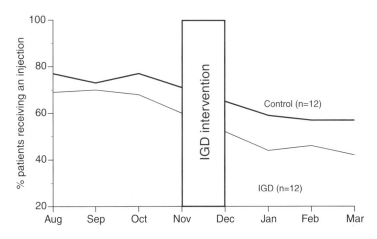

FIGURE 4.1 Use of injection before and after IGDs

the pre-intervention rate of 69.5 per cent to an average of 42.3 per cent during the post-intervention period in the intervention groups. Injection use also declined from 75.6 per cent at baseline to 67.1 per cent at follow-up in the control groups, but the reduction was statistically greater in the intervention groups (Prawitasari Hadiyono et al. 1996). These data were presented to all health centre staff during the feedback seminar in April 1993 in the Gunungkidul District Health Office.

The collaboration with the MO of the Gunungkidul District Health Office continued into a third project to address locally the global INRUD priority concerns of polypharmacy and the over-use of antibiotics and injections. Two members of the INRUD country core group joined the project team. Both are medical doctors. One works with a non-governmental institution and the other at the Department of Health.[4]

Two goals were jointly addressed: the development of self-monitoring procedures for rational drug use (Bimo et al. 1994) and testing the applied field methods manual developed by INRUD social scientists for use in drug utilization studies (Arhinful et al. n.d.). In mid-1993, the INRUD team trained the Gunungkidul district health administrators (DHAs) in developing their own instruments to self-monitor drug prescribing. The training included an initial workshop in the DHA office to orient staff to the urgency of the problem and to quantitative drug use indicators (WHO/DAP 1993) as well as selected applied field methods, such as focus group discussions, in-depth interviews, structured observation and questionnaires. The workshop participants also agreed to conduct a prescribing survey to assess drug use in the health centres. Data were obtained on the use of antibiotics, injections and polypharmacy and the underlying factors identified through applied field methods.

A core DHA team comprised of DHA personnel and a medical doctor from a health centre and another from the district hospital was divided into two groups. One group was trained in developing quantitative drug use indicators (WHO/DAP 1993), while the other was trained in developing instruments based on applied field methods. The core group then trained appointed prescribers at each health centre to use the instruments.

The resulting self-monitoring procedures included: (1) a monthly random survey of 30 cases at each health centre and 30 cases at each of the sub-health centres to measure the use of antibiotics, injections and polypharmacy; (2) monthly observation of clinical encounters between paramedics and patients by the health centre manager; (3) monthly interviews with paramedics and patients done by the health centre's own team; (4) monthly discussion with all health centre staff about appropriate solutions to the problems found; and (5) monthly meetings of health centre managers at the DHA to discuss the centres' self-monitoring results.

In August 1993, four health centres were selected in which the instruments were piloted. Managers of those four health centres and appointed paramedics in each of the facilities were trained to administer the procedures by the district core team. Prawitasari Hadiyono and Suryawati's (1994) follow-up study indicated that within three months of adopting the procedures, there was a significant improvement in drug prescribing as reflected in the reduction of polypharmacy (3.5±0.2 to 2.9±0.1; p<.05), antimicrobial use (45.8 %±9.2 to 28.4 %±2.3; p<.05), and injection (35.8 %±20.9 to 17.4 %±9.7; p<.05). These encouraging results led the DHA to implement the self-monitoring procedures in all 29 health centres in the district, as reported by Sunartono and Darminto (Santoso 1995c).

Interviews with the district medical health officer, district core team members, managers and prescribers involved in the pilot study revealed that, overall, they were pleased with the procedures. They reported that the procedures helped them substantially in managing the use of drugs in their facilities. Questionnaires used to obtain underlying information regarding the use of antibiotics, injections and polypharmacy, however, were found to be less useful than in-depth interviews in terms of the richness of the information they yielded. Additionally, it was found that monthly discussions at the DHA created peer pressure to conform to the targets set by the health centres themselves. Reports must be made prior to this DHA monthly meeting. To avoid embarrassment during the meeting, each health centre strove to meet its monthly targets in compliance with the monitoring procedures, as reported by Sunartono and Darminto (Santoso 1995c, 1995d).

The self-monitoring procedures were subsequently adopted by the Department of Health of the Republic of Indonesia in developing manage-ment guidelines for rational medication use in health (Tjondrowardojo et al. 1996). Discussion, interview and observation methods were included in the monitoring procedures, along with drug use indicators. Clearly, the third project was successful in developing procedures for improving pre-scribing in the national health delivery system.

In 1994, INRUD core group members began a fourth study in collabora-tion with Dennis Ross-Degnan, one of the support group members from Harvard University, to examine drug utilization rates in health centres following the initial intervention in 1992 and the implementation of the self-monitoring procedures in 1993 and 1994.[5] Results of a time series analysis indicated that the use of injections in general, with no specific type of treatment, was substantially reduced from 72 per cent to 16 per cent in health centres that were involved with the IGD, and from 68 per cent to 21 per cent in the health centres initially acting as control groups. There was less of a reduction in the use of antibiotics, but the trend was one of

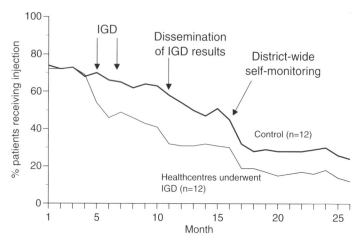

FIGURE 4.2 Time series data on injection use, Gunungkidul District, 1995

decreasing usage. Number of drugs prescribed tended to decrease as well. The time series analysis shows that behavioural interventions (IGD and self-monitoring) have had a substantial impact in improving appropriate prescribing in health centres in Gunungkidul DHA, especially with respect to the use of injections. It is concluded that behavioural interventions combined with managerial interventions are effective in reducing the over-use of injections and improving overall prescribing. Figure 4.2 shows the time series analysis with respect to injection use following behavioural and managerial interventions.

It indicates a decrease in injectable drug use both in the IGDs as well as control groups after the IGD feedback seminar in April 1993. Although both experimental and control groups tended to reduce the use of injections to a minimal level, the experimental groups did so more than the control groups. From this it can be concluded that the dissemination seminar also had a significant effect on injection prescribing in all health centres. While it is not possible to separate the impact of the IGDs from that of the subsequent implementation of the self-monitoring procedures, the existing literature in behavioural sciences offers clues about how each of the strategies might have induced changes in prescribing behaviour.

Influencing Changes in Prescribing Practices

Studies in social psychology indicate that group membership can result in behaviour change by individuals who tend to comply with group norms and peer pressure (Mackie et al. 1990). In addition, cooperation, consensus and conformity are promoted (Orbell et al. 1988; Wright et al. 1990; Jetten et al. 1996). Group membership has important meaning for Indonesians. As a broad cultural generalization, Indonesians believe in harmony. They are described as having a relatively passive attitude towards life, emphasizing quiet security, self-control, conformity and group-oriented behaviour (Hadiyono and Kahn 1985). Joining the IGDs sets up norms to be agreed upon and followed. At the end of each IGD, participants together usually proclaimed their commitment to reducing injection use in their facilities. Patients also committed to share their experience in the group and teach their neighbours about the unnecessary use of injections. This might be why members of health centres involved in the IGDs reduced their use of injections more than did the control groups.

Group norms and peer pressure were likely to have also contributed to the success of the IGD feedback seminar in bringing about change in prescribing behaviour. This seminar was conducted in a semi-formal way at the DHA office. In the first half, data on injection drug use in individual health centres were presented, while the second half was used for open discussion. Suryawati began her presentation by covering the names of the health centres with the highest rates of injection. The audience asked her to remove the cover, which she did with the permission of those assembled. Everyone was able to see which health centres had the highest rate of injection drug use. Audience members started to mock one another. Javanese culture permits the use of humour as a means of modifying behaviour. The rule is that each party accepts the mocking as humour; offence should not be given or taken. Control group members jokingly complained about the fact that they were not invited to the restaurant where the IGDs were held. Food and togetherness for Javanese are very important. Such a group atmosphere is a vehicle for persuading people to follow certain norms.

The impact of self-monitoring on prescribing behaviour may lie in its strength as a technique for modifying self-control. Behaviour modification theory operationalizes behavioural problems as behavioural deficits (the low occurrence of an appropriate behaviour) and/or behavioural excesses (the occurrence of behaviour is too high) (Martin and Pear 1992). Polypharmacy and the over-use of antibiotics and injections can be viewed as behavioural excesses that can be modified by systematically observing one's own behaviour (Kazdin 1994).

Systematic self-observation was employed in the Gunungkidul self-monitoring procedures. First, each month health centres completed observation forms that allowed staff to compare drug use from month to month. The form was also sent to the DHA for review. To ensure that the procedure is carried out, there is a weekly staff meeting of the district core team, to discuss the results of each health centre's monitoring. Second, a monthly DHA level meeting for health centre managers is held to report on and discuss monitoring results. Third, random feedback and supervisory visits are made to health centres by the district core team, as reported by Sunartono and Darminto (Santoso 1995c).

From a transdisciplinary perspective, the success of the interventions in addressing rational drug use in health centres may be largely due to the active participation and broad collaboration of the team members. The academicians provide technical assistance in developing the feedback system and supporting follow-up by sending visitors to observe the health delivery system in Gunungkidul district. The district managers have integrated research methods into their managerial feedback procedures. Managers in health centres facilitate discussions in their own facilities regarding problems arising each month. These monthly discussions allow problems to be addressed as soon as they arise. Sunartono et al. (1997) advise that feedback from the DHA is to be continuously conducted each month to preserve the changes in drug use in the health centres. The resulting transdisciplinary approach parallels the approach described by Albrecht et al. (1998), where all members of the team were actively involved in developing community-based heart disease prevention initiatives.

Impacts of the IGD, Feedback Seminar and Self-monitoring

Interventions may produce intended as well as unintended impacts and cause harm in addition to benefits. Positive impacts of the interventions in Gunungkidul include several changes in health centre clinical practice. The prescribers began to use treatment guidelines more frequently in caring for the patients. Making simplified guidelines available in each of the health centres may support more accurate diagnosis and lead to appropriate drug prescribing. Greater rationality in the use and supply of drugs in each health facility can lead to cost savings.

Prescribers indicated during the IGDs that they feared losing patients if they did not meet patient demands for injection. Their fears proved to be unfounded. Patient attendance at health centres did not decline. In fact, it remained the same in all health centres. In a FGD follow-up study with prescribers in April 1995, some sub-health centres reported that they lost patients after reducing their use of injections. However, they could not provide exact numbers of patients to support their claim.

Another unanticipated, yet positive, impact was an apparent increase in community health education. Consultation time increased from two minutes to five minutes. Providers began to explain how to use the drugs given, the side-effects, and also the nutritional factors that should be considered by the patient. Suryawati and I observed this during follow-up observations and interviews in April and May of 1994 with providers in four health centres involved in the IGD as well as the self-monitoring procedures.[6] We learned in an interview with the medical officer of the district health office that he intended to implement the self-monitoring procedures in all health centres in Gunungkidul district so that his successors might follow it. Although he moved to another district 1995, the system is still in place.

The continued use of the system is also supported by the fact that GMU Centre for Clinical Pharmacology and Drug Policy Studies has served as a WHO collaborating centre since 1995. Guests from India, Myanmar, Nepal, Vietnam and elsewhere have visited the district to learn how the system operates. These visits helped to reinforce the system's merits among district health personnel.

The medical doctors who participated in the follow-up FGDs in April 1995 stated that they had never heard of IGD. When asked about prescribing injections, they said that patients did not ask for specific treatment or injections. We can hypothesize that after the IGDs, patients' awareness improved regarding injection use. The mothers, many of whom were community health cadres, may also have educated community members regarding the unnecessary use of injections. This hypothesis, however, needs to be proved in a further study.

Despite the positive impacts, several unanticipated negative impacts were noted. During the follow-up FGDs in April 1995, paramedics involved in the self-monitoring procedures complained that they had to travel to collect data and take lengthy notes in each health centre. They felt that the process was time-consuming and burdensome with no adequate incentive. The paramedics also commented that more patients now go to other health centres and private practices to obtain injections. Some revealed that paramedics have begun buying their own syringes in order to satisfy patients demanding injections through their private practice. These reports demonstrate an alarming incongruency in the paramedics' health centre and private practice behaviour. The extent to which this practice occurs needs further investigation.

As Figure 4.3 demonstrates, each of the studies to date has led to a follow-up investigation, providing new leverage for subsequent work. Quantitative and qualitative research methods are used in fact-finding as well as impact assessment. Innovations in intervention strategies are tested in each study, providing another leverage point for developing a new procedure. All transdisciplinary team members are active in each study and work together to implement and support the findings in their own capacity.

GMU Rational Use of Drugs TD Team: clinical pharmacologists, behavioural
scientists, district health managers, health centre managers, medical doctors,
paramedics, patients

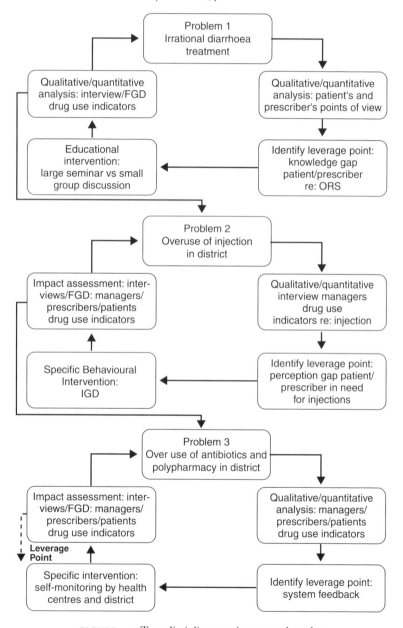

FIGURE 4.3 Transdisciplinary action research cycles

Future Directions

Many tasks lie ahead for our transdisciplinary research team. One is to refine our intervention design and share it with other researchers. We have presented our studies at international conferences, and participants have asked for advice in replicating our study design. We have supported fully such requests by providing necessary assistance, including a request from a Vietnamese group who have replicated the self-monitoring procedures in their health system.

Currently, Suryawati, two other junior team members and myself are developing community education intervention materials to reduce injection use in primary health care facilities. These materials are designed to complement the health education conducted by the health centre staff themselves. In this study, funded by the Ministry of Health, one of the intervention methods pilot-tested is a behavioural strategy using surrogate patients to monitor the use of injections in health centres and present their findings, with the assistance of the manager, to prescribers. This method, called IGD Plus, however, proved too costly and was feared to influence the morbidity pattern if used widely. We decided instead to implement a combined method consisting of brief lecture, IGD and posters, and this was found to be as effective as IGD Plus (Suryawati 1998).

Indonesian early-career researchers in drug use studies have also emerged. They have developed intervention strategies to improve the quality of medications for children used both in hospitals and health centres. Two pre-proposals by senior students at GMU Medical School and a graduate student in the GMU Management and Drug Policy Studies graduate programme were among the best ten, and one was among the best 18 submitted. This competition was held during a joint workshop on drug use intervention proposal development hosted by INRUD Indonesia, the WHO Collaborating Centre for Research and Training on Rational Drug Use and Gadjah Mada University and sponsored by the Applied Research on Child Health (ARCH), the WHO Action Programme on Essential Drugs (WHO/DAP), the Rational Pharmaceutical Management (RPM) Project and INRUD (*INRUD News* 1998; Suryawati 1998). Unfortunately there was no young social scientist interested in submitting a pre-proposal.

In conclusion, the transdisciplinary research team will continue to develop new intervention strategies to improve the use of medicine in Indonesia. Leverage points for engendering change indicated in previous studies will be followed up in subsequent intervention research. Early-career researchers will join the team to sustain existing efforts in improving the use of medicines in the community.

Acknowledgements

I am grateful for financial support from APNET and IFSSH to attend the Social Science and Medicine International Conference in Scotland in September 1996 at which a preliminary version of this chapter was presented. Special thanks are due to Dr Nick Higginbotham, who gave encouragement, intellectual support and insight in writing the paper. Thank you as well to Ms Nancy Johnson for editing the previous draft. Last but not least, my great thanks are due to Dr Budiono Santoso, Dr Sri Suryawati and Dr Dennis Ross-Degnan, who frequently stimulate my thought and creativity to contribute fully to the field of rational use of drugs.

Notes

1. Country core group members are assisted by support groups comprising individuals from MSH (USA); Drug Policy Group, Harvard Medical School (USA); Department of International Health Care Research and Social Medicine, Karolinska Institutet (Sweden); Department of Clinical Pharmacology, Faculty of Medicine, University of Newcastle (Australia); and Action Programme on Essential Drugs and Control of Diarrheal and Respiratory Diseases Programme, World Health Organization, Geneva (Switzerland) (*INRUD News* 1991b). The network is coordinated by MSH and receives financial support from WHO/DAP, Pew Charitable Trusts and DANIDA (Laing 1992).

2. This study was funded by the Applied Diarrheal Disease Research (ADDR) Project of the Harvard Institute for International Development through a Cooperative Agreement with the United States Agency for International Development.

3. Financial support for this study came from the Action Programme on Essential Drugs, World Health Organization through INRUD.

4. This project arose out of the third workshop of INRUD in Badagry, Lagos, Nigeria in 1992. INRUD committed to fund this project fully.

5. This project, entitled *The Use of Time Series Analysis to Evaluate Strategies to Improve Rational Use of Drugs*, was funded by Harvard University and the USAID Applied Diarrheal Disease Research (ADDR) programme.

6. A small amount of funding was received from the Asia Pacific Network (APNET) of the International Forum for Social Sciences in Health (IFSSH) to conduct this study.

References

Albrecht, G., S. Freeman and N. Higginbotham (1998) 'Complexity and human health: the case for a transdisciplinary paradigm', *Culture, Medicine, and Psychiatry* 22: 55–92.

Arhinful, D. K., A. Das, J. E. Prawitasari Hadiyono, K. Heggenhougen et al. (n.d.) 'Applied field methods for use in drug utilization studies', paper submitted to WHO/DAP for publication.

Bimo, S., B. Santoso, S. Suryawati, J. E. Prawitasari Hadiyono and D. Sunartono (1994) 'Development of self-monitoring for drug use in health facilities: a pilot study', *INRUD News* 4: 21.

INRUD News (1991a) 'What is INRUD?', *INRUD News*, 2 December, 2: 20.

— (1991b) 'Support group', *INRUD News*, 2 December, 2: 1.

— (1996) 'INRUD update', *INRUD News*, 6 February, 1: 1.

— (1998) 'INRUD update', *INRUD News*, 8 February, 1: 1.

Jetten, J., R. Spears and A. S. R. Manstead (1996) 'Intergroup norms and intergroup discrimination: distinctive self-categorization and social identity effects', *Journal of Personality and Social Psychology* 71(6): 1222–33.

Kazdin, A. (1994) *Behaviour Modification in Applied Setting* (5th edn), Pacific Grove, CA: Brooks/Cole.

Laing, R. (1992) 'Report on third INRUD meeting held at Administrative Staff College of Nigeria (ASCON) Badagry, Lagos State, Nigeria, 11–24 October', unpublished paper.

Mackie, D. M., L. T. Worth, A. G. Asuncion (1990) 'Processing of persuasive in-group messages', *Journal of Personality and Social Psychology* 58(5): 812–22.

Martin, G. and J. Pear (1992) *Behaviour Modification: What is it and how to do it*, Englewood Cliffs, NJ: Prentice Hall.

Ministry of Health, Republic of Indonesia, Yayasan Indonesia Sejahtera and Management Sciences for Health (1988) *Child Survival Pharmaceuticals in Indonesia Part II: Where Does the Tetracycline Go?*, Jakarta: Ministry of Health of Indonesia.

Orbell, J. M., A. J. C. van de Kragt and R. M. Dawes (1988) 'Explaining discussion-induced cooperation', *Journal of Personality and Social Psychology* 54(5): 811–19.

Prawitasari Hadiyono, J. E. and M. W. Kahn (1985) 'Personality differences and sex similarities in American and Indonesian college students', *Journal of Social Psychology* 125(6): 703–8.

Prawitasari Hadiyono, J. E. and S. Suryawati (1994) *Transferring Qualitative Methods to Self-monitoring Procedure in Health Centres*, Second Asia Pacific Social Science and Medicine Conference, May, Quezon City, The Philippines.

Prawitasari Hadiyono, J. E., S. Suryawati, S. S. Danu et al. (1996) 'Interactional group discussion: results of a controlled trial using a behavioural intervention to reduce the use of injections in public health facilities', *Social Science and Medicine* 42(8): 1177–83.

Rosenfield, P. (1992) 'The potential of transdisciplinary research for sustaining and extending linkages between the health and social sciences', *Social Science and Medicine* 35(11): 1342–57.

Ross-Degnan, D., R. Laing, J. Quick et al. (1992) 'A strategy for promoting improved pharmaceutical use: the International Network for Rational Use of Drugs', *Social Science and Medicine* A35(11): 1329–41.

Santoso, B. (1995a) 'Hospital pharmacy and therapeutic committees in Southeast Asia: role and functions', *Medical Progress*, November: 5–10.

— (1995b) 'Misuse of injections: a serious threat to health care in developing countries', *Medical Progress*, April: 5–10.

— (1995c) 'From research to action: the Gunungkidul experience', *Essential Drugs Monitor* 20: 21–2.

— (1995d) 'From the Indonesia Core Group', *INRUD News* 5(1): 12.

— (1997) 'Problems with drug use and the impact on health care in Southeast Asia', *JAMA SEA*, March: 5–6.

Santoso, B., S. Suryawati and J. E. Prawitasari Hadiyono (1996) 'Small group intervention vs. formal seminar for improving appropriate drug use', *Social Science and Medicine* 42(8): 1163–8.

Sunartono, D., S. Suryawati, J. E. Prawitasari Hadiyono et al. (1997) 'Impact evaluation of self-monitoring of drug use indicators in health facilities: experiences from

Gunungkidul, Indonesia', programme and abstract, International Conference on Improving Use of Medicine (ICIUM), April, Chiang Mai, Thailand.

Suryawati, S. (1997) 'Transdisciplinary action research to improve the rational use of drugs', unpublished paper presented at Yogyakarta College of Education 33th Dies Natalis, 20 May.

— (1998) 'Indonesia Core Group', *INRUD News* 8(2): 15–16.

Tjondrowardojo, A., D. Indrasanto, F. Karim et al. (1996) *Management Guide Efforts to Rational Medication in Health Centres (Pedoman pembinaan upaya pengobatan rasional di puskesmas)*, Jakarta: Republic of Indonesia Department of Health.

WHO (1993) *How to Investigate Drug Use in Health Facilities: Selected Drug Use Indicators*, WHO/DAP/93.1 Geneva: World Health Organization.

Wright, E. F., C. A. E. Lüüs and S. D. Christie (1990) 'Does group discussion facilitate the use of consensus information in making causal attribution?', *Journal of Personality and Social Psychology* 59: 261–9.

5

A Community Approach to Smoking Cessation and Relapse Prevention in a Traditional Fijian Village

Gary Groth-Marnat, Simon Leslie, Mark Renneker,
Sunia Vuniyayawa and Maerewai Molileuu

In his book *The Fatal Impact*, Alan Moorehead (1968) described the introduction of infectious diseases to the South Pacific by Europeans. The phrase 'the second fatal impact' has more recently been coined to refer to the 'introduction' of non-communicable diseases linked to modern lifestyles (Marshall 1991). These include cardiovascular ailments, hypertension, diabetes, cancer, gout, emphysema and bronchitis. Most of these are either primarily caused, or significantly exacerbated, by behavioural factors such as diet, stress, social support, obesity, lack of physical exercise, alcohol consumption, exposure to toxic substances, and smoking. As in Western industrialized countries, the single most preventable cause of premature death is smoking. This issue is particularly urgent in a country such as Fiji, which has seen significant increases in the proportion of smokers over the past 20 years.

The fact that South Pacific countries, including Fiji, have a much higher proportion of smokers than developed countries (although the average number of cigarettes smoked per person per day is lower; see Marshall 1991) is the result of tobacco companies capitalizing on a combination of 'optimal' socio-cultural, economic and political conditions. This has culminated in Fiji being rated among the top three countries for smoking prevalence (WHO 1996). The factors that have led to the current high prevalence of smoking in Fiji include a prior (20 years ago) low rate of smoking, few anti-smoking organizations, little awareness regarding the health consequences of smoking, few restrictions on tobacco imports, a desire on the part of many individuals to appear 'Western', aggressive marketing on the part of tobacco companies, and a collective-oriented society in which accepted behaviours by some individuals are quite likely to be taken up by other members. Tobacco companies, for example, have sponsored village sporting events or raffles that could be entered by saving up empty cigarette packets. One such marketing promotion involved participants exchanging 15 empty packets in return for a T-shirt with the tobacco company's name emblazoned on the front (Marshall 1991). Another strategy employed by tobacco representatives is to distribute cartons of free cigarettes in a village and later arrange to sell the brand at nearby stores. Indeed, American tobacco companies have the power to request that the US government enact enforceable trade sanctions against those countries that refuse to import tobacco products (Barry 1991). Such threats have been used successfully to open markets in Japan, Taiwan and South Korea.

This combination of circumstances has led to sometimes dramatic increases in smoking in South Pacific countries. Smoking in Papua New Guinea, for example, increased by 500 per cent from 1960 to 1980 and Western Samoa saw cigarette imports increase from twelve million in 1965 to 100 million in 1978 (Stebbins 1990; Warner 1987). Adverse health effects related to smoking have increased concomitantly. As far back as 1983, lung cancer was found to be the leading cause of cancer among men in most Pacific populations (Chapman and Leng 1990). Data from 1985 indicate that Maori women, of whom 60 per cent smoke (Chapman and Leng 1990), had the world's highest rate of mortality from lung cancer and coronary heart disease (Hay and Foster 1981; Kent 1985). Research specific to Fiji has connected smoking rates to lung disease (Beecher et al. 1995), mortality from heart disease (Collins et al. 1996), and an increase in respiratory symptoms in children from homes where adults smoked (Flyn 1994).

It is predicted that over the next 10–20 years, negative health consequences of tobacco use will reach epidemic proportions (Marshall 1991; Stebbins 1990; Wigley 1974). Unfortunately, there is often little awareness of the health complications of smoking, which is, in part, due to the few requirements on tobacco companies to include health warnings. For example, at one point in the village we worked with in Fiji, the villagers believed that while native cigarettes could cause poor health, smoking Western imported cigarettes was safe. It is thus crucial to develop compelling, culturally appropriate interventions to reduce smoking rates. In Papua New Guinea, restrictions on smoking in public areas have been recommended, as have intensive education of children, labels on cigarette packets warning of health risks, tight controls on nicotine content, the creation of anti-smoking campaigns, and bans on cigarette advertising and vending machines (Wigley 1974). Similarly, Fijian officials have prohibited smoking in public hospitals and placed limits on cigarette advertising (Kent 1985). While such public health legislation is an effective means of combating large-scale tobacco consumption, it is also important to initiate or facilitate small-scale community-based efforts as well as more fully understand the unique cultural conditions that lead to smoking initiation, maintenance, cessation and relapse. Often, these factors are different from those in developed countries where anti-smoking campaigns have already been established. In the remainder of the chapter, we describe the unique process by which a village in Fiji developed and implemented a highly successful community-based smoking cessation intervention.

Fijian Cultural Values and Health Beliefs

Like other South Pacific countries, Fiji has seen considerable increases in smoking over the past two to three decades. It has minimal import restrictions and few anti-smoking organizations, and the population has had relatively little education regarding the health risks of smoking. In addition, tobacco is an important cash crop accounting for 2.2 per cent of arable land use (Chapman and Leng 1990). Since the typical Fijian villager earns an average of US$2.00 a day, the immediate financial consequences of smoking to the individual and the village are likely to be particularly high. Long-term economic and health consequences can also be anticipated. Villagers may face deteriorating health with either no or minimal medical support.

Fiji has a total population of 600,000, of whom 44 per cent are ethnic Fijians (Melanesians), and 50 per cent Indo Fijians (descendants of indentured servants from India). Two per cent claim dual descent from a parent of European ancestry and a parent of Fijian ancestry. One per cent are Chinese and another one per cent claim European ancestry (largely Australian and New Zealand), while the remaining 2 per cent are mixed. Ethnic Fijians live in relatively cohesive, communally oriented villages. Core values include respect for authority of family and village elders, togetherness and sharing of resources (Ravuvu 1983). The development of a strong sense of community is emphasized more than the development of the individual. This is highlighted by the fact that the villagers with whom our team of visiting health practitioners worked determined early on in our association with them that their highest-priority health need was a community centre. The 'ideal' Fijian is a person who has respect for customs, traditions and other people; who is generous, kind-hearted and good-natured; and who encourages group solidarity (Defrain et al. 1994; Ravuvu 1983). Conflicts are usually mediated through the larger community and may even take the form of ritualized requests for harmony and forgiveness (Hickson 1986).

Fijian beliefs about health, disease and death combine supernatural, interpersonal and biomedical explanations. For example, a Fijian who is physically ill might attribute his or her illness to a rift with another community member, breaking a taboo, disturbing a sacred force, or physiological malfunctioning. Thus Fijian health beliefs are multi-layered and relate to the overall sense of harmony and well-being in the community. Any individual or group attempting to enhance village health must take into account the Fijian need to balance the supernatural forces related to illness or establish harmonious relations within the community. For example, anti-smoking public health messages are likely to be more effective if they emphasize the negative impact cigarettes are likely to have on the community rather than merely warning individuals of the risks to themselves.

One community ritual which has particular significance for ethnic Fijians is drinking kava (*yaqona*). Kava is a mild relaxant, euphoriant and hallucinogen derived from the powdered root of *Piper methysticum* (Ruze 1990). A deep respect is given to kava ceremonies and taboos (sanctions) are sometimes developed during these ceremonies to facilitate change within a community. Taboos are important to ethnic Fijians in that there is usually the accompanying belief that breaking a taboo will result in ill-health or injury.

Developing a Relationship with the Community

In 1986, a group of 20 health practitioners (Surfers' Medical Association), primarily from the USA and Australia, first came into contact with the village of Nabila because of its proximity to a nearby resort. Visits to the village have occurred annually between 1986 and 1997 (except 1994). These visits were in conjunction with a conference on sports (surfing) medicine and gradually incorporated working with the village as part of the conference programme. Initiated by villagers' requests for help with medical problems, a relationship evolved between the health care practitioners and villagers through repeated contact. Each year, between 20 and 25 members of the conference spent two weeks at the resort and four days in the village itself. A wide number of disciplines were represented including medical practitioners (family practice medicine, pediatrics, emergency medicine), dentists, physiotherapists, psychologists, nurses and primary and secondary schoolteachers.

Initially, medical interventions were directed at caring for acute medical problems. It soon became apparent, however, that such 'crisis-based' approaches were likely to have little long-term impact given our relatively brief visits. As a result, we began emphasizing more health education and promotion efforts directed at encouraging community members to become more knowledgeable and active in caring for their own health (Groth-Marnat 1991). These efforts were guided by the philosophy and content of David Werner's book *Where There is No Doctor: A Village Healthcare Handbook* (Werner 1977). Each year we left 10 to 15 copies of the book in the village. Specific achievements have been the establishment of a self-maintaining dispensary, facilitating a semi-autonomous village health committee that makes health-related decisions, education of a village nurse, first aid classes, water catchment for drinking, dental education, and a scabies reduction project.

A key element of our approach was to become knowledgeable about, and sensitive to, village culture and traditions. This involved a particular focus on village members' conceptions of illness. Each member of the medical team read Ravuvu's (1983) book *Vaka i Taukei: The Fijian Way of Life*. Talks on Fijian culture and language were incorporated into the conference and descriptions of past projects and experiences were provided through a journal/newsletter. Of particular importance were briefings by one or a combination of the first three authors (M.R., S.L., G.G.-M. as well as previous coordinators of the health project: Kevin Starr, David McWaters and Bill Jones) to the medical team on appropriate village behaviour and interviewing techniques. After each day spent in the village, members of the medical team would discuss aspects of village behaviour and attitudes, along with what they had learned about themselves as a result of interactions in the village. Examples of culture accommodation by the team included using an appropriate spokesperson to communicate health-related information, partaking in kava ceremonies, and soliciting suggestions from the village health committee about needed services. We shared our concerns related to tobacco's health-damaging effects with the villagers, discussed possible strategies to reduce smoking, and communicated information about the interaction between smoking and diseases such as asthma, diabetes and heart disease. In short, collaboration with village members was highly valued.

Nabila Develops its Own Smoking Cessation Programme

Of 238 village members, 147 were over the age of 16. In 1990, when the smoking cessation intervention was initiated, 31 per cent of the village smoked, with approximately 41 per cent of all adult males being smokers. It is estimated that the above percentages represented nearly a twofold increase over a period of five years. While this was apparently the result of increased advertising by tobacco companies, it is speculated that, in a communally oriented culture (Triandis 1995) such as Nabila, new behaviours would be likely to spread more rapidly than in more individualistic societies. This is consistent with observations that most resources were shared among members of the group. Cigarettes were purchased either in nearby larger villages or in the main city of Nadi located two hours to the north. Cigarette availability did not change during or after the intervention. The smoking-related health and economic impact on Nabila was thought to be considerable for several reasons. Since the average income of community members was between US$2.00 and US$4.00 a day, cigarettes can reduce an individual's disposable income by up to 25 per cent. At the same time, community members frequently stated that one of the major reasons for not seeking medical assistance was that they could not afford it. A village health survey conducted in 1992 and based on both physician assessments and villager self-reports found that common chronic difficulties included asthma, hypertension, diabetes, and vascular and degenerative diseases. The survey further indicated that hypertension had reached epidemic proportions. Each of these diseases is likely to be significantly exacerbated by smoking.

Initially, efforts to bring about a reduction in smoking focused on educating villagers about the health risks of smoking. At one point, American Cancer Society posters were placed in the dispensary. On another occasion, the village minister stopped smoking (the 'exemplar' approach). However, these efforts were clearly unsuccessful in that, between 1986 and 1990, it was estimated that the proportion of smokers nearly doubled. It was evident that the village had neither taken ownership of the problem nor developed initiatives to address it.

In 1990, the medical team members discussed a variety of intervention techniques including further education, rapid inhalation, social contracting, and a reward system for abstainers (Leslie 1992). Despite our acute awareness of both the long- and short-term health and economic impacts of smoking, we were concerned that smoking cessation was more our agenda than that of the villagers. Our reluctance to impose our values on the people of Nabila resulted in our decision not to lay out a concrete plan for smoking cessation. Instead, we shared our concerns with the village spokesperson, who then relayed these concerns to the village elders.

During the ceremony that marked our departure, the village spokesperson announced to the medical team that the entire village had decided to abstain from smoking. He further stated that the money saved from not smoking would go towards completing a partially built community centre. It was explained that the youth of the village had not only endorsed the cessation programme, but initiated it. This was surprising, as it appeared that the youth had been the sub-group most alienated by our anti-smoking efforts. We were told that shortly after our departure there would be a taboo placed on smoking.

We were both surprised and pleased by the village announcement, but also concerned that such a decision might have been overly ambitious. In particular, we were aware that, within developed countries, community-based cessation programmes have resulted in only 20–30 per cent of abstainers being successful upon six- to 12-month follow-ups (Clarke et al. 1993; COMMIT research group 1995a, 1995b; Lando et al. 1995; Lichtenstein and Glasgow 1992). Even successful abstainers typically experience difficulties and relapse several times prior to eventual success. Thus we were worried about the possible negative reaction to individuals who relapsed or the possibility that factions might develop that would undermine the authority of the village elders.

The outcome of the intervention was evaluated in several ways to ensure accuracy and consistency of the information gathered. Data collection included initial postal correspondence between the village health committee and the medical team, followed at nine and 21 months by in-depth interviews with the health committee, a review of dispensary records, and informal discussions with community members. The 21-month follow-up also involved a comprehensive health survey of every adult villager (approximately 170 participants) and included questions related to smoking. The interview was conducted by a physician in conjunction with the village nurse, who acted as a translator when necessary. As part of the interview/ survey a physician clinically assessed each village member, with particular emphasis on blood pressure measurements.

The Impact of the Intervention

Three months after departing Nabila, the medical team received a letter from Nabila indicating that the entire village had stopped smoking. The letter stated that, directly after the 1990 departure of the medical team, the villagers collected many of the cigarettes in the village and destroyed them. Those who had been smokers chain-smoked to the point of nausea. This was followed by a ceremony in which the remaining cigarettes were destroyed. In addition, the entire village signed a pledge stating that they would adhere to their agreement to stop smoking. The pledge was permanently posted on the wall of the dispensary. A kava ceremony was held on 28 July 1990 to formalize the decision, assist in reducing the desire to smoke, and create a taboo. A ritual was performed in which the 'evil' of the cigarettes was placed into the kava and thrown onto the ground. The Fijian media heard about Nabila's accomplishment, reporting it through newspaper stories and radio broadcasts. Nabila became known as 'the village that quit smoking'. This clearly served to reinforce the villagers' decision to abstain. An additional 50 people who had once lived in Nabila also stopped smoking. As a sign of solidarity, three-quarters of the youth in the nearby village of Yaku also quit.

Further correspondence indicated that, once the decision had been made, most community members did not experience difficulties in abstaining. Those who did were encouraged to suck on lollipops as a means of reducing their desire and/or participated in kava ceremonies to reinforce their commitment. It was later reported that four people did relapse, with perceived subsequent negative consequences. The first one stood up after smoking a cigarette and fell down, lacerating his scalp. The second one developed a large testicular swelling and another relapser was bitten by a dog. The fourth person lit a cigarette while drinking kava and immediately lost consciousness. These individuals publicly sought forgiveness at a kava ceremony. Afterwards, they were able to abstain without further difficulties.

Follow-up evaluation at nine (1991) and 21 months (1992) indicated that smoking was almost non-existent in the community. The exceptions were a youth temporarily living in the village but not originally from Nabila and four people over 80 who were allowed to smoke. Additional visits to Nabila in 1995 and 1996 indicated that smoking was still very low to non-existent. It has also been noted that more anti-smoking efforts throughout Fiji have begun to occur.

The intervention thus appears to have been remarkably successful, especially given the long-term maintenance of cessation reported at follow-up. One of the most important elements of this success was that the intervention was framed within the context, and drew upon the decision-making of, the entire village. The community pledge, agreement to comply by all members of the village, and a ceremony to solidify the agreement were consistent with the core Fijian values of harmoniously fitting into the group and deep respect for adhering to community guidelines. Since the village was a cohesive and self-contained community, it is less likely that external influences disrupted either these values or the decision to stop smoking. It has been hypothesized that it is exactly such community-based efforts that might be most successful in relapse prevention within other cultures and contexts (Clarke et al. 1993; COMMIT Research Group 1995a, 1995b; Lichtenstein and Glasgow 1992; Saunders and Allsop 1991).

Other key factors included the medical team's development of a long-term relationship of understanding, commitment and trust with the village. During the first four years of working with the villagers and discussing smoking-related issues, there was no one thing we said or did that triggered the decision to quit smoking. Rather, a series of discussions and deliberations occurred until some critical point was reached. This was in part because the villagers recognized that we were deeply concerned about the consequences of smoking in the community. In addition, the villagers felt a need to repay us somehow for our efforts in the village. Indeed, reciprocity is a strongly felt value in ethnic Fijian culture (Ravuvu 1983). The decision may also have been precipitated by villagers becoming disturbed about the problem through gradually seeing the link between smoking and illness. The decision also required subsequent 'ownership' of the problem and the emergence of culturally compelling measures to bring about change. The knowledge that we would be returning in subsequent years and the media coverage helped to prevent relapse, at least in part, since the villagers knew they would be accountable for the success of the intervention. Ultimately, however, it was not the visiting medical team who initiated, designed or guided the intervention. We were simply the catalyst that allowed it to occur.

What Can be Learned from the Nabila Cessation Programme?

Research on smoking cessation indicates that people who have a high expectation that they will be successful are indeed most likely to abstain (Curry et al. 1987). Cognitive variables may be even more powerful predictors than physiological factors. One of the things that characterized the Nabila intervention was the high expectation of success because of the belief in the ability of kava to create change, the respect accorded to village decisions, and the extensive social support among community members. The negative consequences that occurred when people relapsed served to reinforce further the belief in the taboo. Thus both the power of the community and consequences resulting from breaking a taboo were entirely consistent with, and served to reinforce, the Fijian multi-layered understanding of health and illness.

Research has further indicated that, within Western cultures, the major reasons for relapse are negative emotions (37 per cent of relapsers), interpersonal conflict (15 per cent), and acquiescence to social pressure (32 per cent) (Marlatt and Gordon 1985). Each of these is often associated with stressful events (Oldenberg and Pope 1990; Wewers 1988). In contrast to most Western cultures, many of the above stress-related factors were likely to be minimized in a Fijian village or at least be subjected to highly developed social mechanisms for mediating their impact. For example, anger and interpersonal conflict are mediated by the group, sometimes through a formal ceremony of forgiveness referred to as *isoro* (Hickson 1986). Furthermore, there is little sense of time urgency and a feeling that tomorrow will take care of itself (Ravuvu 1983).

A further factor to consider is that the dominant discourse in Western society about smoking and some other forms of substance abuse does not draw heavily upon notions of morality. In contrast, the more value neutral concept of 'addiction' is used. Peele (1987) argues that this is unfortunate in that the addiction (disease) model is likely to perpetuate and reinforce cognitions that are conducive to relapse ('it's the disease that has control of me'). In contrast, Nabilans sometimes referred to the desire to smoke as being tempted by 'evil' or the 'devil' in cigarettes. The kava ceremony was perceived as a means of dispelling this 'evil'. The strength of such moral judgements was thus likely to be a powerful motivator for smoking cessation and abstinence.

A number of community-based smoking cessation programmes have been developed in the USA with varying degrees of success. They have each used a variety of techniques including adult education, self-help materials, multi-media presentations, targeting specific sub-groups, and workplace interventions (Lando et al. 1995; Schofield et al. 1991). While some of these programmes have been effective, others have been somewhat disappointing. For example, the COMMIT project was found to have little or no impact on heavy smokers and produced only a slight reduction on the part of light to moderate smokers (COMMIT Research Group 1995a, 1995b). The most successful community-based programmes are those that take cultural considerations into account, provide long-term support, and rely on the community itself for decision-making (Clarke et al. 1993; Hunkeler et al. 1990; Perez-Stable et al. 1994).

While these elements were present in the Nabila project, a far higher proportion of abstainers was found. This may be largely attributable to the small size and cohesiveness of the village, along with the strong belief in the taboo initiated at the kava ceremony. Indeed, kava has a long history in Fijian society of being used to create change. Additionally, reciprocity towards the medical team, a reduction in the economic drain on the community, social contracting (media, pledge), the community rapid in-halation ceremony, a public ceremony used to forgive the relapsers, the negative consequences occurring to persons who relapsed, the use of moral judgements, the absence of a disease model, and an on-going, committed relationship between the medical team and Nabila were key to the success of the project.

Findings concerning the efficacy of the intervention may have been strengthened by contacting people who left the village after the taboo was initiated to determine their smoking status. Similarly, useful information might have been obtained on the cessation success of villagers originally from Nabila but who lived elsewhere at the time of the taboo. This would have provided an assessment of the relative degree to which on-going influences from within the village itself were crucial to success.

Although many of the above factors were unique to the Nabila inter-vention, the following general guidelines are relevant for researchers and health care practitioners from 'outside' the local culture wanting to engage in community-based initiatives to improve health status.

1. Take time to develop a relationship. Often initial efforts are unproductive or even counterproductive and are best viewed as adding to a slowly emerging process that may eventually lead to change.

2. Learn relevant customs and beliefs (explanatory models) associated with illness behaviour. In Nabila, for example, there was a belief at one point that Western-produced cigarettes were not harmful. In addition, there were initially few beliefs connecting smoking to illness.

3. Work to ensure that health promotion efforts are congruent with the values of the people within the culture. Specifically, public health efforts in a communally oriented culture might be best framed by demonstrating how a desired behaviour change contributes to the community (i.e., reduced economic and health burden on family and village).

4. Find out how decisions are made and change occurs in the community and be flexible in working with and blending into these processes. This might involve members of a medical team participating in various ceremonies and rituals, collaborating with key people in the village (elders, minister), monitoring changes in explanatory models of health and illness, and being willing to evaluate the impact of their own behaviour on the village.

5. Encourage the community to design and initiate the intervention themselves. This often means letting go of one's own agendas and time frames. Specific lessons from Nabila included using a spokesperson to communicate important information, collaborating with the village health committee, focusing on the community itself (rather than individuals), and working with the elders.

6. Search for unique features, ceremonies or rituals of the culture that can be used to initiate, consolidate and maintain change within the community.

7. Smoking cessation interventions should include not only 'top-down' mass media and public health approaches, but also 'bottom-up' grassroots endeavours. Such an approach might include training of village health care workers, indigenous healers, village elders, community nurses and medical practitioners.

Despite its limitations, the Nabila project is unique to the smoking cessation literature because of its high rate of success. This is particularly noteworthy given that the follow-up intervals extended well beyond the typical 6–12 months found in most studies and included two formal follow-up surveys at nine and 21 months and informal annual follow-ups for five years following the intervention. Moreover, the study clearly defines the optimal conditions within the Fijian context that allowed such a success to occur.

Acknowledgements

Our thanks to the villagers of Nabila, who allowed us to learn so much from the health project, essentially designed and implemented the smoking cessation programme, and gave us permission to publish this article. Thanks also to the following past directors of the Nabila Health Project: Kevin Starr, David McWaters and Bill Jones. Portions of this chapter were previously published in *Social Science & Medicine* and presented at the XIVth International Conference on the Social Sciences and Medicine, Peebles, Scotland, 2–6 September 1996.

References

Barry, M. (1991) 'The influence of the U.S. tobacco industry on the health, economy, and environment of developing countries', *New England Journal of Medicine* 324: 917–19.

Beecher, G. R., F. Laudon and E. Baque (1995) 'An ecological study of diet and lung cancer in the South Pacific', *International Journal of Cancer* 63: 18–23.

Chapman, S. and W. W. Leng (1990) *Tobacco Control in the Third World: A Resource Atlas*, Penang: International Organization of Consumers Unions.

Clarke, V., D. Hill, M. Murphy and R. Borland (1993) 'Factors affecting the efficacy of a community-based quit smoking program', *Health Education Research* 8: 537–46.

Collins, V. R., G. K. Dowse, S. Cabealawa, P. Ram and P. Z. Zimmet (1996) 'High mortality from cardiovascular disease and analysis of risk factors in Indian and Melanesian Fijians', *International Journal of Epidemiology* 25: 59–69.

COMMIT Research Group (1995a) 'Community Intervention Trial for Smoking Cessation (COMMIT): I. Cohort results from a four-year community intervention', *American Journal of Public Health* 85: 183–92.

— (1995b) 'Community Intervention Trial for Smoking Cessation: II. Changes in adult smoking prevalence', *American Journal of Public Health* 85: 193–200.

Curry, S., A. Marlatt and J. R. Gordon (1987) 'Abstinence violation effect: validation of an attributional construct with smoking cessation', *Journal of Consulting and Clinical Psychology* 55: 145–9.

Defrain, J., N. Defrain and J. Lepard (1994) 'Family strengths and challenges in the South Pacific: an exploratory study in Fiji', *International Journal of Sociology and the Family* 24: 25–47.

Flyn, M. G. (1994) 'Respiratory symptoms of rural Fijian and Indian children in Fiji', *Thorax* 49: 1201–4.

Groth-Marnat, G. (1991) 'A survey of health behaviors in a Fijian village: implications, limitations, and future directions', *Surfing Medicine* 8: 18–20.

Hay, D. R. and F. H. Foster (1981) 'The influence of race, religion, occupation and other social factors on cigarette smoking in New Zealand', *International Journal of Epidemiology* 10: 41–3.

Hickson, L. (1986) 'The social contexts of apology in dispute settlement: a cross-cultural study', *Ethnology* 25: 283–94.

Hunkeler, E. F., E. M. Davis, B. McNeil, J. W. Powell and M. R. Polen (1990) 'Richmond quits smoking: a minority community fights for health', *Health Promotion at the Community Level*, London: Sage.

Kent, D. (1985) 'Ending the social acceptability of smoking and tobacco advertising in New Zealand', *New York State Journal of Medicine* 85: 422–4.

Lando, H. A., T. F. Pechacek, P. L. Pirie et al. (1995) 'Changes in adult cigarette smoking in the Minnesota Heart Health Program', *American Journal of Public Health* 85: 201–8.

Leslie, S. (1992) 'Smoking cessation in the village of Nabila', *Surfing Medicine* 9: 6–7.

Lichtenstein, E., R. E. Glasgow (1992) 'Smoking cessation: what have we learned over the past decade?', *Journal of Consulting and Clinical Psychology* 60: 518–27.

Marlatt, G. A. and J. R. Gordon (1985) *Relapse Prevention*, New York: Guilford Press.

Marshall, M. (1991) 'The second fatal impact: cigarette smoking, chronic disease, and the epidemiological transition in Oceania', *Social Science and Medicine* 33: 1327–442.

Moorehead, A. (1968) *The Fatal Impact: An Account of the Invasion of the South Pacific 1767–1840*, London: Penguin.

Oldenberg, B. and J. Pope (1990) 'A critical review of determinants of smoking cessation', *Behavior Change* 7: 101–9.

Peele, S. (1987) 'A moral vision of addiction: how people's values determine whether they become and remain addicts', *Journal of Drug Issues* 17: 187–215.

Perez-Stable, E. J., B. V. Marin, G. Marin (1994) 'A comprehensive smoking cessation program for the San Francisco Bay area Latino community: Programa Latino Para Dejar de Fumar', *American Journal of Health Promotion* 7: 430–42.

Ravuvu, A. (1983) *Vaka i Taukei: The Fijian Way of Life*, Suva, Fiji: University of the South Pacific.

Ruze, P. (1990) 'Kava-induced dermopathy: a niacin deficiency?', *Lancet* 45: 1442–5.

Saunders, B. and S. Allsop (1991) 'Alcohol problems and relapse: can the clinic combat the community?', *Journal of Community and Applied Social Psychology* 1: 1–9.

Schofield, M. J., S. Redman and R. Sanson-Fisher (1991) 'A community approach to smoking prevention: a review', *Behavior Change* 8: 17–25.

Stebbins, K. R. (1990) 'Transnational tobacco companies and health in underdeveloped countries: recommendations for avoiding an epidemic', *Social Science & Medicine* 30: 227–35.

Triandis, H. C. (1995) *Individualism and Collectivism*, San Francisco: Westview Press.

Warner, K. E. (1987) 'Health and economic implications of a tobacco-free society', *Journal of the American Medical Association* 258: 25–47.

Werner, D. (1977) *Where There is No Doctor: A Village Health Care Handbook*, Palo Alto, CA: Hesperian Foundation.

Wewers, M. E. (1988) 'The role of postcessation factors in tobacco abstinence: stressful events and coping responses', *Addictive Behaviors* 13: 297–301.

WHO (1996) *Tobacco Alert 1996*, online: http://www.who.ch/programmes/psa/toh/Alert/abr96/fulltext.html

Wigley, S. C. (1974) 'Lung cancer and the Melanesian: an impending problem?', *PNG Medicine* 17: 296–303.

Part III

Africa

Introduction

Layi Erinosho

Although there were just a handful of scholars in health social science in Africa some two decades ago, the situation has now changed, judging by the periodic surveys of the Social Science and Medicine Africa Network (SOMA-Net). There are now a number of active scholars in the area in Africa, some holding doctorate degrees in sociology, demography, geography and psychology. While a few are working in medical schools and other health-related research institutions, many more are based in faculties of social and management sciences.

Training in health social science in Africa is now localized, unlike in the past, when Africans had easier access to postgraduate education in Europe and North America. The most developed departments in Africa in health social science are sociology, psychology, demography, geography and economics. The most developed programmes in English-speaking Africa are in Nigeria, Kenya, South Africa and Cameroon (a bilingual country), while programmes in Ghana, Malawi and Zimbabwe are making gains. These countries have full-fledged social science faculties with ample pioneer scholars who received their training abroad. Of course, South Africa stands out with a well-developed university education for health social science.

Various responsible national authorities (such as ministries of health) and international agencies gave support to health social science in the wake of a number of initiatives associated with essential national health research. Of note are the Applied Diarrheal Diseases Project (ADDR), the International Health Policy Program (IHPP), Combating Childhood Communicable Diseases (CCCD), the Operations Research Program, Health System Research (HSR), INCLEN, and the UNICEF Partnership Projects, which have facilitated the participation of Africans in health social science research, policy and programme development.

The uneven development in health social science across countries may be attributed to a dearth of indigenous scholars teaching or conducting research in some countries as well as to decisions by bilateral and multilateral agencies to target a few countries with their research programmes. For example, health social science was galvanized and given further impetus by the inclusion of Nigeria, Kenya and Uganda in the IHPP and also by the activities of the WHO Health System Research Program in the Southern African Sub-Region.

Despite the growth in the number of African scholars in health social science, their contributions to research, policy initiatives, health care promotion and medical education are still constrained. This is because many of them are far removed from contexts in which their contributions can be recognized, harnessed and used by responsible authorities. A gulf between social and biomedical scientists remains because African biomedical scientists only grudgingly accommodate social scientists working within medical schools. The result is that substantive contributions in health social science in Africa are still produced outside medical schools and largely from a single disciplinary standpoint, rather than from an interdisciplinary one.

Perhaps the most important factor that acts as a barrier to the contribution of health social science to programme development, medical education and a proactive research programme in Africa is the absence of an appropriate institutional framework. Contributions from the context of existing frameworks such as faculties of social and management sciences, clinical departments in medical schools, and/or non-government organizations have had a feeble impact. The most appropriate framework is perhaps an interdisciplinary centre, with faculties of social and medical sciences jointly assuming a supervisory role. The mandate of such a centre would cover teaching and research, and its staff members would hold cross-appointments outside their disciplinary departments. This type of institutional framework would give a higher profile to health social science as well as promote true partnership between social and biomedical scientists. Thus far, there is no relatively autonomous department that incorporates a mixture of scholars who work side-by-side as partners in any university in Africa. The Inter-faculty Collaboration Programme on Health and Behaviour Studies through the Centre for Health and Behaviour Studies at the University of Nairobi and the Social Science and Medicine Program (SOSMED) at the University of Dar es Salaam and the Muhimbili Medical Centre stand out, however, as examples of interdisciplinary programmes. Funded by the Carnegie Corporation of New York and established by Fellows from the Harvard East African Health and Behavior Fellowship Program, these cross-faculty programmes encourage and support training, collaborative research and dissemination of information on priority health problems.

The future of health social science in Africa holds great promise. African societies are still confronted by challenges in health that demand collaborative research involving multiple stakeholders – namely, social and biomedical scientists, policy-makers and programme managers – if they are to be effectively addressed. Consequently, an interdisciplinary research orientation is the key to a fruitful health social science in Africa. In order to move health social science forward in Africa in the twenty-first century there is a need for renewed efforts and increased funding to:

- advocate the application of health social science approaches to health policy and programmes;
- promote the teaching of health social science within medical curricula;
- stimulate interdisciplinary research in health social science; and
- hold regular regional/continental meetings for stocktaking by African scholars in health social science.

SOMA-Net, the African regional network of the International Forum for Social Sciences and Health, has made progress on all four of these fronts. To create a forum for the exchange of information and ideas and to foster closer collaboration between health and social scientists, SOMA-Net has organized four biennial international conferences. The first, on 'Africa Health and the Economic Recession of the 1990s', was held in August 1992 in Nairobi, Kenya. In October 1994, SOMA-Net convened a second conference in Douala, Cameroon, the theme of which was 'African Health in Crisis: Which Way Out?'. The third conference, held in Harare, Zimbabwe, focused on 'African Health in the 21st Century: Social Sciences in Health Approaches'. In August 2000, the fourth conference was held in Gaborone, Botswana. Its theme was 'Africa Health at Crossroads: Challenges for the Next Millennium'. SOMA-Net has also compiled a directory of individuals and institutions working in the field of health social science and an inventory of donor funding priorities and interests.

Recently, SOMA-Net has been involved in training interdisciplinary research teams of scientists and programme managers working in the area of nutrition in operations research. With support from the United States Agency for International Development (USAID), through the Academy for Educational Development (AED) and Sustainable Approaches to Nutrition in Africa (SANA), a three-week workshop was held in Mombasa, Kenya. At the close of the workshop, participants had developed proposals on improving child feeding in their respective countries. The teams were provided with seed funds to enable them to initiate the projects.

SOMA-Net is currently collecting and analysing curricula and training materials from medical schools and faculties of social sciences in selected African universities to determine their health social sciences content. The aim of the exercise is to identify gaps, weaknesses, strengths and opportunities that will enable the Network to advocate, where necessary, more health social science content. In addition, SOMA-Net promotes best case examples of how social sciences have been used to improve health in Africa. Three such cases are showcased in this section of the book. Each demonstrates an interdisciplinary approach to health research, which enhances the scope and quality of data gathered as well as the potential for retooling received knowledge on illness and health behaviour in Africa.

Health problems are, by and large, multi-faceted, and much more so in Africa, where ubiquitous socio-cultural factors loom large in the aetiology, course and management of illness. That the African is a man or woman of two worlds is a case in point. He or she is often deeply rooted in spiritualism and wont to attach great importance to the role of spirits and mystical and unseen forces in the affairs of humankind. On the other hand, she or he is essentially a part of a world of novel ideas, technology and inventions, made possible by globalization. It is not surprising that the world view of the African, even at the beginning of the twenty-first Century, is characterized by a certain degree of pluralism.

Consequently, traditional/spiritual healers and their therapeutics still play a significant role in health care delivery, despite the introduction of Western medicine to Africa a little over a century and a half ago. This is because the incidence of illness is usually linked to mystical forces or the evil machination of the enemy through sorcery or the practice of witchcraft. The widely accepted antidote for various disorders incorporates medicinal herbs, symbolic rituals and, most importantly, spiritual warfare against unseen malevolent forces. Indeed, so pervasive are such beliefs that even Western-educated Africans resort to traditional concepts and management of disease during personal crisis or when their disorders fail to respond to biomedical therapeutics.

Traditional/spiritual healers still hold sway over the populace in Africa because they are: (i) greater in number than Western-style health care providers; (ii) more accessible to the population than biomedical practitioners; and (iii) fill the gap created by the dearth of Western-style health care agents in underserved rural and urban areas. No less important is the fact that Africans tend to feel more 'at home' in the company or facilities of traditional/spiritual healers than in those of Western health care practitioners. Finally, the power that traditional/spiritual healers exert on the populace stems from a mutually shared concept of disease rooted in magic and religious factors. This in turn accounts for the greater confidence of the populace in the diagnostic and therapeutic skills of these healers than in those of Western-style practitioners, despite the power that the latter exercise over the formal health care delivery system.

These observations notwithstanding, the Western biomedical and traditional concepts and therapeutic systems of care co-exist and compete in

Africa today. Patients shift from one system to the other, with the largely non-literate portion of the population seeking the help of traditional/spiritual healers at the onset of illness before seeking care from Western biomedical practitioners and facilities. Consequently, the widely shared magico-religious concept of disease that transcends all social groups in African societies does not necessarily deter patients from utilizing formally trained Western biomedical health care agents.

Western-trained practitioners in Africa today are confronted in their practice by patients whose perception, evaluation and behaviour patterns through all the stages of ill-health traverse and transcend the two world views and systems of health care. This reality has evoked a mixed reaction from observers, scholars, Western biomedical health care practitioners, programme managers and policy-makers in Africa. To some, African patients stand to benefit and are indeed already benefiting from the continent's plural system of health care delivery because they are continuously taking advantage of the therapeutic skills and practices of both the biomedical and traditional systems of care. It is no wonder that there have been strident calls in some quarters for the integration or conscious promotion of some sort of collaboration between the two systems, as has been the case in India and the People's Republic of China. Yet according to others, the traditional therapeutic regime should be banned or its use discouraged because it is primitive, bereft of scientific efficacy and inimical to patients' well-being.

These standpoints have led to the emergence of two schools of thought, which can be described as the *culture-bound vis-à-vis* the *non-culture-bound*. The proponents of the former recognize the importance of accommodating and harnessing both the Western biomedical and traditional therapeutics, while those of the latter often ignore indigenous healing techniques in the hope that faith in them will disappear as more and more of the citizenry receive formal Western education.

These standpoints have tended to shape health policy and programmes as well as the orientation of research. Some African countries have formulated concrete state policies for the promotion of traditional medicine and have sought ways of accommodating or integrating it into the formal system of health care – other countries have not. Similarly, some researchers recognize the need to develop health intervention programmes that accommodate socio-cultural contingencies, while others either dismiss or are oblivious to them. Nevertheless, it has become increasingly evident that culture-bound approaches hold much promise for community-based, action-oriented health care programmes. This is because a culture-bound orientation offers a window of opportunity for: (i) a perceptive understanding of health problems; (ii) developing appropriate interventions; and

(iii) harnessing the material and human resources of both biomedical and traditional medicine for the overall well-being of the population.

An awareness of the utility of a culture-bound approach seems to have provided the *raison d'être* for Chapter 6 on a community-action intervention to improve medical services in the Democratic Republic of the Congo; the use of genograms as a visual complement to ethnographic and epidemiological evidence in the study of HIV/AIDS transmission in Uganda described in Chapter 7; and the study of AIDS prevention among Zimbabwean traditional healers in Chapter 8.

There is a certain degree of convergence in these three chapters, despite the fact that they are products of diverse research interests and studies conducted in countries with dissimilar historical antecedents, cultures, systems of health care, ethnic composition and geography. They draw attention to the importance of magico-religious explanations of ill health in Africa, highlighting as well the interplay between traditional and biomedical medicine in community health care. As stories of successful intervention outcomes, the Congo and Zimbabwe studies underscore the point previously made about the potential of a culture-bound or, to use the expression of Willms et al., 'culturally compelling health interventions' to produce positive results in Africa. The three chapters also demonstrate the utility of the ethnographic method in effectively capturing the underlying social processes in illness and health behaviour, which might have been easily missed had the researchers resorted to more rigid and less inductive quantitative methods.

6

A Community-action Intervention to Improve Medical Care Services in Kinshasa, Congo: Mediating the Realms of Healers and Physicians

René Devisch, Lapika Dimomfu, Jaak Le Roy and Peter Crossman

The vast African capital city of Kinshasa, with its estimated five million or more inhabitants, offers a bewildering picture of medical pluralism. Patients circulate between three different health care systems: the medical health care establishment and pharmacies; folk healers (including initiated cult healers, self-promoted healers and herbalists); and faith or spiritualist healers of the independent charismatic healing churches. These three systems operate according to different transactional practices and are embedded in different understandings of the human body and the aetiology of health and illness. Until the early 1980s, the state funded public health care. Since then, preventive health care and curative health care have entirely been supported by the European Union, as well as by multilateral Belgian, Dutch and German governmental funding, Christian churches and/or NGO financing. To date, cooperation between the various fields of therapy choice has been lacking.

In the past, Kinshasa's medical health care service was widely recognized as one of the best in sub-Saharan Africa. Over the last decade, the sanitary infrastructure as well as the medical preventive and community health care services in Kinshasa and the hinterland have severely declined due to the total collapse of state services. A small number of well-staffed and well-stocked private clinics continue to serve the well-to-do minority and expatriate personnel in the downtown and affluent residential areas. In contrast, the squatter zones have been completely neglected while the older suburban townships have only a minimum of good primary care centres and a few efficient polyclinics. Numerous forms of folk healing, however, are available throughout the city from both initiated cult and self-promoted healers (Bibeau et al. 1979; Corin 1979; Creten 1996; Devisch and Mbony-inkebe 1997). Charismatic faith healing is offered by numerous Pentecostal

church communities and hundreds of independent churches often designated as churches of the holy spirit (Devisch 1996; Lapika Dimomfu
1984; Le Roy 1994a, 1996, 1998).

The relationship between the three health care systems is complex and
poorly understood, as are the factors that determine why health-seekers
switch from one health care setting to another. Aside from a medical
anthropological study carried out in 1976 by Bibeau et al. (1979), a
considerable gap remains in our knowledge concerning the daily health
behaviour and health-seeking practices in the capital. The knowledge and
socio-cultural dynamics that inform therapy choice decisions may depend,
in part, on the particular aetiology of an illness offered by family elders
or significant others. The social stigmatization of particular health problems
or injuries and the client's expectations or economic and family situation
may also influence therapy choice.

This chapter describes a multi-disciplinary[1] action-research project
directed at the plural health-seeking practices of the residents of two
poverty-stricken suburbs of Kinshasa. Begun in December 1994, the research intervention pertains to the situation in the Congo (formerly Zaire)
before the May 1997 takeover of state power by the Alliance of Democratic
Forces for the Liberation of Congo (AFDL), and therefore before the new
government and civic culture in the Democratic Republic of Congo had had
a chance to impact upon urban public health policy and its implementation.

On the research level, the project sought to gain a better understanding
of the specific character of cult healing practices in relation to the prevalent
conceptions of illnesses (in particular, those of 'closure' versus 'effusion').
In addition, an attempt was made to answer the following questions:
1) Does urbanization promote secularization – that is, an inherent shift in
the explanation of misfortune, accidents, and illness *from* ethic, mythic,
sacral dimensions (ancestors, spirits, deities, supernatural sanctions,
sorcery) and social dimensions (seniority, group solidarity and sanctions)
towards a more mechanistic and secularized image of the body and more
cognitive and subject-related dimensions of experience (fear, fatigue, stress,
risk behaviour, malnutrition, infection)? 2) When and why do people resort
to cult/folk healing? If Kinshasa had a sufficient and financially accessible
medical health care infrastructure, would the population still consult the
cult/folk healer? 3) Is biomedicine capable of replacing the African medical
traditions completely? In which instances are African traditional healing
practices effective? In which cases are they harmful or even dangerous?

Addressing such questions enabled us to develop an action-intervention
approach aimed at improving the quality of overall health service through
increased coordination of the various systems. We hypothesized that the
more any communitarian health programme entailed a plurality of resort,

and the more its accessibility and therapeutic value were openly assessed by people at the neighbourhood level, the more motivated health-seekers would be to make improved use of preventive and curative health services. A key objective was to identify the community networks or core groups of delegates of such networks (such as local healers, women's action groups and community councils of elders) to take active part in a reflection on the focus and concern of the action-research.

Specifically, in the action phase of the project, we sought to mobilize the communities, at the neighbourhood or residence network level, for the purpose of setting up community support networks. Such networks, or lay therapy management groups, were seen to reflect the current process of *villagization of town* – that is, a return by suburban residents to the local community-like behaviours, social organization, and solidarity of village life. In collaboration with the research team, two committees or core groups of delegates from community networks took the lead in defining and negotiating practical forms of exchange and coordination between the three health care systems. Patients and lay therapy management groups also jointly developed specific health-seeking strategies on the basis of culturally informed attitudes, beliefs and explanatory models concerning health and illness. Finally, with medical doctors and community health-planners within the Ministry of Health, the committees worked to define ways of optimizing available community resources so as to develop lasting health improvements.

The Action-research Setting

Two shanty towns, considered representative of the poverty-stricken suburbs of Kinshasa, were selected for the action-research: an older quarter, Ndjili XII, and a newer neighbourhood, Mbanza Lemba. The several hundred thousand residents of both shanty towns are culturally closely related, the majority originating from the adjacent provinces of Bandundu and Lower Congo. Immigrants and their descendants from these two provinces constitute more than half of the city's inhabitants. The peoples of rural Lower Congo province are well documented in anthropological studies regarding the Kongo ethnic group, many of whose members inhabit Congo-Brazzaville as well (Bockie 1993; Buakasa 1973; Hagenbucher-Sacripanti 1989; Jacobson-Widding 1979; Janzen 1978, 1982, 1992; MacGaffey 1986; Mahaniah 1982; Van Wing 1959).

Mbanza Lemba, a village-like slum quarter with crowded households, is located on the fringes of the city and occupies the hillsides of the University of Kinshasa campus. A squatter zone of recent origin, it developed rapidly over the 1980s in the absence of any formal urban planning. Its inhabitants thus enjoy very few of the public services and infrastructural amenities available in the older suburbs and the city centre. Education levels are exceptionally low. Fewer than 5 per cent of Mbanza Lemba's inhabitants earn regular wages. Houses are rudimentary shelters with two or three rooms constructed of breeze-block walls and tin roofs. Hillside construction leaves homes vulnerable to erosion: heavy rains often wash away whole plots and the dwellings on them. For many of its inhabitants, kerosene lamps are the only source of lighting; cooking is done on charcoal fires and water is drawn from shallow wells dug near dwellings. Although the major streets were connected to electric and water lines around 1986, only a few homes along these streets have electricity. No paved roads, sewerage or sanitary systems exist. Mbanza Lemba has the appearance of an immense village with its unfenced lots, numerous unfinished homes, and many lanes inaccessible to motor vehicles. Most households keep some poultry and have a small garden with a fruit tree.

Ndjili suburb – of which only the old and impoverished Quartier XII in the vicinity of the international airport is the focus of this study – was built in the 1950s as a 'modern' township. It represented an attempt at what colonial authority defined as a 'harmonious association' between members of the upcoming generation of white-collar workers and urban middle-class families, both European and Congolese. It aimed at housing the new individual, in line with the Utopian reformist preoccupations that, in the former decades, had inspired the architectural, hygienic and educational modernization of suburbs in Belgian towns such as Gent or Liège. The spacious suburb of Ndjili originally enjoyed a well-equipped infrastructure with a diversity of community services such as schools, health care, markets, entertainment, sports and sanitation. Its development was administered with the aim of raising a so-called Congolese Elite to the European standards of rationality, work, family, marriage, hygiene and health care, in contrast with the so-called underdeveloped illiterate villagers.

Compared with Kinshasa as a whole, Ndjili XII shows high indices of educational qualification. An apparent increase in single female inhabitants over the last years, however, reflects both men's loss of status and their reluctance to engage in egalitarian marriage relations. As in many other parts of Kinshasa, most parents in this suburb are no longer able to provide for their children the levels of education and health care they themselves enjoyed in their youth. This deterioration reinforces their awareness of being destitute. They are increasingly confronted by their exclusion from the social privileges and material comforts enjoyed by the leisured class living in the downtown areas and propagated by modernization discourses and transnational television programmes.

Research Methods

A combination of qualitative research techniques, including participant observation, case studies, structured and semi-structured interviews, and focus groups were employed as well as quantitative research methods such as random sample studies with questionnaires and sociological surveys. The initial stage of the exploratory investigation involved selection of key and lay informants. Unstructured individual and focus group interviews were conducted with people in the local community, primary health care professionals, and cult and faith healers regarding the research objectives and methods. All the medical health care facilities in the target communities were identified and visited. Discussions concerned: 1) local health needs and available care facilities; 2) health-seeking and treatment practices regarding a number of common somatic and psycho-social complaints and culture-bound illnesses; 3) existing networks and family dynamics that direct community members to various health care resources; 4) explanatory models, therapeutic practices and group psycho-dynamic processes with regard to various types of illness and care facilities; and 5) changes and variations in patients' therapy management and reasons for alternatively resorting to medical care, healers or healing churches.

Next, a culturally and locally adapted survey questionnaire was prepared and carried out by RIAGG (see note 1). The core of the questionnaire represents a synthesis of the Bradford Somatic Inventory (BSI) and the Help-seeking Behaviour and Explanatory Questionnaire (HBEQ).[2] The latter is specifically designed for medical and psychiatric health care research in developing countries. Drawing on the information obtained in the in-depth and focus group interviews, a series of questions was added to investigate further family narratives and dynamics around the illness experience. The questionnaire was translated into the vernacular liNgala language and a series of preliminary interviews was carried out to test and improve its linguistic, conceptual and sociological relevance.

Part 1 of the survey questionnaire enables the interviewer to explore and clarify, in an open-ended way, how the family has dealt with the present or most recent illness of one of its members. Eliciting information about previous or parallel treatments allows for a longitudinal and case-study perspective on the illness. Part 2 investigates types of somatization and different bodily and subjective expressions of an illness, while Part 3 explores the extent to which the family context influences the patient's (self-) understanding at the onset of the illness.

The survey questionnaire was administered in the form of a semi-structured interview. Interviews were conducted with a random sample of 65 families or households (each counting an average of eight persons) from the 1,182 registered dwellings in Ndjili and with 60 of the 2,374 households in Mbanza Lemba. Two years later, in 1997, 120 of the 125 families were revisited in order to obtain additional information on family composition and socio-dynamics, the patient's ethno-cultural background, and the relationship between the Kinois household and its extended family in the rural hinterland. The follow-up interviews assisted us in developing a longitudinal perspective of families' help-seeking strategies. Half the families contacted originally in 1995 were experiencing cases of chronic or lasting illness. The return visit in 1997 permitted us to enquire as to how the problem was now, what steps the family had undertaken in seeking treatment, new aetiological explanations, and whether the patient had experienced a relapse or come down with another illness.

Finally, sociological, anthropological and medical-psychiatric enquiries were carried out from a multidisciplinary perspective by CERDAS, ARC and RIAGG respectively, with patients and their families as well as medical personnel, cult/folk healers and faith healers from the Mbanza Lemba and Ndjili XII neighbourhoods. A series of more specific questions regarding the therapeutic landscape was put to three samples of 50 patients drawn from the medical, cult therapy and faith healing spheres. These questions provided further information on the classification of symptoms, idioms of distress, explanatory models, culture-sensitive diagnostic and aetiological discourse, and people's perceptions of the three approaches. Similar questions were addressed to 50 cult healers and 35 faith healers.

From the survey questionnaire, the 1997 follow-up visits and the series of questions related to the therapeutic landscape, 70 case histories were compiled for patients accessing the cult or faith healing spheres, as were a further 90 case histories for patients at the polyclinic of the Neuro-Psycho-Pathology University Hospital of Kinshasa. Particular attention was paid to the mental health dimension of the illnesses under study and their relationship to psychiatric categories of psychosomatic disorder, anxiety, depression, psychotic states and epilepsy. In the majority of cases, clinical interviews with patients residing with healers took place during their treatment, something that enabled us also to investigate diagnostic procedures, individual and group processes, and the healer–patient or healer–family relationship.

Local and expatriate sociologists, anthropologists and medical-psychiatric researchers involved in the project participated in both its investigative component and the subsequent action-research component. The sociologists assembled the survey data and the physicians prepared and applied the survey questionnaire. Local social anthropologists began with a broad remit, spending the first months establishing their role as participant-observers and becoming part of the local scene. While they gradually developed a narrower focus of investigation, a great deal of time and energy was spent establishing mutual trust and respect, without which suspicion towards members of public institutions such as the university may have undermined data collection. In addition, the anthropologists assisted in continually adapting the research methodology and the therapeutic landscape questionnaire, as new insights came to light. Intensive joint seminar meetings, held when several co-investigators were in Kinshasa, helped to interrelate the various data collection events in a stepwise fashion including 1) selection of key informants; 2) identification of the ecological situation in the respective communities in relation to a limited number of common psychosocial health problems; 3) setting up of a culturally and locally adapted methodology consisting of questionnaires, interviews and rating instruments; 4) investigation of symptoms, expressions of distress, family psychodynamics, explanatory models used, different forms of treatment and coping mechanisms, and aetiological and therapeutic rationales; 5) definition of a new set of integrated interventions; and 6) the adaptation of the original psycho-social intervention programme.

A subsidiary component of the research involved an investigation of the impact of the Ebola epidemic (De Boeck 1998, 1999) in Kikwit, the town in southwestern Congo where the outbreak occurred. The study found that folk understanding of the disease, which several dozens of people either contracted in hospital or died of in hospital, led to widespread distrust of public hospitals and biomedical treatment. This brought about massive abandonment of the formal medical institutions and, as a result, the informal health care settings of folk and faith healing are flourishing as never before.

Findings

At the time of the investigation we identified, in Ndjili XII, six cult healers handling 30 'in-patients' (patients spending at least several days per week, over several weeks, in the healer's compound) as well as ten faith healers who, along with six assistants, cared for a total of 48 patients. In the Mbanza Lemba quarter we enumerated seven cult healers treating 23 in-patients, and six faith healers, aided by four assistants, caring for a total of 16 in-patients. All the cult and faith healers were more than 30 years old. Among the cult healers, of whom ten were men, eight were 50 or older. More than half the faith healers were women; their average age was somewhat lower.

The best-known cult and faith healers appear to be of the same ethno-cultural origin as the overall population in the respective suburbs; the composition of the clientele served by these healers reveals the same tendency. Approximately eighteen faith healers and assistants came from the Lower Congo compared with two from the Bandundu province, two from northern Kivu, and two from Angola. Half had begun secondary education but none had earned final diplomas. Apart from two healers who were housewives by profession, another two who were fully employed, and five who declared themselves to be occasionally employed, the remainder considered faith healing to be their principal activity.

With respect to health-seekers, 60 of the 90 patients resorting to faith healing were under 34 years old (two-thirds of this group were 25 and older); 29 of these patients making recourse to faith healing had begun secondary school but only 7 per cent completed this level of education. Eighteen of the 53 cult healing clients were in their thirties, while 25 were older than 45. (Strikingly, a great number of these clients complained of haemorrhoids and/or sexual deficiency.) On the whole, more than half of the cult healing patients were men, the majority of whom were in their forties or older; one-fifth of this group declared themselves to be employed while one-third stated that they found occasional work.

Some of those seeking cult healing believed that sorcery accounted for symptoms such as extreme anaemia, breast tumours, hernias or chronic venereal disease. In comparison, the majority of culturally defined complaints submitted to faith healing were attributed to sorcery, a fear of evil spirits, abortion, harmful substances ('that sorcerers have thrown into the body'), conjugal conflict, incurable wounds, irritability, or sexual or reproductive illness (most often reported as impotence, cysts on the ovaries, excessive menstrual flow, or acute rectal piles – the latter being considered an ominous and polluting substitute in post-menopausal women for menstrual discharge, because of the loss of blood from the rectum).

Cult healing was the preferred recourse for states of depression and anxiety, epileptic and convulsive conditions, and a number of common culture-specific idioms of distress labelled as illnesses of 'effusion or openness' versus those 'of disabling closure'. Among the illnesses of openness that we most frequently encountered, the majority were first submitted to biomedical diagnosis and treatment and only later to either cult/folk healing or faith healing practices. These culturally defined illnesses may include complaints such as (1) weak fontanelle as well as severe headaches, in particular at the spot of the fontanelle, which patients and healers define as a feeling 'as if the head were splitting' (called *yata* in kiKoongo or yiYaka) and (2) skin rashes caused by sorcery (called *mpese*). Still other illnesses of openness entail some humoural imbalance: (3) states of excessive heat or fire, producing fever or itching; (4) chronic diarrhoea; (5) various culturally defined 'gynaecological' ailments, including excessive menstrual flow, miscarriage and acute rectal piles (see above), all supposed consequences of sexual misdemeanours; and (6) mental disturbances, such as that of an adult patient with an impatient heart that is no longer able to keep cool and easily bursts out in fits of rage. Similar forms of excessive heat are also exhibited in general irascibility, frenzy, wild cursing, obscene speech, sexual harassment, physical violence or other forms of a lasting inability to get along with others. The patient is seen as a repository of disturbed or overheated relations in the family group.

With such cases, cult healing consists of expelling the evil and cooling down the patient, refashioning his or her corporal boundedness and modes of transaction with others and the world. Herbal therapy with cold potions, enemas and ointments seeks to 'produce some shade or coolness for the body'. There are strict space–time regulations for the use of each and the precise recipe is specific to each illness. Further, the element of group treatment in the healing churches offers additional support, containment and meaning.

Among the illnesses of disabling closure (*yibiinda, biindama*) – namely those of contraction, deflation or withdrawal in a state of coldness (in which the body boundaries act as fences or lines of cleavage) – the complaints most frequently addressed to faith healers include: (7) *lukika*, a gnawing pain in the blood vessels of the head and in particular the temples, as well as (8) *kibeka* or 'burst of the spleen', a name for severe and chronic cramps, infant convulsions and epileptic-like fits, especially those suffered by people in bereavement. The spleen is popularly seen as the seat of sorcerous spirits or forces, causing one to become morose and impassive (as opposed to impetuous or irritable). Because the spleen, like the liver, is considered the seat of the humoural balance in the person, it is feared that a child suffering *kibeka* may later experience fertility problems.

Other ailments involving symptoms of closure include (9) those described by a state of coldness or frigidity or a 'cooling down of the blood'. A backache, for example, that confines a person to the house or to sitting or lying down the whole day is associated with coldness. Breathing difficulties (10) may be indicative of the body's closure, as may rheumatism, pains in the joints, or even impotence. (In these cases the victim's body and vital flow are said to be turned inward 'like a fermenting cassava paste bound in leaves'.) Children (11) who fail to crawl or stand upright at an appropriate age are assumed to suffer closure, as are those (12) who experience various gynaecological ailments (amenorrhoea, frigidity, barrenness) and impotence or (13) anaemia and chronic constipation. As well, there are (14) various interrelated mental expressions of closure: an individual closes up in deafness or blindness; withdraws from social contact; turns inward in a state of helplessness, torpor or weary resignation; or no longer responds when spoken to. The sufferer appears to be afflicted by apathy, extreme timidity, sorrow, grief, or prolonged anger, or refuses to speak or to share his or her income; the patient is stiffened by despair, apathy and melancholy.

Health-seeking strategies may originate with the individual health-seeker or with his or her lay therapy management group. When first confronted with an ailment or disease, the individual usually begins by practising some form of self-medication, using herbs obtained from the garden, a herbalist or a pharmaceutical shop. After this initial attempt at self-treatment, the large majority of those who participated in the household survey, in particular those with a school education and a Christian outlook, went on to consult a public or private medical service. Advice by relevant others was influential in this choice. The household survey data indicated that the type of symptom or complaint is not predictive of the decision to seek out medical treatment over cult or faith healing, except with acute and life-threatening symptoms necessitating hospitalization. Health-seekers may use both medical and culture-specific terms (such as *lukika*) to name an affliction. The use of a culture-specific illness term does not imply that health-seekers rely on a 'traditional' aetiology and cult healing.

Unsuccessful treatment was interpreted in almost half of the cases as resulting from incompetent care, prompting health-seekers to turn to another medical practitioner. The longer the illness resists medical cure, however, the more readily health-seekers and their advisers come to suspect sorcery, evil spirits or a family conflict as having hampered the medical intervention. As in the minority of cases in the household survey for whom medical care was not the starting point in the health-seeking pathway, many health-seekers, disillusioned by medical therapy, joined a healing church community in search of emotional support or exorcism.

Since cult healing fosters the involvement of the patient's family and recognizes the importance of the patient's life world, only advice by a family member or a reliable person within the support network can authorize a decision to seek out this form of healing. Most urban health-seekers feel reluctant to consult a folk healer for fear of malpractice, uncontrolled medicinal doses or high prices. Indeed, the most frequently cited reasons for seeking cult/folk healing were: 1) suspicion or worry – most often induced by significant others – that the underlying cause of the affliction may be sorcery, ancestral wrath and/or a family conflict; 2) the presence of particular symptoms such as skin disease, deformity, epilepsy, infertility, dementing illness, dysphoria and other affective illnesses, which threaten social functioning; and 3) the occasional referral of the patient, by a physician or nurse, to a healer because the type of symptom, the patient's anxiety or his or her violence requires close kin group support and culture-specific ritual treatment integrating identity discourse and family history.

With respect to both cult and faith healing, 83 per cent of the patients expressed their satisfaction with the therapy, perceiving either some improvement or complete healing. Only 3 per cent unambiguously expressed dissatisfaction. At the time of the investigation 14 per cent were still in therapy and preferred not to influence the cure by publicly expressing any evaluation of its effectiveness. Clients valued easy access to, and dialogue with, their cult/folk healer as well as the ability of the healer to inspire confidence in the therapies offered. Numerous health-seekers and their family members stated that they would more readily and frequently consult cult/folk healers if the efficacy of their practices were guaranteed by some formal control system.

In short, it appears that therapeutic pathways are shaped mainly by patients and their families in connection with the neighbourhood support network and in interaction with their care providers. Most health-seeking choices and pathways are idiosyncratic and fragmentary, and reflect short-term care goals. The often scant information that patients have at their disposal, in particular regarding types of treatment, their efficacy and cost, orients the choice of treatment. Doctors, paramedical personnel and healers seem, by and large, unfamiliar with individual patients' actual health-seeking strategies. Moreover, care-providers within a given health care system know little about the other systems. Although they may acknowledge receiving patients from another system, they make no effort to cooperate with healers from other systems. The issue of earlier treatment or referral to other care-givers is rarely discussed openly in the therapeutic encounter. The only exception to this finding is that cult and faith healers at times may send a patient to a hospital for diagnosis or specialized medical treatment. Above all, in the collective representations, health is not first and foremost a matter of the individual's mastery or control. Rather, Kinois people are concerned with preventing or healing the illness within their vital social network.

From Data to Interpretation: Parallel Consultation to Reintegrate the Plurality of Worlds

Given the widespread practice of parallel consultation, we hypothesize that by interlinking, in their own idiosyncratic manner, various health care settings and healing resources, health-seekers aim to overcome the conflicting plurality of mental landscapes, their anxiety or vulnerability, and the disorders that accompany the fragmented urban ecology they inhabit. Although we have not been able to establish a causal relationship between the urban ecology, the (lost) sense of place (in particular affecting the adult males), morbidity and the health-seeking pattern under consideration, it strikes us that, for their part, healers and healing churches do acknowledge specific ways in which urban conditions have an impact on their clients' wellness and illness. They refer to a particular range of symptoms brought on or exacerbated by a rapid and massive transition to life in a city such as Kinshasa, including skin rashes, dysmenorrhoea, convulsive states, various gynaecological ailments, substance abuse, aimless wandering, frenzy and violence, as well as states such as dysphoria, identity diffusion, vagrancy, weary resignation and torpor.

Plural health resort or therapy choice fits with the multiplicity of identity models and symbolic landscapes in the city. Compared with the rural environment, the urban ecology entails, especially for the immigrant from the hinterland, a bewildering variety of ethno-cultural scenarios and logics, educational differences and many new and diverse psycho-dynamics. The transition to a radically different cultural context, which often entails a rupture in familiar cultural perspectives, may have a profound impact on the individual psyche, bodily awareness and the family group (Douville 1996; Le Roy 1994a, 1994b; Rouchy 1995). The impact differs depending on the particular dynamics determining relations between the family and the patient as well as on the coping and supportive capacities of the group. The resulting changes in the organization of family life and of gender relations are at the origin of identificational predicaments and vulnerabilities (cf. Audisio 1994; Cadoret 1994; Douville et al. 1999). Each therapeutic setting provides partial and transitory solutions for the health-seeker. It contains and reflects the processes of fragmentation and reconstruction that take place on the social and individual levels (Le Roy 1994a, 1996).

Our investigation revealed a high and increasing rate of dissatisfaction with biomedicine, in contrast to correspondingly high levels of satisfaction with informal health services – in particular, cult/folk healing. The sociological survey showed that most patients are comfortable with the parallel consultation of formal medicine and cult/folk healers, or formal medicine and faith healing. These patients do not find the two forms of care incompatible; on the contrary, they see them as offering some complementarity.

It is apparent that, in moving from one health care system to another, patients submit their various experiences of illness to several tests: besides seeking to restore their physical health, they also seek to neutralize the evil causing the illness or misfortune in order to remove the social stigma associated with the ailment. Only cult/folk and faith healing, however, respond to culturally determined, and predominantly relational, folk aetiologies of illness. Within the context of the therapeutic arts in western Congo, as in the wider Bantu-African therapeutic traditions (Janzen's expression: 1989), healing means making whole, and often entails a kind of homoeopathic self-healing. In other words, cult healing aids both the patient and support group to re-embody as well as to re-experience in culture-specific sensory and emotional ways one's predispositions (*habitus*, see Bourdieu 1980) and symbolic landscapes of healing and health experience. As with kinship relations, healing practices are largely governed by a reciprocal logic of the gift, of openness and flow, and set the scene for a co-participative therapeutic relationship embedded in culture-specific symbols. Whereas misfortune and sorcery entail closure or blockage of flow, gift exchange and ritual performance vitalize social relations, making them visible and personalized. The underlying metaphors of healing are those of tying or intertwining and of knotting or weaving the threads of life (Bekaert 1998; De Boeck 1991, 1994, 1996; Devisch 1993: 23ff, 255ff; Devisch and Brodeur 1999).

Illness and health derive from life-bearing and life-harming 'forces' at work in the social domain and in the life world. Thus, in the perspective of western Congo cultures, to be in good health depends on the relations between people, or between the individual, the social group and the life world. Good health results from the vital integration of elements, rules and processes (such as one's relations to named spirits; behavioural rules; rules of descent, filiation or hierarchy; space–time coordinates; humoural logic; double-sided processes of fate and anti-fate, good fortune and misfortune, destruction and regeneration, or deceiving and redeeming) that also determine the life world and the physical and material well-being of both the individual and his or her family or residential group as a whole. Symptoms and illness, on the other hand, are signifiers of socio-moral lesions or disruptions both within the sufferer and with respect to the embracing contexts of physical, social, moral and cosmological components. Cult therapeutic interventions thus aim at reassuring the patient's being-in-the-world through the ritual creation of a new integrative order in which the physical and social bodies are once again attuned to one another and brought into line with the space–time and cosmological orders.

We argue, therefore, that successful health care must involve an interconnection of, or some negotiation between, the different fields of therapy choice in a manner that sustains the patient's basic search for healing – that is, for appropriating therapeutic good and restoring wholeness. Consequently, neither the cult/folk sector nor the medical sector is capable of independently supplying a satisfactory and encompassing answer to disease, sickness and illness. Thus, in terms of its action-intervention component, the project encouraged the two study communities to explore the possibilities of improving the interconnection of community health programmes and promote cooperation on a neighbourhood level such that patients and their support groups receive more timely and objective advice regarding their care strategy.

From Research to Action

Towards the second half of the research period, specific intervention steps were designed. The action or intervention phase of the project aimed generally at defining, setting up and implementing health services that would meet the most critical health needs of the communities concerned. The following principles served as guidelines: 1) resources available in the neighbourhoods were to be employed; 2) only a bare minimum of financial support could be made available for the purpose of organizing the intervention; 3) the action would be directed to linking together health care providers from the three different health systems; 4) the final responsibility for networking would fall to a core group or committee of community representatives to be formed; and 5) committee members and researchers would be considered partners in the intervention and mutually carry out decision-making.

Given the current process of villagization, we postulated that the most realistic way of working towards some form of practical coordination of services between the various health care fields was to start at the neighbourhood or residence network level. Meetings were held in the community (namely with the most capable matrons, elders and healers) to assess the focus and concerns of the action-research as well as the community support networks and their influence on illness careers and health-seeking behaviour. The delegates then formed committees, in both Mbanza Lemba and Ndjili XII, who worked side by side with the researchers. The initial plan foresaw that the researchers and respective committees would organize bi-monthly meetings with as many healers as possible in order to determine the latter's healing specializations as well as the health needs of their clients. It was then the task of the committees to provide health-seekers with informal advice with regard to the appropriate medical aid, healers and therapies available. Since we intended to mobilize the dynamics of local networks, we avoided offering any training to the committee members with respect to advising or counselling patients.

Throughout the process, contacts were maintained with the Ministry of Health. Several of the community meetings took place in the presence of health policy-makers, medical inspection authorities responsible for primary health care in Kinshasa, and researchers from the university departments of public health, mental health and sociology–anthropology. The medical inspection authorities showed a keen interest in the project for several reasons. In their duties they had often been confronted with contradictory reports from both patients and physicians about 'indigenous' treatment. They were indeed puzzled by the recent and growing under-utilization of public health care facilities, despite their low cost and accessibility.

The medical inspection authorities found themselves in the unfamiliar and unprecedented situation of being invited by (some unschooled) folk healers and users of health care to discuss local health policies. This unusual and asymmetrical situation, which ignored the hierarchy within the public health organization, paved the way to mutual understanding of a number of salient public health issues. The physicians' presence in the community meetings gave a biomedical turn to the discourse, for example, by raising the issue of scientifically demonstrated therapeutic efficacy. Usually, health-seekers do not assess folk or faith healers in these terms since their legitimacy derives from their initiation and embodiment of healing imagery, or from the charismatic performance witnessing of divine action.

Another primary objective of the action-research was to inspire greater sensitivity on the part of the medical and psychiatric health service providers to patients' aetiological repertoire, to their socio-behavioural rationale in health-seeking, and above all to their social capital or relations of trust and day-to-day cooperation that provide them with a source of support. In view both of sustaining the biomedical services' curative impact and of helping powerless health-seekers to be understood, we sought to develop culture-specific communicational and observational skills. The committee members had to practise skills of informing, dialoguing and decision-making in culturally appropriate ways. They had to avoid the positivist mindset of the physicians, and to adopt people's multifarious views, epistemology and aetiology.

Using methods similar to those recommended by David Bell and Lincoln Chen (1994), the action-research thus worked towards improving the quality of medical care and health resource allocation in Kinshasa through more comprehensive recognition of the range of health problems particular to the urban context and the culture-specific forms of expressing distress and bodily discomfort. This required a reciprocity between caregiver and patient of a type that, in a context of great social disparity, provided for greater equity, among other values, by differentially attending to the health risks and cultural rationale characteristic of the poverty-stricken suburbs and shanty towns. More concretely, the project attempted to help the medical care institutions to develop more appropriate responses to individual patients' lived experience and cultural perspectives, as well as to the importance of the support network – or, more precisely, lay therapy management groups – at the community level.

From the outset of the action component of the project, very different styles of therapy management were adopted by the target groups – in fact, they were so different that the very initiative was called into question. The Mbanza Lemba committee chose to select only cult/folk healers of one social and ethno-cultural origin. The initiators, who wished to put themselves forward as professional community workers, perceived the project as a source of income and local power. Above all, they saw the project as formal legitimization of the freelance health centre they intended to set up. In this particular case, it was clear that the initiative was an attempt to revive an earlier but unsuccessful enterprise led by a local nurse and a midwife. We opted, however, to take the side of the committee and follow the self-promoting experience on its own merit, meanwhile comparing its group dynamics with that of the committee coordinating the intervention programme at Ndjili. The committee there, composed largely of healers and representatives of local community networks, was more oriented to informing, counselling and advising health-seekers (Le Roy and N'situ 1998). Granting power and institutional prestige to the support network proved, in effect, to be sufficient compensation for healers and committee members by the project.

Further development of the programme, and in particular efforts to empower the committee and local healers, has been hampered by the overall deterioration of public services in the city and the political upheaval in recent years. Consequently, we abandoned the discourse of empowerment and community action and redirected our attention to the following issues.

Quality of care In the committees, the cult/folk healers were invited to specify their competence, in the presence of colleagues and clients, and the means by which they would seek to assure and assess good and efficacious treatment. They agreed on a simple means of evaluating their claims – namely a committee member interviewing one of their patients. This procedure sorted out the occasional and less experienced healers and helped the more experienced ones to continue focusing their practice on illnesses they knew well. The resulting selection and specializations of the healers clarified and strengthened their position in the community. The committees felt reassured that they could promote the work and specializations of these healers within the local community in general as well as provide appropriate advice to those seeking help. The emphasis on, and recognition of, the healers' specializations signalled two developments: on the one hand, a return to the more classic situation, with healers addressing only those illnesses for which they had been initiated and, on the other hand, a sort of professionalization of healers, who were gradually able to turn their art into a full-time profession. Healers initiated into the same cult and thus treating the same illnesses came to a point where they were able to exchange some of their skills and herbal knowledge. By comparing their practices and learning from each other, they gained greater confidence in their own skills.

Organization of the healers In Mbanza Lemba the committee opted to bring the collaborating healers together in one *ad hoc* health centre. Upon arrival, the patient would be seen by a healer who was responsible for dispatching health-seekers to the appropriate healer and/or therapeutic setting. Although this process allowed for simplified administration, control over the quality of service provision and increased hygiene, it prevented the practice of some ritual procedures and the usual gift exchange between healer and patient. In Ndjili, lay persons, healers and community elders making up the committee limited their role to one of offering advice to health-seekers. The committee initiated, moreover, forms of collaboration between clients and care-providers, and between the care-providers themselves. This dynamic interferes with neither the therapeutic relation and procedures nor the form of payment. It allows, however, only minimal control over the quality of services provided. This type of organizational structure allows health-seekers to obtain personal and other relevant information regarding healers while leaving treatment decisions entirely to patients and their lay therapy management groups. Our regular and structured supervision of the committees' activities proved important for their survival. The researchers involved have taken on the role of facilitators in helping to solve problems while encouraging the group to find its own solutions and sustainable forms of therapy management.

Benefits for the community Patients commented on how the committees' advice shortened their search for effective care. During the two years of the experiment, no case of intoxication or major mistake in the treatment offered by the healers has been reported. The healers themselves initiated modes of reciprocal referral by referring some patients, during intake, to a colleague more specialized in the problem at hand. Key observers in the communities have emphasized how the committees offer reliable supportive networks. Complementary to the tasks performed in the health committee, initiatives were taken to enhance financial and moral support for families confronted with major accidents and losses. Possibilities were envisaged of setting up cultural and other activities to improve the quality of life in the neighbourhood.

Collaboration with medical care-providers Although the project did not encounter institutional resistance from the medical establishment, ignorance and suspicion regarding cult/folk therapies still typify the attitude of most representatives of the medical services. From the outset, the project teams established good working relationships with the public health officers responsible for Ndjili and Mbanza Lemba. Furthermore, attempts were made to collaborate in some manner with the private polyclinics in the respective neighbourhoods. These contacts set the scene for developing, in the longer term, an institutionalized mode of referral, and hence collaboration between medical practitioners, healers and patients.

Additionally, initial steps have been taken to remedy the need for a shift in approach and attitude on the part of the medical establishment, by implementing plans for an Institute for Medical Anthropology at the University of Kinshasa. Considering that virtually all physicians and nurses are university-trained, interdisciplinary training during the medical curriculum with regard to the cultural rationale underlying people's actual health-seeking behaviour is deemed a priority. Phytotherapeutic research on medicinal herbs at the Kinshasa Faculty of Pharmacy, to determine their organic or chemical curative properties, has merely contributed to the subordination of cult/folk healing practices, reducing their value to that of a singular vegetable cure.

Co-operation with faith healers Faith healers and healing churches have, to this date, not been included in the committees' actions. Faith healers openly accuse cult/folk healers of relying on the forces of (evil) spirits and *sataani*; healing churches also view healing as a mode of proselytism. This conflict represents the most significant practical setback for the project. Whereas cult/folk healers and most patients highly prize some recourse to medication, most healing churches practise only a form of purification through aspersion and ingestion of holy water and laying on hands, as well as through family council, collective prayer, song and other ritualized therapeutic actions. Although the local committees were initially reluctant to collaborate with faith healers in any way, a dialogue has been initiated to foster trust with several faith healers.

With the establishment of a basic level of communication between cult/folk healers and formal health services, it is quite likely that further coordination may develop under its own steam. New insights and strategies, and in particular new learning and communicational skills, have emerged from the on-going action-research. These should gradually be shared to devise new forms of interaction or collaboration between health providers and government officers, between action-research and policy-making, and between multilateral funding organizations and their Congolese counterparts. It is unlikely, however, that the healing churches will quickly move beyond the present level of understanding and informal collaboration reached between the researchers and the individual leaders of these healing communities. An exception may lie in those instances where a small minority of leaders acknowledge working with elements of cult healing.

Discussion

Having taken the challenge of helping to coordinate competing health systems as its point of departure, the project encountered several stumbling-blocks in reaching its action-research aims. Esotericism, craft-related or technical knowledge and different underpinning ideologies or world views were found to stand in the way of mutual understanding, recognition and cooperation. This class of epistemological difficulties not only bears consequences for relations between cult/folk healing, faith healing and biomedicine, but equally determines the behaviour of, and relations between, project researchers and participants. From the standpoint of the sociology of knowledge one quickly perceives in the parallel health systems a struggle between a universalizing, positivist and modernizing knowledge and traditional, local and pluralistic attitudes and practices. In sum, different historical and socio-cultural contexts have led not only to competing care systems but to competing health discourses. To grasp this fundamental difficulty in the project's realization better, it is necessary to describe in greater detail how the contemporary mindset in urban Congo, affecting both the researchers and the target group, is dominated by rationalistic and universalizing conceptions propagated by formal education, Christianity and mass media.

Local knowledge and modernity in contemporary Congo: shattered mirrors From the late colonial period (the Congo attained political independence in 1960), the models offered as 'mirrors' to the (urban) people for evaluating their health were founded on optimistic developmental theories inspired by Western evolutionary visions of legal-rational authority and good government, social well-being and the political economy of modern health for the new nation. Through these mirrors, the urban Congolese in the intervening decades first assimilated new ideals of health and health care and later partially rejected them. We maintain that the populace, through the widespread pillaging of the so-called modern institutions and enterprises (in a kind of Luddite uprising) that took place in the early 1990s, has broken down the mirroring process and false hopes stemming from the (post-) colonial legacy (Devisch 1995, 1996, 1998).

Beginning in the 1950s, modernization discourse characterized the village as a negative space. It was to be converted or abandoned; its paganism, polygyny, healing practices and sorcery, as well as the oppressive conservatism of the elderly, were to be eradicated. Development rhetoric focused on conditions of inadequate food, unclean water, poor hygiene and inferior shelter, which left villagers defenceless in the face of natural disaster, perils and infectious disease. Mortality, fertility and vaccination statistics were nearly always the first items mentioned in colonial administrative reports, as if hygienic, obstetric and medical action were adding new frontiers to rational modernity's imperium of progress. In this modernist vision of reality, the world of the village was reduced to a realm of untamed and unsafe nature. Life 'in the bush', as colonial discourse defined it, was considered to have little social or cultural existence, isolated from the civilizing function of the school, written word, hospital, administrative post, capitalist enterprise, market or church.

Since the late 1960s, under President Sese Seko Mobutu, a Eurocentric rhetoric of modernization has been integrated into the party-state's nationalist cause and presented under the guise of a Return to Authenticity politics. The underprivileged immigrant to the city was defined as a *citoyen* (a citizen), namely a typical member of the new nation. This identity was happily and positively contrasted with the colonial and ambivalent label of *évolué* or *acculturated*, which suggests a hybrid identity (rendered by the colloquial term: 'black white'). The new characterization, however, continued to be seen in contrast to that of the *villageois* (villager), a term replacing the *indigène* (the indigenous person), one who was still devoted to subsistence farming and the traditional world view.

The process of acculturation to the urban context was seen as a passage towards civilization, as an upward movement within the social scene, providing access to new territories of citizenship, instruction and information. The acculturated Kinois had advanced from the village context to the urban, from tradition to modernity, from insalubrious life conditions to a new space under the dominion of so-called modern hygiene and biomedicine, or from local connections with a tribal culture having its own distinctive characteristics to more globalizing and diversified scenes of foreign meanings, multiple norms and hybrid ideals. Similarly, moving from suburban to urban space (from *la cité* to *la ville*) was understood to be a vertical progression: the more a person's life involved *going up* to the city (*monter en ville*), to an elite school, business office, central hospital or church, the higher he or she had ascended on the civilizational ladder. Being uprooted from the rural locale in order to attend school, be converted to Christianity, consult a medical specialist or engage in an urban profession was a precondition for social climbing in terms of initiation and access to the higher social space of the city. Many Kinois would not have admitted to *going down* to the village (*descendre au village*) except for business or the funeral of close kin. How often one heard or read from Congolese *évolués* that as long as the emigrant families 'believe in all these outmoded things, they will be incapable of assuming their proper role in modern society; better that they had remained in the village!'

A lack of adaptation to the new nationalist scene orchestrated by

President Mobutu's Return to Authenticity movement was considered a fault or a mark of the non-adaptive villager still bound to the traditional space of ancestral law. The individual who persisted in not fitting into modern urban life, remaining out of step, or even rebelling against its lifestyle was soon marginalized and ostracized as a villager. Until late in the 1980s, the city-dweller spoke disdainfully about rural modes of life and especially initiatory practices (such as circumcision rites), divination, the ancestral cult and the world of sorcery, which traditionally link a person with an ancestral lineage and a source of ethno-cultural belonging and identity.

Kinshasa, with a population of about five million at present, is one of the largest urban centres of tropical Africa. With fewer than half a million inhabitants in 1960, the city expanded rapidly at a rate of approximately 10 per cent annually in the 1970s and 1980s. Massive immigration and high childbirth rates among a young population, for whom having many children constitutes a mark of wealth and a social security strategy, has deepened the division originally drawn by the Belgian colonists between the European sections of the city, called *la Ville*, and the ever-expanding African settlements that surround it, called *la Cité*. The former includes the downtown area with its places of employment, stores and neatly planned neighbourhoods where the privileged minority reside. The latter covers more than three-quarters of the total area of the capital. Most Kinois live here, either in older, somewhat planned districts or in newer, poorer zones or shanty towns where successive waves of immigration have inscribed themselves onto the urban terrain. Many of the shanty towns that comprise the expansion zone are inhabited by members of the same ethno-cultural community or group and share a common language, making Kinshasa a microcosm of Congo. In the last 15 years, there has been such stress on every aspect of the city's infrastructure, along with a lack of maintenance and mismanagement, that public schools, medical and administrative services, transport, roads and telephone communications have deteriorated considerably, if not broken down altogether.

Today, many Kinois find themselves in the thick of the struggle for survival, human dignity and decent housing. Half of the estimated jobs (de Maximy 1984: 20–8ff; Pain 1984: 105ff) are thought to have been lost because of the looting and destruction which took place in September 1991 and January 1993 (Devisch 1995). While the cost of living continues to rise, the labour market shrinks and, since 1990, the average daily salary for a civil servant has covered less than one-fifth of a family's basic daily necessities. Today, it is estimated that more than 90 per cent of Kinois do not draw a regular salary.

While the burden of economic responsibility falls primarily on the women who eke out an existence on the slim profit margins of street vending or by selling sex, the predatory economy of the street has become an informal and increasingly widespread means of survival for a growing number of young men in the shanty towns. Survival in most of the *Cité* is now more than ever defined by the infamous 'Article 15', as people have nicknamed the fictitious legal code that regulates the life of the deprived. We suggest that the predatory economy of the street is an urban version of the rural economy of hunting or collecting. This is a crafty, even malicious, sort of predatory behaviour, but not a violent one. For the oppressed, petty thievery acquires the status of a common mode of survival; it is their version of power, under the sign of Article 15. Men and boys refer to Article 15 with both self-conscious laughter and pride when in the presence of a stranger, for it at least brings them virile honour, if not at times providing more benefits than regular employment.

The villagization of town and lay therapy management Congolese have now begun to discover how much they have become foreigners to their original culture, family group, mode of life, education and communalism. Matri-centred households and female-centred networks operating at the core of suburban society sustain the process that Kinois people have called 'villagization of town'. Since 1993, neighbourhood, religious and residential associations have engaged in basic communal support activities such as improving neighbourhood security or providing basic amenities such as tap water, appropriate sanitation and electricity. Their leaders, including clever matrons, insightful elders and charismatic leaders in healing churches, increasingly inspire the revaluation of their residence connections or networks of communal belonging and support. Economically destitute, the populace today increasingly mobilizes its social capital as well as the will to temper the power of the state by exercising grassroots democracy and civic culture. These civic networks now counter the tendency of the masses to submit passively to the bureaucratic state and have succeeded in gradually arousing sentiments of communal empowerment. This new communal dynamic, which to a large extent is the outcome of women's daily struggle to assure the nutrition, health and education of their children, involves no less than a rehabilitation of one's place of belonging in the urban fabric.

A new sense of solidarity and communitarian ethical duty has thus developed at the neighbourhood and township level. Although the villagization of town does not actually entail a physical return to rural village life, urbanites' growing sense of rootedness in their residence networks draws on the collective and largely unconscious predispositions or *habitus* that somehow echo the socio-logic of village family structure and its communitarian economy of exchange or gift. When facing misfortune and bereavement, Kinois of the suburbs tend to reinforce the ethics and communal practices of matri-centred solidarity among kinsfolk in line with seniority and descent rules. They thereby tie in with dispositions at the core of age-old aetiologies, communal healing and ritual enactments of life changes. In Kinshasa, the major healing rites are performed in the language and style of the culture of origin and are thus adapted to the kinship allegiances and cosmology of the given group. Clients, however, can easily cross cultural boundaries because the cults possess a common cultural substratum, especially with regard to treatment strategies, metaphors related to the human body, and other preverbal symbols at play in the therapeutic setting: dances, mimes, body decorations, ritual objects, massage, fumigation, medicinal substances and, above all, trance-possession.

Kinois remain convinced that the current crisis will last for a long time. At the moment, they are unprepared to put their faith in the state's capacity to develop a new era of prosperity and greater justice. The populace has become increasingly aware that, in all matters of survival, health, security of the family, or school education, individuals can count only on themselves and the solidarity of brothers and sisters in their church or residence network. For the masses, participation in the moral revaluation of collective issues at the household or residence level – in communal prayer and sharing in the economy of divine grace and spiritual knowledge offered by the healing churches – is as much a source of social respectability as one's status by birth or professional achievement. For this reason, critics now state that, in the long term, community health care should tie in with this revitalized social capital and new moral fabric, and become less dependent on governmental agendas and external agencies or funding.

To put the matter in terms proposed by Veena Das (1994: 163–4), although she writes in relation to the plight of the victims of the chemical poisoning at Bhopal, India, in turning to healing churches, healers and local health centres, Kinois seem to be 'discard[ing] paternalistic notions by which health is handed down to the poor through a paternalistic and bureaucratically defined rationality'. Omnis, the NGO coordinating health care action throughout Kinshasa, has become alarmed by the decreased use of biomedical and sponsored health initiatives. Dispensaries and maternities in the townships have witnessed a significant decline in consultations, while the overall health situation in the urban areas has deteriorated significantly due to epidemics and malnutrition. The financial factor does not explain people's current withdrawal from, or dissatisfaction with, biomedical help since usually only token payments are required for treatment at most clinics. Instead, many patients complained of the low socio-moral satisfaction gained from biomedical consultation and treatment.

An externally sponsored tuberculosis vaccination programme, carried out in early 1996 and intended to reach the entire populace of the capital, has experienced a turnout of only 70 per cent in some zones. Parents and neighbourhood elders explained that they have deliberately boycotted the campaign in an attempt 'to defame the state, for in so doing, it deliberately sought to infect their children'. Widespread rumours have led to an attitude of deep suspicion towards paramedical personnel because many have turned their services into private businesses. (It is common for medical staff to treat patients only after they have received something in the way of personal payment, called 'beans for the children'.) These rumours increasingly associate clinics and primary care centres with the discredited kleptocratic state establishment, which people now wish to avoid altogether.

Under the present circumstances, health-seekers increasingly access ethno-culturally more familiar networks of health care in their own neighbourhoods for their minor ailments. Here they find an expanding informal sector of small and non-subsidized, often religiously inspired, health centres run by paramedics or even quacks of some sort. Clients acknowledge that the service offered by these people or centres may be of low quality, yet they find it largely reassuring and positive insofar as it helps them to look after themselves. Pharmaceutical shops, often kept by untrained personnel, can be found in every street and self-medication (especially with ampicillin, Cibalgine or Indocid) for minor ailments is widespread. People often claim that, in view of the high rates of inflation, 'buying a pill from time to time remains a cheap substitute for the more costly daily bread'.

At first, Kinois health-seeking practices and attitudes towards medical practice seem to entail a series of contradictions. They may be understood, however, as strategies for coming to terms with unsettling and conflicting social, cultural and economic realities. In the current processes of villagization and endogenization (or cultural re-rooting of health care in people's own cultural soil), neighbourhood networks seem to domesticate (literally, bring home or turn into a family place or network) culturally alien institutions, such as biomedical views on health, disease and cure. These on-going processes remobilize the kin and/or solidarity relations that underpin people's health-seeking behaviour and cult or faith healing practices. In the coming decades, neither the state nor NGOs will have the material resources or moral capital to coordinate community health care. People's growing resourcefulness with respect to self-medication will draw increasingly on folk healing traditions rather than on biomedicine.

The current general state of dysphoria, the struggle for survival, and educational and health care opportunities have had other direct influences on the present action-research programme. On the one hand, collaborators themselves often felt distressed by material, funeral or health problems. As researchers in the field, they met doctors or healers and their patients in the thick of economic and institutional hardships and, like them, suffered the same vagaries of life in the post-colony. For their part, informants often lacked the motivation necessary to carry out interviews, or were tempted to turn them into opportunities for personal gain. Since October 1996, the severe political unrest in Kinshasa has slowed or hampered research in the field and has disrupted the programme of seminar meetings scheduled with public health-planners and doctors. On the other hand, Kinois colleagues and collaborators have confirmed time and again how much their partnership with European researchers, even if short-term, provided them with essential and critical support. It enabled them to foster an attitude of self-criticism in their work with patients who, in their contact with representatives of the medical or university institutions, habitually glossed over or suppressed the cultural rationale in their experience of illness, and felt unable to express their symbolic means of coping with respect to the sheer brutality of the struggle for survival.

The researchers are convinced that the project's involvement with local urban networks of lay therapy management is indeed significant, all the more since the action-research takes local health needs, strategies and social distress or anomie as its point of departure. Moreover, the project aims to strengthen the communities' available resources, in terms of persons, relationships, responsibilities or goods, while fostering people's culture-specific agency and views – elements that otherwise tend to be ignored in community health programmes. On the other hand, the culture-specific character of people's agencies and views in health-seeking has confronted the researchers with their own culture-specific mindset, thus laying bare an epistemological paradox – which we will now examine – that the action-research has not fully been able to solve.

Healers accommodating to the mindset of the researchers The vehemence and persistence with which many healers proclaim that the efficacy of their healing practices work solely on the basis of the medicinal properties of the plants they use provided an initial clue to a key epistimological difficulty encountered by the project. Similar affirmations are even more common among the faith healers. Though only a few faith healers use plants in therapy, they all attribute their powers of healing to the Holy Spirit. Alongside their plants, they claim that it is their prayers and the power of the God that ultimately heals. To the casual researcher, it might then appear, on the basis of the testimony of the healers themselves, that their therapies have nothing to do with ancestors, the spirit world, symbolism, group or ritual.

Echoing the testimonies of many of her colleagues, for example, one faith healer (Prophetess Ngadi, Ndjili-Kinshasa, speaking in the vernacular liNgala) informed us: 'Tata azalaki kosala na makambo yo kala ya bakoko. Ngai nazali kosalela na tino ya Biblia, ya priere. Tobongola makambo ya bakoko tokoma na Biblia, na losambo. Ngai nayebi Nzambe nasalisaka naboyi nzete na kombo ya Nzambe. Bukoko ya kala tobwaka.' ['My father worked according to the old customs of the elders. I am working through the Bible and through prayer. We changed (*kobongola*: transform, modify but also disfigure) the customs of the elders and we arrived at the Bible and at prayer. I know God and work with him, and I refuse "plants" (*nzete*, that is, healing with plants in the way the elders did) in the name of God. We have thrown away the old ways of the elders.'] This type of response poses both methodological and theoretical problems even for the dedicated and forewarned researcher. The anthropologist familiar with African medicine can safely assume, for example, that the vegetal substances for a particular treatment have probably been 'revealed' in dreams to the cult or faith healer, collected in a particular, ritually determined place and manner – including the offering of prayers to the spirits – and prepared according to specific procedures determined by the healing tradition. When a healer denies that this is the case, the researcher is hardly in a position to contradict the informant or attempt to demonstrate an inconsistency. On the theoretical level as well, the observer-researcher has no right to contest the explanation of the healers when they themselves deny that their capacity to heal has anything to do with non-empirical, non-organic properties or forces.

We have undoubtedly encountered here a limitation of the social sciences as well as psychiatric and group psychotherapeutic approaches in dealing with health perceptions and behaviours. Looking at the phenomenon more closely, we discover two levels at which scientific investigation encounters resistance. The first is a sociological phenomenon, one that could have been anticipated in the context of the present project. In the target neighbourhoods, approximately fifty cult and fifty faith healers were identified. In the process of organizing community committees, nearly half of the cult/folk healers showed interest in joining or cooperating with a local association, but many of these eventually dropped out of the process. At this time, after approximately two years of implementation, only five or six cult/folk healers in each of the neighbourhoods continue regularly or actively to participate in cooperative efforts. While one can understand that many factors might diminish a healer's enthusiasm for 'going public' with his or her vocation, including the unwillingness to risk disclosure or competition, we understand this phenomenon in fact to represent a form of 'auto-censure'. As implied by other studies (Bekaert 1998; Creten 1996; De Boeck 1991, 1994; Devisch

1993, 1995, 1996; Devisch and Brodeur 1999; Lapika Demomfu 1984; Van Wolputte 1997), this means that the only healers who were ultimately willing to cooperate with the initiative were those who were prepared to adopt a quasi-medical and Christianized discourse. In our presence, they all affirmed working strictly with medicinal plants, while at the same time some attributed their healing capacities to 'God' or the 'Holy Spirit'. A number of healers may even pray together at the opening of their formal meetings.

One might surmise that this form of discourse does not reflect their actual practice, and indeed in most cases it does not. Does the researcher then assume that the healers are inconsistent or dishonest? And here we reach another, more subtle, limitation of social science and psychiatric research – what we refer to as a matter of 'competing discourses'. Verbally at least, these cult/folk healers would seem to be reducing their therapies to vegetable and organic principles (they themselves are fond of speaking of the *principe actif* residing in the plant substance), just as the faith healers relegate any therapeutic efficacy to the work of the Holy Spirit. According to our socio-cultural perspective on informal therapies, however, patients would find little satisfaction in healing practices that do not take account of an essentially relational and group aetiology.

It is worthwhile here to look again at how issues of cultural aetiologies and therapies, on the one hand, and epistemologies, on the other, relate. There can be no one-sided thrusting of scientific (medical) criteria (originating from a written culture with a visual logic) upon the cult/folk healers to evaluate their fundamentally oral and even gestural ways of gaining and transmitting therapeutic knowledge in the healing cults and folk practices. Each cult plays on the emotions, and engages the totality of sensorial corporeality, cosmology or life world (that is, beliefs and horizons of meaning) and relevant kinship relations in the process of healing. The patient's symbolic death and rebirth takes place within a group drama and on the basis of complex symbolic processes. Each cult offers its own chain of metaphors and metonyms in order to remodel the specific syndrome into a vital consonance between body, group and life world. A sphere of initiatory secrecy and sacralization underpins the therapeutic relationship between healer and patient or neophyte. Of course, the ways in which such multilayered and predominantly non-verbal semantic drama leads to physical, affective and cognitive changes, which not only heal but also give a new identity to the patient, escape a more positivist medical understanding. By definition, folk/cult healing cannot be evaluated by means of criteria commonly used for positivist scientific knowledge or applied by governments as standards for medical and therapeutic professionalism. The healers' therapeutic success with the patient equally functions as a test of their authenticity.

There remains a question to which we alluded earlier regarding the logical consistency of a haphazard appeal to presumably contradictory explanatory theories, where a cult/folk healer may shift from one discourse to another depending on his or her audience or the context. Indeed, the use of local language is telling: one speaks liNgala or French to the researcher or in a community meeting, but during the serious business of healing, the only effective speech – whether spoken or paradigmatic – is the healer's mother tongue. The urban healer has been forced to carry his or her skills beyond ethno-cultural boundaries and is thus necessarily faced with a problem of translation, at least where legitimation of the practice is at stake. To a certain extent, recourse to an otherwise foreign discourse is only a form of extension of one's professional sphere. But that is not all. Healers grasp very well the efficacy of modern drugs and surgery, just as they recognize the value of medicinal plants. Yet this acknowledgement in no way diminishes their 'knowledge' and ability to manipulate other forms of 'power'. In their acceptance of epistemological categories and logic that surpass the primitive and exclusive distinction between the material and the immaterial, they are indeed pluralistic and intellectually honest. We can only raise the question as to whether the appeal – at different times and in different contexts – to equally valid discourses actually constitutes self-contradiction. What does it mean when one discourse (modernist, objective, drawing on the authority of science and the medical order) claims to be exclusive while the other (experiential, relational, drawing on the authority of cult traditions) does not?

For the healers, then, adopting a scientific discourse is simply a natural step or strategy in the effort to organize and improve both the quality and quantity of their services, and thus to legitimate their practices. In this way, they can only be said to be responding perfectly to the aims and objectives of the researchers who have sought their collaboration. The phenomenon of externally initiated social projects and their agents raising expectations, paralleled by the solicitation (conscious or unconscious) of particular behaviours, among the target group is well documented. This project was no exception. In this sense, requiring that healers practise in a building belonging to the centre (something that some healers themselves decided upon, ostensibly to improve hygiene, presumably because of the added status) raises fundamental questions with regard to the integrity of cult therapy practice. We have not yet been able adequately to assess the consequences of this development. Again, it is important here to recall the impact on urban Congolese society of the rationalizing and modernizing project that has been felt and absorbed, to varying degrees, by all levels and classes of the population.

The mindset of the researchers Our reflections cannot be addressed solely to the healers, for the researchers themselves are subject to the same sociological forces and epistemological conditions. It was our experience that, despite our vocation as social scientists and psychiatrists, most of the researchers were either unable, or found it extremely difficult, to pierce the veil of the universalizing and rationalistic knowledge we all shared by virtue of our Western education. This made it nearly impossible to uncover precisely the culturally particular elements of illness and healing in the suburban populations of southwestern Congo. There are aspects of therapy dynamics that are shared by many cultures across the world, and discovering these was in fact part of the challenge of observing health behaviour among a mixed ethno-cultural population. But comparative and generalizing theories are clearly inadequate to explain the deepest, to a large extent unconscious, levels of local conceptions and practices related to illness and healing.

The fact that a dialogue between healers and researchers was possible at all is, in part, due to a mutual recognition of the other's vocation. Acceptance by others in our roles as researchers was determined by our negotiation of trust in order to overcome the biases of gender, ethno-cultural identity, educational and middle-class status, or, for example, to avoid being perceived as a member of a state institution. But trust and the possibility of dialogue is not a sufficient condition for mutual comprehension. As we have already shown, the adopted (we do not wish to imply 'affected') modernizing discourse and behaviour of the healers, particularly in the presence of the researchers, constitutes an added obstacle that only the researcher who is familiar with the healer's mother tongue, local culture of origin and age-old hermeneutics proper to the healing cults, is able – with any credibility – to circumvent.

If the researcher does not possess a thorough grasp of the healer's mother tongue, it is all but impossible to carry on a serious dialogue on therapeutic practice with him or her, much less explore the culturally bound aetiologies underlying the practice at hand. It is one thing if researchers simply have not had the opportunity to develop the necessary linguistic skills to deal with a particular informant and need to resort to translation. It is yet another when systematically, in the course of interviews, questionnaires and organizational meetings, the default language is never a mother tongue but the lingua franca (liNgala) or that of formal schooling (French). The limitations and dangers of translation are well known. Nevertheless, we do not intend to imply that the culturally determined aspects of aetiology and therapy are exclusively verbalized or communicated through language; we would argue that the non-verbal and gestural level, which may be even more culturally conditioned, is, in fact, predominant.

This alone would explain the marked capacity of cult and faith healers to work in an inter-ethnic context, although we are dealing with Bantu populations who share many cultural characteristics.

Rather, we observe that the use of a 'non-ethnic' language (French or the vernacular liNgala) is often either the unconscious choice of the researcher, who no longer masters the subject's mother tongue, or the conscious choice of the researcher who feels the necessity of communicating a certain status, education and distance from what the (post-) colonial discourse commonly designated as *indigène* (indigenous), meaning backward, ignorant and typical of village life. The informant or counterpart is equally willing to attempt at least to speak in the 'modern' language in order to affirm his or her own modernity.

The researcher, a product of secularistic Western science, is often reluctant to appeal to Christianity – as some cult/folk healers seem to do – to communicate their status as a university researcher. Rather, for the sake of research, he or she may participate fully in a healing service for which, according to the criteria imposed on participants by the faith healers themselves, one must 'have faith' or 'be pure'. Given Christianity's omnipresence in the capital and southwest, it is no surprise that anyone can easily resort to Christian discourse without necessarily being a practising believer. The problem resides more in the fact that Christianity has been at the forefront of the civilizing mission, particularly where local 'religious' beliefs and practices were concerned, for they were considered, *a priori*, 'pagan' or pertaining to magic and fetishism (depending on whether the dominant discourse is religious or scientific). Even the 'modern educated' Congolese is anxious to avoid too close an association with those local cultural spheres, which smack of backwardness and ignorance, for fear that their affirmation – or mere contiguity – will make him or her appear equally backward and ignorant.

It is not that the researcher has abandoned the right to plural discourse – except to the extent that his or her education and urban life have caused him or her to forget his or her culture of origin – but that he or she is all too often anxious to impose that discourse which confirms his or her modern status, power and education, at least in contexts where such behaviour is socially indicated. This means that the researcher is often unmotivated to revalorize a local knowledge or practice, which he or she has forsaken. Without passing judgement on the researcher's personal motivations and conscious intentions (indeed a Western problem), it seems that the impact of the civilizing mission is such that dealing seriously with indigenous culture requires not only significant effort (in terms of studies focused on indigenous knowledge and practices) but also a break with prevalent attitudes.

Conclusion

The way in which healers are capable of dealing with the dictates posed by city life, medicine and the market economy, and of creatively transforming and metabolizing these influences, or the way in which they succeed in voicing the aspirations of the people amid the current institutional crisis in the Congo, are of vital importance for their continued practice. At the same time, this is one of the key problems in our applied research. Our contribution lies in the mediation between the world of healers and formal health care institutions as well as on the level of acquiring critical insight and knowledge. Among other things, this means that researchers must constantly be aware of the sociological and cultural factors impacting on their epistemological practice in order to minimize the limitations and maximize the potentialities of the social sciences, psychiatry and group psychotherapy.

Acknowledgements

The project (TS3 CT94-0326, entitled Therapy Choice, Management and Satisfaction in Kinshasa) and financed by the European Union (DG XII B4 STD Medicine; coordinator and contractor, Professor R. Devisch; subcontractors, Professor Lapika Dimomfu and Dr J. Le Roy) was originally designed to cover Kinshasa alone. The four extensions that it has meanwhile undergone are partly being reported on in separate studies. The first of these is the research by Professor Filip De Boeck (K. U. Leuven Africa Research Centre) on Culture and trauma in the aftermath of the Ebola epidemics in Kikwit, Southwest Congo (De Boeck 1998; 1999). Second, Dr Mubagwa Kanigula (K. U. Leuven Faculty of Medicine) tested our questionnaire on 'Therapy management, choice and satisfaction', by applying it in the city of Bukavu in eastern Congo in January 1996. Third, with regard to the integration of the plural health care systems in Tropical Africa, Dr Daniel Grodos and Professor Emeritus Pierre Mercenier (Royal Institute of Tropical Medicine, Antwerp) have provided a report (Grodos and Mercenier 1996) on their lengthy experience in that domain. Fourth, Steven Van Wolputte developed a survey (1997) on recent medical anthropological research in Africa south of the Sahara.

We also gratefully acknowledge the contribution to the research proposal by our colleague Filip De Boeck in theorizing the dialectics between gift logic and monetary commodity exchange in view of understanding the new socio-logics involved in health-seeking in Kinshasa. The hypotheses he has helped to put forward in that regard are in line with those of De Boeck 1996. In 1996, Walter Six made some initial contributions to the empirical research in Kinshasa. Among the authors of this chapter, Peter Cross man contributed as the first author of the final sections on 'Healers accommodating the mindset of the researchers' and 'The mindset of the researchers'.

Notes

1. The Inter-regional Centre for Training, Research and Documentation in the Social Sciences at the University of Kinshasa (CERDAS), under the supervision of

Professor Lapika Dimomfu, coordinated the sociological investigation regarding utilization of the various health centres. Mr Kiyulu N'yanga Nzo, Mr Mulopo Kisweko and Mr Matula Atul Entur were responsible for carrying out the study. Professor Lapika coordinated the action-research in Mbanza Lemba. Psychiatrist and psychotherapist Dr Jaak Le Roy, of the Academic Regional Institute for Community Health Care (RIAGG) in Maastricht, and psychiatrist Dr A. Nsitu, of the Neuro-Psycho-Pathology University Hospital of Kinshasa (CNPP) focused their research on the therapeutic work and explanatory models used by care-providers, patients and families in the various health care systems as well as interconnections between these systems. Dr Le Roy was involved in the definition of the research project and was responsible for the medical-psychiatric and psychodynamic part of the overall action-research design and its implementation in Ndjili XII. He acknowledges the advice of Professor Joop de Jong, of the Transcultural Psycho-Social Organization (TPO) and the Free University Amsterdam. The Africa Research Centre (ARC) at the University of Leuven, CERDAS at the University of Kinshasa, and RIAGG Maastricht were the three institutional partners in this joint research project. A dialogue has been set up between those involved in the on-going action-research and two professionals of the Ministry of Health: Dr Bimamisana MD, director of the Mount Amba Health Centre at the University campus, and Dr Masaki MD, who is general health inspector for Kinshasa.

2. Both the BSE and HBEQ have been used in a mental health research programme by IPSER (Institute for Psycho-Socio-Ecological Research), directed by Professor M. de Vries, University of Maastricht and Professor J. de Jong, TPO (Transcultural Psycho-Social Organization) and the Free University Amsterdam. The questionnaire and database, which aim at a statistical and qualitative analysis, are the work of Dr J. Le Roy. Inspiration stems from J. de Jong (1994) and his 'Collaborative TPO–WHO Programme for the Identification, Management and Prevention of Psycho-Social and Mental Health Problems of Refugees and Victims of Organized Violence within Primary Care'. Data retrieval was carried out with the help of Dr I. Komproe, TPO.

References

Audisio, M. (1994) 'Modernité et événement, trauma et défense', *Connexions* (Paris) 63: 147–58.

Bekaert, S. (1998) *Culturen van binnenuit leren kennen*, Antwerp: EPO; Mechelen: CIMIC.

Bell, D. and L. Chen (1994) 'Responding to health transitions: from research to action', in L. C. Chen, A. Kleinman and N. C. Ware (eds), pp. 491–502.

Bibeau, G., E. Corin, M. H. Buganza, M. Mandela and M. M. Mvunzi (1979) *La Médecine traditionnelle au Zaïre: fonctionnement et contribution potentielle aux services de santé*, Ottawa: CRDI/IDRC.

Bockie, S. (1993) *Death and the Invisible Powers: The World of Kongo Belief*, Bloomington: Indiana University Press.

Bourdieu, P. (1980) *Le Sens pratique*, Paris: Minuit.

Buakasa, Tulu kia Mpansu (1973) *L'Impensé du discours: kindoki et nkisi en pays kongo du Zaïre*, Kinshasa: Presses Universitaires du Zaïre.

Cadoret, M. (1994) 'La question de l'identité, transmission, dette, ritualité', *Connexions* (Paris) 63: 189–98.

Chen, L. C., A. Kleinman and N. C. Ware (eds) (1994) *Health and Social Change in International Perspective*, Boston, MD: Harvard School of Public Health/Harvard University Press.

Corin, E. (1979) 'A possession psychotherapy in an urban setting: *Zebola* in Kinshasa', *Social Science and Medicine* 13B: 327–38.

Creten, P. (1996) 'Gender en identiteit: een medisch-antropologisch onderzoek bij de Nkanu in Kinshasa en zuidwest Zaïre', doctoral thesis in anthropology, Catholic University of Leuven.

Das, V. (1994) 'Moral orientations to suffering', in L. C. Chen, A. Kleinman and N. C. Ware (eds), pp. 139–70.

De Boeck, F. (1991) 'Therapeutic efficacy and consensus among the Aluund of Southwest Zaire', *Africa* 61: 159–85.

—— (1994) 'When hunger goes around the land: food and hunger in Luunda land', *Man* 29: 257–82.

—— (1996) 'Postcolonialism, power and identity: local and global perspectives from Zaire', in R. P. Werbner and T. O. Ranger (eds), *Postcolonial Identities in Africa*, London: Zed, pp. 75–106.

—— (1998) 'Beyond the grave: history, memory and death in postcolonical Congo/Zaïre', in R. P. Werbner (ed.), *Memory and the Postcolony: African Anthropology and the Critique of Power*, London: Zed, pp. 21–57 (in French translation: 'Au-delà du tombeau: histoire, mémoire et mort dans le Congo/Zaïre', in J.-L. Grootaers [ed.] [1999], *Mort et maladie au Zaïre*, Tervuren: Institut Africain-CEDAF; Paris: Harmattan, pp. 129–72).

—— (1999) 'Domesticating diamonds and dollars: identity, expenditure and sharing in Southwestern Zaire (1984–1997)', in B. Meyer and P. Geschiere (eds), *Globalization and Identity: Dialectics of Flow and Closure*, Oxford: Blackwell, pp. 177–209.

de Jong, J. T. (1994) 'Prevention of the impact of man-made or natural disaster at the (inter)national, the community, the family and the individual level', in S. E. Hobfoll and H. M. de Vries (eds), *Extreme Stress and Communities: Impact and Intervention*, Dordrecht: Kluwer.

de Maximy, R. (1984) *Kinshasa, ville en suspens: dynamique de la croissance et problèmes d'urbanisme; approche socio-politique*, Paris: ORSTOM.

Devisch, R. (1993) *Weaving the Threads of Life: The Khita Gyn-eco-logical Healing Cult Among the Yaka*, Chicago, IL: University of Chicago Press.

—— (1995) 'Frenzy, violence, and ethical renewal in Kinshasa', *Public Culture* 7: 593–629.

—— (1996) '"Pillaging Jesus": healing churches and the villagisation of Kinshasa', *Africa* 66: 555–86.

—— (1998) 'La violence à Kinshasa, ou l'institution en négatif', *Cahiers d'études africaines* 38(2–4) nos 150–2: 441–69.

Devisch, R. and C. Brodeur (1999) *The Law of the Lifegivers: The Domestication of Desire*, Amsterdam: Harwood Academic Publishers.

Devisch, R. and Mbonyinkebe Sebahire (1997) 'Medical anthropology and traditional care', in P. G. Janssens, M. Kivits and J. Vuylsteke (eds), *Health in Central Africa Since 1885: Past, Present and Future*, Vol. 1, Brussels: King Baudouin Foundation; Leuven: Peeters, pp. 47–64.

Douville, O. (1996) 'Cliniciens et anthropologues: vers un dialogue possible?', in O. Douville (ed.), *Anthropologie et cliniques: recherches et perspectives*, Rennes: ARCP, pp. 53–94.

Douville, O., J. Le Roy and A. Blondin-Siop (1999) 'A propos du parcours de soin de patients africains séropositifs en France', *Cliniques Méditéranéennes* 59–60, Paris: Eres.

Grodos, D. and P. Mercenier (1996) 'Le Problème de la méthodologie dans la recherche sur les systèmes de santé', manuscript prepared for the European Commission DG XII-B4 STD *Medicine*, project TS3 CT94-0326 (40pp.).

Hagenbucher-Sacripanti, F. (1989) *Santé et rédemption par les génies au Congo*, Paris: Publisud-ORSTOM.

Jacobson-Widding, A. (1979) *Red-White-Black as a Mode of Thought: A Study of Triadic Classification by Colours in the Ritual Symbolism and Cognitive Thought of the People of the Lower Congo*, Stockholm: Almqvist and Wiksell.

Janzen, J. M. (1978) *The Quest for Therapy: Medical Pluralism in Lower Zaire*. Berkeley: University of California Press.

— (1982) *Lemba, 1650–1930: A Drum of Affliction in Africa and the New World*, New York: Garland.

— (1989) 'Health, religion and medicine in Central and Southern African traditions', in L. Sullivan (ed.), *Healing and Restoring: Health and Medicine in the World's Religious Traditions*, New York: Macmillan.

— (1992) *Ngoma: Discourses of Healing in Central and Southern Africa*, Berkeley: University of California Press.

Lapika Dimomfu (1984) *L'art de guérir chez les Kongo du Zaïre, discours magique ou science médicale?*, Brussels: CEDAF – Institut Africain, *Les Cahiers du CEDAF*, 1(3).

Le Roy, J. (1994a) 'Processus thérapeutiques groupaux dans les églises de guérison à Kinshasa', *Connexions* (Paris) 63: 101–24.

— (1994b) 'Group analysis and culture', in D. Brown and L. Zinkin (eds), *The Psyche and the Social World*, London: Routledge, pp. 180–201.

— (1996) 'Sur les institutions thérapeutiques dans les églises de guérison', in O. Douville (ed.), *Anthropologie et cliniques: recherches et perspectives*, Rennes: ARCP, pp. 53–94.

— (1998) 'Relier la personne et le social: fonction sociale de la maladie et le travail thérapeutique dans les églises de guérison au Zaïre', *PTAH* 1(1) (Paris).

Le Roy, J. and A. N'situ (1998) 'Le groupe, opérateur de changement et de recherche: recherche action communautaire pour l'amélioration des soins de santé à Kinshasa (Congo)', *Connexions* (Paris), 71.

MacGaffey, W. (1986) *Religion and Society in Central Africa: The Bakongo of Lower Zaire*, Chicago, IL: Chicago University Press.

Mahaniah, K. (1982) *La Maladie et la guérison en milieu kongo*, Kinshasa: Centre de vulgarisation agricole.

Pain, M. (1984) *Kinshasa: la ville et la cité*, Paris: ORSTOM.

Rouchy, J. C. (1995) 'Identification and groups of belonging', *Group Analysis* 28: 129–42.

Van Wing, J. (1959) (first edn, vol. 1: 1921, vol. 2: 1938) *Études Bakongo: sociologie, religion et magie*, 2 vols, Paris: Desclée de Brouwer.

Van Wolputte, S. (1997) *Gezondheid en genezen in Afrika*, Amsterdam: Het Spinhuis.

7

Representing HIV/AIDS Concerns in Uganda: The Genogram as a Visual Complement to Ethnographic and Epidemiological Evidence

Nelson K. Sewankambo, Patricia A. Spittal and
Dennis G. Willms

The magnitude of reported incidence and prevalence rates of HIV infection in sub-Saharan Africa is staggering, and to many people in the
Western world the statistics are difficult to comprehend and accept. At the
end of 1999, UNAIDS estimated that out of a global total of 34.3 million
adults and children living with HIV/AIDS, 24.5 million were living in sub-
Saharan Africa. In Uganda alone, there was a reported estimate of 820,000
adults and children living with HIV/AIDS and 1.7 million AIDS orphans
(UNAIDS 2000: 124). Rakai district in southwestern Uganda, the setting
of the research results reported on in this chapter, represents one example
of 'a mature HIV-1 epidemic, with a prevalence of the infection of 15.9%'
(Wawer et al. 1999: 525, 533). Yet in the early 1990s, sero-prevalence rates
were as high as 35 per cent in the general population (Wawer et al. 1991;
Sewankambo et al. 1994). With strong prevention programmes and an
openness about the reality of HIV/AIDS, Uganda has brought its estimated
prevalence down to around 8 per cent (UNAIDS 2000: 9). And yet 'the
suffering generated by HIV infections acquired years ago continues to
grow, as millions of adults fall ill and die and as households, communities
and whole sectors of the economy stagger under the burden' (ibid.).

While struggling to come to terms with the statistical reporting, it is
even more difficult to imagine the impact of HIV/AIDS on families,
communities and nations in sub-Saharan Africa. This chapter attempts to
address the issue of how we, as people living in the West and North, can
understand more authentically and concretely the devastating consequences
of this disease (HIV/AIDS) on persons living in sub-Saharan Africa. As
such, this chapter argues for more compelling representations of the impact
of HIV/AIDS on people and communities, whereby the genogram visually
complements ethnographic (illness and disease narratives and case studies)

and epidemiological evidence (numerical reporting of the incidence and prevalence of the disease). As health researchers, it is imperative that our reporting of HIV/AIDS realities is done responsibly and fairly. It is therefore incumbent upon us to ensure that we are morally accountable to those people whose lives we represent.

For the people reported on in this chapter, however, the numbers are not the issue. These people experience the harsh reality of living with HIV/AIDS every day. Their stories are expressions of denial, hopelessness, despair and suffering. Their world is made real through case studies, narratives and life histories that uncover the emotional intensity of 'giving up their lives' to this disease, of losing hope, of voices dimmed through death and the destruction of family desires. Numbers quantify a certain reality and provide evidence of 'how bad it is'. Stories, on the other hand, dynamically demonstrate the relational tensions, dilemmas and contingencies of 'being without hope'. In this chapter, we explore the visual evidence that graphically demonstrates the reality of suffering – the genograms that complement ethnographic and epidemiological evidence.

Our research team lived and worked in the town of To-Day for more than eight years.[1] Influenced by epidemiological studies that report on the seriousness of the HIV/AIDS problem in Rakai district, the initial objective of Phase 1 of our research was ethnographically to uncover social-cultural understandings of HIV/AIDS, and interpret the impact of this disease on people living in the town. At this preliminary stage in our research, we were naive in thinking that we were prepared to deal with the consequences of what we would learn. As we reported at that time, not only were we surprised by the extent and depth of the suffering, we began to wonder how to communicate the reality of HIV/AIDS to the outside world.[2] At present, in the midst of our Phase 2 participatory intervention research, we are compelled to find ways to represent the experience of living with HIV/AIDS to a variety of stakeholders – academic, donor and government constituencies.

Furthermore, as we incorporate participatory methodologies into the process of our intervention research, there is a critical need to find ways to represent these risk realities (cf. Willms and Sewankambo 1995) to the community itself, particularly to those vulnerable groups in To-Day affected by HIV/AIDS. In a fatalistic social-cultural environment, people need resources that will enable them to solve problems related to lifestyle (such as issues pertaining to sexuality, gender communication, safe sexual practices). We maintain that the genogram – a clinical tool typically used in family medicine and family-based therapy (cf. Ebell and Heaton 1988; Friedman et al. 1988; Gerson and McGoldrick 1985; Halliday 1985; Herth 1989; Like et al. 1988; Mengel and Mauksch 1989; Rogers and Cohn 1987;

Rogers and Holloway 1990; Rogers et al. 1993; Shellenberger et al. 1988; Shore et al. 1994; Waters et al. 1994) – can be used to help represent the reality of HIV/AIDS to these different stakeholders. As a graphic research and educational tool, it complements ethnographic data, usually in the form of narratives and stories, and epidemiological data that report HIV/ AIDS incidence and prevalence in statistical and numerical formats. In short, we suggest that communicating the reality of HIV/AIDS to varieties of communities and sectors requires these three approaches: quantitative representation (numbers and trends reflected in incidence and prevalence rates), qualitative and ethnographic representations (case studies, narratives, stories), as well as visual representations (in this instance, the genogram). We argue that this configuration of representations is needed in order to provide a more compelling and persuasive appreciation of the impact of HIV/AIDS on communities in sub-Saharan Africa such as To-Day.

Study Background

This study was designed with the hope that ethnographic methods and perspectives would bring to light more grounded understandings of the social and cultural context of high-risk behaviours relating to HIV transmission. The study was conducted in To-Day, a rural town devastated by HIV/AIDS in Rakai district, southwestern Uganda.

To-Day was chosen as the location for our ethnographic research for a number of reasons. The town has developed over the years as a trading centre and truck-stop. It is located on the infamous trans-African highway, which extends from the Indian Ocean port city of Mombasa, Kenya, through Uganda to other land-locked countries such as Rwanda, Burundi and Zaire. At the junction of To-Day, there are also feeder roads leading deep into the villages. Many people converge on To-Day from other districts to complete trade transactions, which include coffee, *matooke* (plantain banana) and cattle marketing. It is recognized as a very popular stop-over point servicing the needs of lorry and transport truck drivers. These services may include lodging and commercial sex.

To-Day's history of being a prostitution 'hot-spot' has also contributed to its reputation as being a place of HIV/AIDS. The period, 1984–86, is vividly remembered by people because 'that is when things started to change ... people started to die'. To-Day is not the only place where these statements apply. There are many other towns much like this in East and Central Africa.

The members of our research team – comprising four Makerere University graduates – were trained in ethnographic data collection techniques, data management, analysis and interpretation (cf. Willms and Johnson

1997). The project began in February 1992. At the time of writing, the team is still living and working in To-Day.

It has been observed that people know how they can avoid infection, yet, in spite of this awareness, participate in sexual behaviours that place them at high risk for HIV transmission. This is an enduring public health conundrum, and worthy of intensive social science theorizing. Through massive HIV/AIDS primary prevention campaigns (made accessible through the television, radio and print media), people have come to know the risk behaviours associated with HIV transmission. Yet *knowing* – what persons say are the risk behaviours they should avoid – does not necessarily translate into *believing*, the concomitant experience of being vulnerable to, and adopting health behaviours that minimize or reduce the risk of, HIV transmission. Theorizing in the area of emotions (Jenkins 1991), aesthetic anthropology (Good 1996), and the notion of 'mindful bodies' (Scheper-Hughes and Lock 1987) may edge us towards a conceptual framework for understanding the dissonance in mind–body, and/or belief–action, eventually leading to theoretically useful intervention processes. The team's primary objective was, therefore, to study the meanings, nature of vulnerability and risk experiences of people living in such a place. We felt that learning about how people personalize and 'talk about'[3] risk of HIV/AIDS would assist us in strengthening existing prevention programmes as well as constructing better ones.

Methodology

Initially, we studied those groups of peoples identified through epidemiological and sentinel surveillance studies conducted at the district level. In To-Day, this meant interviewing bar girls or waitresses, their clients, and truck drivers. At that time, it was commonly presumed that such groups were responsible for perpetuating the heterosexual route of HIV infection from high-risk groups into the community (Piot et al. 1987). We decided to study these previously identified individuals and groups using a variety of complementary methods: unstructured and semi-structured in-depth interviews, focus groups, 'chance' discussions with informal groups and participant observation. Using this combination of ethnographic methods, we have generated a non-numerical, experiential kind of evidence. Life stories, illness narratives and observations of critical events (for example, the rituals observed at a funeral for a person who died of HIV/AIDS) are a kind of evidence that represents the community members' personal and collective suffering, coping strategies and rationalizations of the disease. In short, we have endeavoured to represent authentically what is real, true, and reflective of the everyday lives of the people of To-Day.

How do we know that we have accurately represented the reality of HIV/AIDS in their lives? One reason is that we have sampled to redundancy – that is, our research team has interviewed approximately one hundred people to the point where the same modes of communication and vernacular expressions emerge in the discussions. We have triangulated the evidence three ways: through different methods (in-depth interviews, focus groups, participant observation); different researchers and interviewers (the team of four research assistants recording, interpreting, talking and 'walking through the results' on a daily basis); and over time (conducting interviews with the same person numerous times and in different situations).

In a profound sense, we were not emotionally and intellectually prepared for the magnitude of the risk and vulnerabilities associated with HIV/AIDS, or the extent of the suffering that exists for people in To-Day. We were shocked into the realization that the lives of many people are characterized by sexual compromise, hopelessness and despair. To-Day is a place where hunger, poverty, sickness and death are common experiences. Virtually unknown are experiences of hope!

A poignant, almost extreme fatalism is characteristic of most conversations and is certainly evident in many, if not all, of the risk narratives compiled. People have seen their friends, relatives and children die horrible deaths. In fact, given the ubiquitous reality of death from HIV/AIDS in To-Day, many persons have resigned themselves to believing that 'there is nobody who can escape this disease'. This ethos of fatalism extends beyond the individual person to the community, pervading all aspects of life in To-Day (cf. Spittal 1995). With this ethnographic realization, we now have a better appreciation of the moral dilemmas and contingencies experienced by people living there, confronting the fact that even though people do know how they can protect themselves, they continue to 'give up their lives'.

The more in-depth our ethnographic assessments, the more we were immersed in human suffering. We came to recognize the prevalence of abuse in sexual relationships, and were assailed by an overriding sense of hopelessness and despair (cf. Spittal et al. 1997). With this emerging knowledge came confusion, ethical dilemmas and concerns as to whether the traditional intervention and programme processes that were to follow our Phase 2 research would be appropriate.

What do these data mean for us and for the people of To-Day? What is our responsibility with respect to interpreting, interacting with and disseminating these data? What are the consequences of certain dissemination strategies? Also, addressing the central question of this chapter, how do we appropriately, and in the spirit of moral accountability, *represent* this kind of research evidence to community members and policy-makers alike, in a manner that demonstrates the magnitude of the impact of HIV/AIDS on the lives of people, households and the larger community?[4]

The Genogram: A Graphic and Visual Complement to Case Studies

In the initial stages of our ethnographic research, each team member began with a study of the town itself, recording daily various details about ethnic composition, political economy, religious affiliations, gender relations and tensions, and indigenous organizations and associations. This part of the research has provided important background information to understanding how HIV/AIDS is experienced in To-Day (Sewankambo et al. 1993). Approximately eight months into the study, the team was advised by the two co-investigators (DW, NS) to move away from the general description of life in To-Day to more selective interviewing geared to generating case studies of people representative of the population. It was felt that a life history approach (eliciting narratives of risk and vulnerability to HIV/AIDS) was an appropriate and worthwhile approach for documenting more specific dimensions of personal risk. The team followed the lives of more than twenty people over a period of eight months. Because of the intricacies and complexities of people's relationships, family histories and sexual networks, the research assistants in the field were additionally asked to display visually, using the genogram, the trajectory and chronology of illness and death in the family of the people they were interviewing.

We thought that the genogram, primarily used in family systems medicine, might contribute in some way to HIV/AIDS intervention design, dissemination and evaluation (cf. Willms 1998). From an anthropological perspective, the genogram is analogous to kinship diagrams for individual, families and clan groups. Working in partnership, the researcher and the subject of the case study generated a picture of the subject's family structure. The skeletal form of the genogram was often completed on the first visit. However, several follow-up visits were required to corroborate patterns of sickness and death in the family. Case study participants even consulted with their parents or siblings in the village in order to get as accurate a picture as possible. The results of this simple exercise changed the very nature of our involvement in this research, our present and future accountabilities to the people of To-Day, and our methodological approach. We could not anticipate the impact this would have on us as people and professionals working in the field of HIV/AIDS (cf. Spittal et al. 1997).

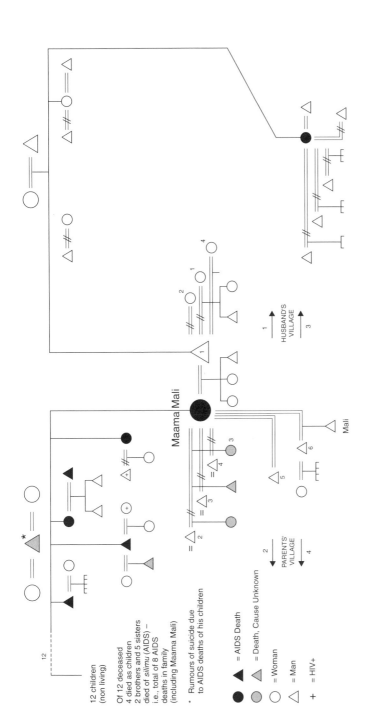

Maama Mali

12 children
(non living)

Of 12 deceased
4 died as children
2 brothers and 5 sisters
died of *silimu* (AIDS) –
i.e., total of 8 AIDS
deaths in family
(including Maama Mali)

* Rumours of suicide due
  to AIDS deaths of his children

◀ = AIDS Death

◩ = Death, Cause Unknown

○ = Woman

△ = Man

+ = HIV+

HUSBAND'S VILLAGE

PARENTS' VILLAGE

Mali

FIGURE 7.1 Maama Mali, alcohol seller

Results

After eight months of interviewing and constructing genograms, the research team left the field and retreated to a place where they could think, write and reflect, far away from the devastation of To-Day. During the retreat, as we discussed one case study after another, we posted the genograms of those people being discussed around the room. The effect was overwhelming. In this safe place, we were suddenly surrounded by another reality, the reality of a disease that was systematically taking the lives of individuals and, in its wake, divesting households, clans and an entire community of their moral and spiritual capacity to deal with and survive this disease. We knew, of course, that the impact of HIV/AIDS on this community was significant. Surveys had produced rates of prevalence, incidence and mortality that were staggering in their own right. These figures, while numbing, were difficult to grasp. Our accumulated ethnographic evidence had produced a different level and kind of evidence – troubling, even horrific understandings of vulnerabilities and risks in To-Day. And yet, regardless of what we already knew from the statistics and the ethnography, the pictorial, visual and graphic representations of sickness and death posted on the walls, left us staring in stunned silence.

What was accomplished at this moment in the research? In addition to confirming the stories, the genograms put a human face to the suffering. Most studies on the impact of the HIV epidemic in Africa focus on the individual. By actually visualizing how this disease has affected household, extended family and community, we came to understand the risk reality of this place more deeply.

What follows here are portions of a case study of an alcohol seller called Maama Mali, who, before she died, resided in To-Day. This is a story of a family's tragedy resulting from HIV/AIDS, and the complementary genogram (see Figure 7.1) vividly provides a visual representation of psycho-social and cultural impacts of the individual case, and in addition, offers to the reader a poignant testament to the suffering experienced by women and children in To-Day.

Maama Mali: The Story of an Alcohol Seller

Much of Maama Mali's adult life was transient in nature, shifting her household and family to and from To-Day and her father's village, Mawo-gola, in Masaka district. We met her when she was living in town, a time in her life when she was enduring the combined assaults of relapsing illness, relative poverty, and the uncertainty of knowing what to do with her children. Maama Mali supported herself and her infant son, Mali, by selling alcohol and charcoal out of her room in Kiyeye. She yearned for a stable future, but that was not meant to be. One of the very first things she said to us was: 'I have been very sick with fever for so long. I think it is because of the mosquito bites on my skin. But I do not think these are mosquito bites; it is a rash and I have seen people with *silimu*[5] with this rash ... What I have is *silimu*.'

Both of her parents resided in the village and were overseers of sizeable banana and coffee plantations. Her father had two wives (Figure 7.2). The first wife had only daughters, so after the divorce she moved to Kooki, where some of the daughters married. Maama Mali's own mother, the second and last 'formal' wife, had twelve children. Only five of these twelve children, including Maama Mali, were then living. Four died when they were young and three daughters have died of *silimu* after having a child each.

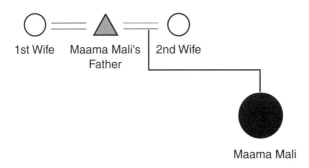

1st Wife   Maama Mali's   2nd Wife
Father

Maama Mali

FIGURE 7.2

Maama Mali left school at the age of 16 and was married the very next year. By then, her husband, who was a mechanic and considerably older than she – 'way above 30' – had already been divorced from two other women. These women left him with two children, a boy and a girl, who became Maama Mali's responsibility when she married (Figure 7.3). Later she was to bear him three children – two girls and a boy (Figure 7.4). It was after the birth of the first child that Maama Mali felt 'forced' to leave her marriage. She explained the situation this way: 'When some women fail in marriage they return home ... they usually mistreat the wives of the married brother, they want the brother to remain single so they can be supported by him.' For Maama Mali, mistreatment meant cooking, cleaning, and doing laundry for everyone living in the compound. Tired of the burden and getting no support from her husband, Maama Mali packed up, weaned the last-born, and left.

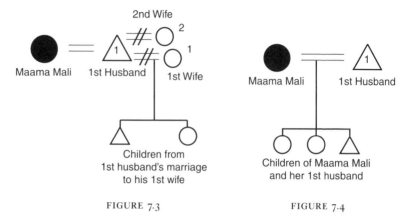

FIGURE 7.3   FIGURE 7.4

She went back to her father's village. Later, while helping her parents cultivate in the village, she met a man.

> I lived in a big house, but separate from my parents. Three of my sisters were there, all divorced. We all had our own rooms; each was free to bring a man. Those days was there anything to fear? We just used to enjoy our-selves; if you got tired of a man you would just leave, change and get another … it is not like these days … these are bad days … these men were already married with children … the women in the village knew about me … there was no way someone could have an affair in the village and the wife not know … at least they did not attack me, neither did I go to their homes.

The next three children she conceived were fathered by these different men in the village, and all three of these children died, at three, three and a half, and the last at eleven months (Figure 7.5). Maama Mali said she was unaware of the cause of death of the first two, but the last was measles. All the children were buried in their fathers' village.

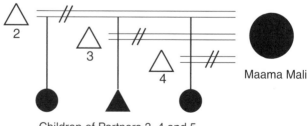

Children of Partners 3, 4 and 5

FIGURE 7.5

The unexplained deaths made her extremely nervous. Her fear was that the deaths were related to a curse from the husband. Although she was very angry, she returned to the husband. By the time she conceived the fifth child, her former ex-husband had married another wife, and also had another child.

> I used to quarrel with the new wife every day ... she had cultivated all of the land, so when I got there she did not want me to take any of the land to grow food for my children ... the houses we lived in were just opposite each other ... we would quarrel in the courtyard ... every day we would work in the garden, meet on the path and quarrel for the rest of the day ... there was so much jealousy that whenever he would sleep in my house ... we would hear her walking around the house at night, around and around and around.

According to Maama Mali, whenever he bought her cloth, something for her house, or even just sauce for *matooke*, there would be an explosion, and on many occasions the women would physically fight. The neighbours would have to separate them. Eventually it became apparent to Maama Mali that the co-wife was visiting a traditional practitioner.

> She would go very early in the morning instead of going to the garden, and come back with something wrapped in leaves ... I do not know how she was doing it but he used to find the witchcraft things and always quarrel with her. This went on for a month and finally I started feeling like I hated the man ... so I went back to my parents ... He followed me there.

She left, despite the fact that she was previously happy in her marriage and her husband treated her well.

> He really liked me ... we did not have a big plot to have a *matooke* plantation, so we had to buy ... but he made sure the food was always there ... I hear of women eating *ntula* (bitter tomato, considered a poor people's food), but I only knew meat ... never ground nuts, it was just the problem of the compound ... a small plot, with a few houses. I was sharing the same kitchen with the co-wife ... The sisters really made me work.

So in 1991, Maama Mali came to stay with her brother, a cattle trader in To-Day. It was in To-Day that her last-born, Mali, was conceived. He was, however, born in her parents' village, in February 1992 (Figure 7.6). She returned to town in January, and had been living in To-Day ever since.

With a dry smile, Maama Mali told us that it was not possible for her child to have a clan if she really did not know who the father was.

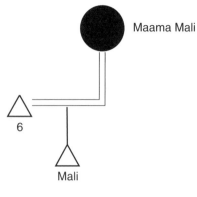

FIGURE 7.6

Children born out of *magendo* (a sexual affair with a businessmen) cannot have a clan ... if you have sex with a trailer driver who you met for one day, makes you pregnant, and the next day goes away, without ever coming back, how would you know the clan of your child. Of course in one day you would not have talked about his tribe and his clan!

Maama Mali did meet the child's father doing business, but he was not a trailer driver. She had moved to To-Day after years of living in the village, and immediately began selling alcohol out of her room on Kijjukizo Road, just a short distance from the centre of town. Initially, her brother provided her with the needed credit (cash, soda and bottled beer) to get her business off the ground. To maximize profits, she took her alcohol on the market circuit. Taata Mali was a tailor, so when business was good, he rented a sewing machine, and took and filled orders right there in the market.

I could not manage village life any more ... so I returned to town ... I was having difficulties finding money to buy things for the house and the things I needed to look after myself, so I got this man to look after me ... but that was the work of Satan, and how I got pregnant.

It was Maama Mali who alerted us to the reality of sexual relations in the markets. Sex is commonplace. In fact, semi-permanent structures are erected to provide lodging for those who are willing to pay for it.

A woman cannot fail to get thirty minutes to go with a man unless she does not know if he has money or not ... we never slept together in the markets ... while others coupled, I slept under plastic bags I shared with three other women ... but he could have had other women when I did not know ... I did not care much ... if I had done what other women were doing, I would not be here now ... I would have already died ... at that time they looked healthy ... of all of us [alcohol sellers] I looked the most sickly ... people used to say I was slimming [had AIDS] and I was going to die, but instead, these women died first.

According to Maama Mali, most women who trade in the market are unmarried. However, there are a few married women who have permanent partners – *safari* men – and at the same time have an occasional partner, a trader, in the markets. They meet up on market days.

Those who slept there, they wanted to get money and nice things so that they become very rich ... but most were single unmarried women ... Even in the market, women had more than one man ... they are surrounded by bushes ... during working hours, when everyone is busy, a woman can take off and go to the bush with another man and come back and continue working, and her permanent partner [in the market] would not know she was just trying to get more money.

At that time, market activity had lessened due to the cattle ban.[6] The Bahima would come, sell their cattle, and in turn buy goods. 'The traders would get a lot of money, and then they used their money to get women.' Maama Mali lamented that she knew only one woman left from the market days.

Most of them have died of AIDS ... so many have been sick ... I do not know if they got it from the market or ... if they brought it with them from the village to the markets ... could they not take it from there to the markets? ... Some people say that AIDS is in towns yet some can still come from the villages to go to the markets when they have AIDS ... it is difficult to know because it takes a long period in one's body.

In her experience, sickness does not necessarily affect the business.

Unless they are very weak and dying, and cannot stand to work ... most of the people who still have their own customers will bring others ... even if she's looking thin they would not go and drink elsewhere because she is thin.

Maama Mali said she could no longer go into the markets because she was so sickly.

My life is very little ... I know I will never get well, I know there is no treatment for my sickness, my biggest problem is headache. When I get frightened or a shock, it just pains ... in the market people shout ... I am no longer comfortable there. There's no treatment that I am going to get to make my headache go.

Like many other people, the father of Maama Mali's infant, Mali, also

Partner 6

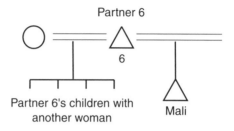

Partner 6's children with
another woman

Mali

FIGURE 7.7

decided to leave the market after the implementation of the cattle ban. He set up a permanent shop on Kooki Road. Mali's father has a wife and family in a village called Kalegero, a kilometre away from To-Day (Figure 7.7). His wife, Maama Mali said, knew about her but did not harass her. In fact, she went to his home for treatment money while she was pregnant, and even slept there after she delivered. Ties were severed with that man soon after the birth because he was not providing consistent support.

> He would sometimes buy food but never bought a dress, Vaseline, or helped me pay the rent … it's like I had him [Mali] alone … I really did not want a man … I had three children who died, so I did not want any more … they would just all suffer and then they would die … what came for me was just the work of Satan.

Maama Mali claimed it was because of her problems that she had to sell *waragi* (alcohol) out of her room.

> Alcohol selling is not a good job … if that's the only way I can feed myself there is nothing that I can do … it is a job for people who did not go to school … it is so bad some women who sell alcohol have ended up being beaten … he comes to your room, he drinks, gets drunk … she asks for her money … he refuses … if she insists, he just slaps her.

And sex is definitely a part of the trade.

> There are some who drink with their customers … the men are drinking and they also drink … when they get drunk they act in a way that attracts these men … some of them get drunk before the men do … they even do not know what they are doing … my neighbour when she drinks she plays [flirts] and invites them to sleep with her … she often ends up having sex with every customer that comes there.
>
> I do not play, I do not drink alcohol, I'm good to them because they are my customers … sometimes when they are drunk there is no getting them out of the house … they do not joke with me … but no man would want to

sleep with me anyway, which man cannot see that I am sick? Very many men have disturbed me ... but when they suggest [sex], I tell them there and then that I do not want ... but of course they insist, but so do I ... men usually bring in things for a woman when she has not shown her side ... these days you cannot eat a man's things for nothing, you have to pay for it ... sometimes a man will come with sugar and bread ... but it is very dangerous to eat these things if you are not going to accept the man.

Although she continued to sell alcohol out of her room, there were days when she became paralysed by fear. Fever, prolonged periods of diarrhoea, weight loss and eventually tuberculosis made her uncertain about the illness of both herself and her child. This uncertainty was exacerbated by the tension stemming from the belief that her immediate family was the target of a revenge-related illness called *omutego*.[7] According to Maama Mali, the way people die 'with the virus' mirrors the course of suffering caused by 'terminal witchcraft'. This belief adds to the fear, uncertainty and confusion that accompany an episode of illness.

I am not even sure that it is AIDS that I am suffering from ... what kind of disease is this that cannot kill even the partner ... all of the partners who I was with that time are still alive ... I just say it is AIDS because of the way I get sick.

Omutega is extremely fatal if not caught in time.

If it comes in the house, it would not kill just one, it would shake down the whole house ... it is sent in revenge, it comes in the wind searching for the person who owes ... if someone borrowed money and failed to pay it back ... if a woman is pregnant and has had many partners, and she does not know the paternity of the child, she gives it to one man and yet another man wants to claim it, he sends *omutego* ... if a family fails to pay for the bull they borrowed to put on the funeral rites ... it kills the first person, the second person, and unless someone catches it and gets treatment ... the person who sends it will tell it to keep looking for the debt ... that is why it usually clears the family line.

At different times in the course of our friendship, Maama Mali told us that three of her siblings had already died of this disease – that is, AIDS – but she also told us three of her siblings of the same mother and father had died of *omutego*. And many more in her family, including step-sisters and brothers, were rumoured to be sick.

I do not think there is anybody here who does not have AIDS. Now everybody here has this disease. The problem is we did not know about it, and by the time we knew about it, we had already been moving.

Maama Mali observed that AIDS – unlike *omutego*, which actually chooses its victims – chooses bodies arbitrarily. And in her family, people were falling sick almost systematically, again beyond reason.

Maama Mali initially fell really sick in town. She decided to give herself three weeks, and if she did not recover, she would pack up her things and go to the village. She decided, therefore, to take her daughter out of school in the village and bring her to town. Born of Maama Mali's first marriage, Namukasa was 13 years old and put in charge of the care of her mother and her brother Mali, as well as cooking, collecting water, washing soiled bed sheets and so forth. Namukasa, a well-behaved child, was a big help to her mother. But Maama Mali's business was increasingly compromised because of this relapse.

> I thought it would be more economical for me to send the children to the village ... I put together some money for the baby's sugar and her school fees ... we all went to the village together ... and after a few weeks I returned.

A fortnight later, at dusk, Namukasa arrived on her mother's doorstep in town, with Mali and a seven-year-old. Maama Mali quarrelled with her young daughter. Business had not yet picked up: 'At least when I was alone I could eat one meal ... but children do not understand that.' Besides, Namukasa had used the money to be used for school fees on transport for the three of them. The child complained that Mali cried all day and she could not leave him unattended to go to school. Her daughter had brought the other child with her to care for Mali, so she could return to the village to go to school. And of course, Maama Mali quarrelled with Namukasa as the child was far too small to cater for both of their needs.

> At 6:30 the next morning, Mali woke crying for food ... I woke the child so she could cook porridge for him ... she carried him to the verandah ... I was sleeping but I heard the child crying, I did not mind so much ... I knew Namukasa was around ... his cries increased so I went to check myself ... I found him alone ... the girls had disappeared.

And they were never found. She sent a message to her step-sisters in Kaliro to see if they had found their way there. Her father's village was too far to go by foot: 'But maybe out of frustration they walked and will be sleeping on the way for two nights before they get there.' To stay sane, Maama Mali convinced herself that a woman must have lured her to become a housegirl in Masaka or Kampala. She chose to ignore the possibility that a man could have just as easily tempted her away.[8]

It was Maama Mali's wish to be buried in the soil of her fathers, so she and all her things – bed, saucepans, mattress, charcoal stove, basins – were loaded on a pick-up truck and taken to the village a few months later.

Maama Mali died soon after. Her daughter, Namukasa, never returned, and if she was alive, was presumably not aware that her mother had died.[9]

Maama Mali's Genogram

In order clearly to visualize the implications of Maama Mali's life's story, it is important that the family system be seen from her point of view. She is indicated on the diagram by a large blackened circle (representing female, and now dead); other triangles (men) and circles have inserted within them a positive sign (signifying being HIV-positive). As the reader can see, the genogram reflects different facets of Maama Mali's social and reproductive life history. For example, the numbers to the left represent the men she 'married' (or subsequently divorced) and the numbers to the right represent the order of marriage in her first husband's life. The diagram was also constructed to elucidate her movements back and forth between her parents' village and her husbands' village and the children she had in each place.

Most importantly, however, the genogram demonstrates the complex pattern of sickness and death that characterized her family history. The documentation of Maama Mali's life took place over a period of a year. During that time, the team of researchers watched her condition slowly deteriorate. When they first met her, there was some confusion over the cause of death of three of her sisters – whether it was *silimu* or *omutego*. The subsequent death of the rest of her siblings make it easy to understand how families become confused over cause of death. Both HIV/AIDS and revenge-related illnesses have the ability to wipe out whole families.

By the time the researchers attended Maama Mali's burial in September 1994, one more sister had died. Late the very next month, the family buried yet another son. He was a successful businessman in town and was mainly responsible for supporting his parents back in the village. He left a wife and five children in To-Day. In January 1995, the family lost yet another brother. Maama Mali, when she was still well and living in To-Day, was this man's primary caretaker. Finally, late in 1995, her very last sister died, and was buried beside her in the family's burial place. It was rumoured that Maama Mali's father had tried to take his own life soon after the death of his last son.

Discussion

Promoting 'Sexual Health' in To-Day, Uganda: A Participatory Action Research Proposal, was a research study initiated with the expectation that ethnographic methodologies might offer richer, more robust understandings of the meanings of risk and vulnerability for people living in To-Day. It was our hope that by learning how people understand, construct and talk about their concerns, we would be given the experiential evidence that would allow us to create and implement more effective prevention initiatives.

Initially, with only epidemiological and clinical evidence at our disposal, we were compelled to study previously identified 'target groups', including those people involved in the commercial sex trade. Our emerging ethnographic evidence not only confirmed the realities of risk for bar girls, waitresses and their clients (truck drivers, mobile market men), but, in addition, exposed previously unidentified groups of people. We realized that understanding the risk realities of cattle loaders, mobile market traders, alcohol sellers and adolescent girls was critical to understanding which people in To-Day were most vulnerable to HIV/AIDS, thus requiring effective prevention programming. Maama Mali's case study, for example, exposed us to the domains and dimensions of HIV/AIDS risk for women who sell alcohol in town and in the markets. On a daily basis, these women are challenged by difficult 'deadly decisions' (see Spittal 1995; Spittal et al. 1997).

From an academic perspective, the process of collecting and designing genograms was very successful. We knew that in clinical settings, genograms are useful tools in helping clients reflect upon biomedical and psycho-social determinants for illness and disease, seeing at a glance risk patterns that characterize their immediate and extended family. We wondered, however, how useful they would be when made available in a community-based, intervention-research setting.

The results are very clear. Genograms highlight issues that are embedded, though perhaps not accessible in written case studies. By offering a bird's-eye view of the extended family in the context of culture, it is possible to trace visually which family members are dead, infected or not infected with HIV.

When we look at the genograms, we wonder what will happen to the children. What is the psycho-social impact of the death of children on the elderly, people who often become responsible for the care of orphans? Where does the money come from to treat HIV-related illness and opportunistic infection? Who provides palliative care? By highlighting such concerns and questions, the genogram demonstrates the emotional and material burdens of this disease on not only the individual, but the family and the community.

We have taken these ethnographically derived understandings of risk – evidence that emerged during the study called 'Talking About AIDS' – and generated the Risk Reality Model, a contextual theory about risk

(Willms and Sewankambo 1995). With the ethnographic data (evidenced in risk narratives, summaries of data, and now the genograms that complement individual cases), and using the Risk Reality Model as a conceptual framework, we are currently in the process of designing, disseminating and evaluating participatory educational resources for people in To-Day at risk of contracting HIV/AIDS. The genogram, as a visual tool and analytic device, has been very useful in representing some of the findings of our study. Our current challenge is finding out how useful the genogram will be in the participatory planning and prevention phase of Phase 2 of the project.

Early in the data collection phase of the ethnographic study, it became apparent that the success of any subsequent community-directed intervention would depend on people's ability to reflect critically on the HIV/AIDS-related problems that emerged in the research. Because genograms are an accessible and visual representation of the impact of such high mortality rates on family and community, we are now testing their utility as a mechanism for reflection in the participatory, programme-planning process. Although we have yet to demonstrate how appropriate it is in this context, we believe that the genogram might be used to help facilitate discussions and generate ideas for problem-solving in the community.

Conclusions

Promoting 'Sexual Health' in To-Day, Uganda: A Participatory Action Research Proposal is a product of a multidisciplinary research collaboration between social scientists, clinicians and clinical epidemiologists. Classical ethnographic methods – including participant observation, in-depth interviews, focus groups and life history research – have generated deeper understandings of the meaning, experience and reality of risk for people living in a truck-stop trading centre in rural Uganda. Genograms, clinical tools typically used in family systems medicine and family therapy, have proved to be effective in complementing both ethnographic and epidemiological evidence. They communicate to the participant, and demonstrate in an immediate, intimate and even visceral way, the impact of HIV/AIDS on the individual, the extended family and the community.

Acknowledgements

Funding for Phases 1 and 2 was generously provided by the International Development Research Centre (IDRC), Ottawa, Canada: IDRC Dossier 3-P-90-0204, Health Sciences Division, 'Understanding High Risk Sexual Behaviour' (Uganda) and IDRC Dossier 03018-02 and 01, Programmes Division. The Salama SHIELD Foundation provided additional funding for Phase 2. We are grateful to Nick Higginbotham, Nancy

Johnson and Susan Walker for their critical review, constructive editing and helpful comments on the chapter.

Notes

1. To-Day is a pseudonym for the town in Rakai district, Uganda, where the ethnographic and participatory intervention research is currently being conducted. Rather than using the actual name, To-Day is used to protect the identity of persons living there.

2. See Spittal et al. (1997) for a discussion of our research dilemma on how to represent the evidence, and, in turn, how varieties of representation would influence programmatic planning (e.g., quantitative, qualitative and, in this instance, visual representations).

3. Since everyone in To-Day talks about HIV/AIDS, the office in town was called 'Talking About AIDS, the To-Day Study Project'. Opening the office in a public place was intentional. It was designed as a participatory strategy for persons to drop by and talk about the impact of the disease on their lives, to corroborate ethnographic research findings and to demonstrate how the ethnographic data were being utilized in prevention and programme planning.

4. Recent theoretical work in representational and visual anthropology considers the kind of knowledge ethnographic work produces – by what method, for whom, about whom, by whom, and to what end (see Gupta and Ferguson 1997; Walker 1999; Wallman 1997).

5. *Silimu* is a Kiswahili vernacular expression for 'slims' or the 'wasting disease'. People dying of HIV/AIDS – before the disease was known as such – were described as having 'slims' because they become extremely thin in the last stages of their illness.

6. Between 1991 and 1992, there was an outbreak of bovine pneumonia. Movement of cattle was banned so as to enforce a quarantine of sorts in the region. It was feared that cattle would become infected at auctions in the marketplace. These auctions were at the core of the market economy; without them other market activities suffered.

7. *Omutego* is a revenge-related illness that pre-dates HIV/AIDS. According to Mama Mali, the way people die of HIV/AIDS mirrors the course of suffering caused by 'terminal witchcraft'.

8. Namukasa was probably 'picked' (up) by an older man and taken as a housegirl, wife or sexual partner. She was about 13 or 14 at the time.

9. An expanded version of Maama Mali's life history may be found in Patricia Spittal's PhD dissertation entitled 'Deadly choices: women's risk for HIV infection in a truck stop-trading centre in rural south-western Uganda', Hamilton, Ontario, Canada: McMaster University, 1995; reference is also made to Maama Mali in Spittal et al. 1997.

References

Ebell, M. H., C. J. Heaton (1988) 'Development and evaluation of a computer genogram', *Journal of Family Practice* 27(5): 536–8.

Friedman, H., M. Rohrbaugh and S. Krakauer (1988) 'The time-line genogram: highlighting temporal aspects of family relationships', *Family Process* 27 (September): 293–303.

Gerson, R. and M. McGoldrick (1985) 'The computerized genogram', *Primary Care* 12(3): 535–45.

Good, B. (1996) *Medicine, Rationality, and Experience: An Anthropological Perspective*, Cambridge: Cambridge University Press.

Gupta, A. and J. Ferguson (1997) 'Discipline and practice: "the field" as site, method, and location in anthropology', in A. Gupta and J. Ferguson (eds), *Anthropological Locations: Boundaries and Grounds of a Field Science*, Berkeley: University of California Press, pp. 1–46.

Halliday, L. (1985) *The Silent Scream: The Sexual Abuse of Children*, Toronto: Guidance Centre, Faculty of Education, University of Toronto.

Herth, K. A. (1989) 'The root of it all: genograms as a nursing assessment tool', *Journal of Gerontological Nursing* 15(12): 33–7.

Like, R. C., J. Rogers and M. McGoldrick (1988) 'Reading and interpreting genograms: a systematic approach', *Journal of Family Practice* 26(4): 407–12.

Jenkins, J. H. (1991) 'Expressed emotion and schizophrenia', *Ethos* 19: 387–431.

Mengel, M. B. and L. B. Mauksch (1989) 'Disarming the family ghost: a family of origin experience', *Family Medicine* 21(1): 45–9.

Piot, P., F. A. Plummer, M. Rey et al. (1987) 'Retrospective sero-epidemiology of AIDS virus infection in Nairobi populations', *Journal of Infectious Disease* 155: 1108–12.

Rogers, J. C. and P. Cohn (1987) 'Impact of a screening family genogram on first encounters in primary care', *Family Practice – An International Journal* 4(4): 291–301.

Rogers, J. and R. Holloway (1990) 'Completion rate and reliability of the Self-Administered Genogram (SAGE)', *Family Practice – An International Journal*, 7(2): 149–51.

Rogers, J. C., M. Rohrbaugh et al. (1993) 'Can experts predict health risk from family genograms?', *Family Genograms* 24(3).

Scheper-Hughes, N. and M. Lock (1987) 'The mindful body: a prolegomenon to future work in medical anthropology', *Medical Anthropology Quarterly* 1: 6–41.

Sewankambo, N. K., M. J. Wawer, R. H. Gray et al. (1994) 'Demographic impact of HIV infection in rural Rakai District, Uganda', *AIDS* 8: 1707–13.

Sewankambo, N. K., D. G. Willms, E. Kirumira et al. (1993) *No Longer Strangers: Participatory Evidence and the Development of Culturally Appropriate HIV/AIDS Interventions in To-Day, Uganda*, technical report of the study 'Understanding High Risk Sexual Behaviour, Uganda', submitted to the International Development Research Centre (IDRC), 30 October.

Shellenberger, S., K. W. Shurden and T. W. Treadwell, Jr. (1988) 'Faculty training seminars in family systems', *Family Medicine* 20(3): 226–7.

Shore, W., H. Wilkie et al. (1994) 'Family of origin genograms: evaluation of a teaching program for medical students', *Family Medicine* 26(4).

Spittal, P. (1995) 'Deadly choices: women's risk for HIV infection in a truck stop-trading centre in rural South-western Uganda', PhD dissertation, Hamilton, Ontario, Canada: Department of Anthropology, McMaster University.

Spittal, P., J. Nakuti, N. Sewankambo and D. G. Willms (1997) ' "*We are Dying...It is Finished!*": linking an ethnographic research design to an HIV/AIDS participatory approach in Uganda', in S. Smith, D. Willms and N. Johnson (eds), *Nurtured by Knowledge: Learning to Do Participatory Action-Research*, New York and Ottawa: Apex Press and the International Development Research Centre (IDRC).

UNAIDS (2000) *Report on the Global HIV/AIDS Epidemic: June 2000*, Geneva: Joint United Nations Programme on HIV/AIDS (UNAIDS).

Walker, S. H. (1999) 'Many voices in dialogue: translating research evidence into community-based HIV interventions', MA thesis (Anthropology), School of Graduate Studies, McMaster University, Hamilton, Ontario, Canada.

Wallman, S. (1997) 'Appropriate anthropology and the risky inspiration of '"Capability Brown": representations of what, by whom, and to what end?' in A. James, J. Hockey and A. Dawson (eds), *After Writing Culture: Epistemology and Praxis in Contemporary Anthropology*, London: Routledge, pp. 244–63.

Waters, I., W. Watson and W. Wetzel (1994) 'Genograms: practical tools for family physicians', *Canadian Family Physician* 40: 282–7.

Wawer, M. J., D. Serwadda, S. Musgrave et al. (1991) 'Dynamics of spread of HIV-1 infection in a rural district of Uganda', *British Medical Journal* 303: 1303–7.

Wawer, M. J., N. K. Sewankambo, D. Serwadda et al. (1999) 'Control of sexually transmitted diseases for AIDS prevention in Uganda: a randomised community trial', *The Lancet* 40 (13 February).

Willms, D. G. (1998) *Translating Evidence to Community-Based Health Interventions*, workshop, International Clinical Epidemiology Network Global Meeting (INCLEN XV), Queretaro, Mexico, 18 February.

Willms, D. G. and N. A. Johnson (1997) *Essentials in Qualitative Research: A Notebook for the Field*, Hamilton, Ontario, Canada: Department of Anthropology, McMaster University.

Willms, D. G. and N. K. Sewankambo (1995) 'The risk reality model: an ethnographically-derived model for eliciting and explaining social-cultural determinants of risk for HIV/AIDS', oral presentation to the IXth International Conference on AIDS and STDs in Africa, Kampala, Uganda, 13 December.

8

AIDS Prevention in the *Matare* and the Community: A Training Strategy for Traditional Healers in Zimbabwe

Dennis G. Willms, Nancy A. Johnson, Alfred Chingono and Maureen Wellington

The design and implementation of *culturally appropriate* health interventions has been a focal point, over the past decade, of action-oriented health social science research. Such interventions are sensitive to the language, idioms, expressions and nuances of meaning of the targeted socio-cultural group (Nichter and Nichter 1996; Were 1992). Individuals and communities may respond favourably to them; the messages communicated may be appreciated, understood, and, at the very least, not offend culturally. Yet persons may not necessarily feel vulnerable or at risk. The challenge now confronting health social scientists is to create interventions that are *culturally compelling* – that is, interventions that are not only culturally appropriate in language, idiom and expression, but persuasive in their ability to make persons feel vulnerable, alter the nature of their assumptive world, and become compelled not only to think, but also to feel and act differently (Willms and Sewankambo 1995).

Designing a culturally compelling HIV/AIDS educational intervention for Zimbabwean traditional healers required transcending conventional conceptual categories and merging models, frameworks and reasoning processes across culturally distinct worlds. This would seem an impossible task considering the difference in understanding about HIV/AIDS between Western medical practitioners and the healers. Biomedical explanations of HIV and how it is transmitted are based on a scientific understanding of physiological and immunological processes as well as the natural history of disease and illness. Indigenous or lay explanations of the disease may derive from spiritual, interpersonal, natural (VanBuren n.d.) and social beliefs, which are empirically grounded, but largely based on moral principles. Nevertheless, we undertook to collaborate with the healers in identifying therapeutic practices that pose a risk to themselves and their patients and in searching for and applying solutions (see also Bischoff and Ostergaard

1994; Courtright et al. 1996; Green 1988, 1997, 1999; Green et al. 1995; Groce and Reeve 1996; Tessendorf and Cunningham 1997; Van der Geest 1997).

There are a number of examples of collaboration between government, traditional healers and their associations in addressing the curative, therapeutic and supportive counselling needs associated with HIV/AIDS (Baleta 1988; King and Homsy 1997). Few, however, are based on the extensive sort of ethnographic research that allowed us to gain an in-depth understanding of what is culturally appropriate, not always achievable through the use of rapid assessment procedures (RAP) or knowledge, attitude and practice (KAP) surveys. Such methods, while useful in ascertaining the breadth of perceived understandings of risk of contracting HIV/ AIDS in certain populations, do not necessarily provide health educators or clinicians with the necessary instruments and vehicles of communication to promote health messages – messages that may best be communicated through metaphor, narrative, analogy, vernacular expressions and other suitable idioms.

In this chapter, we describe the process used to develop a culturally compelling HIV/AIDS intervention that combines biomedical and indigenous understandings of the disease. In addition, we demonstrate the importance of ethnographic research in uncovering the complex web of understandings about HIV/AIDS, thus making such an endeavour possible.

Traditional Healers, Therapeutic Practices and Risk of Contracting HIV/AIDS

Traditional healers were legally recognized by the government of Zimbabwe in 1981 through the Traditional Medical Practitioners Act, No. 38 (Chavunduka 1994: 13). By 1986, the Zimbabwe National Traditional Healers Association (ZINATHA) reported that there were approximately 35,000–50,000 licensed traditional healers in the country, comprising a variety of traditional healing sub-specialities: herbalists, midwives, spirit mediums and diviners (Chavunduka 1986). Traditional healers remain an important source of primary health care for many Zimbabweans, particularly those in the rural districts (Arkovitz and Manley 1990). In the more urban areas, they are often consulted prior to, or in conjunction with, biomedical practitioners. As Neumann and Lauro (1982) note, 'many of the practices of traditional medicine practitioners are designed to preserve cultural institutions and to help the patient live at peace with family, clan, village, tribe and inner self'. Care is directed at the social, psychological, spiritual and physical aspects of the person (Hewson 1998). Traditional healers, therefore, also act as marriage counsellors, moral advisers, social workers and legal and political consultants (Chavunduka 1986) and are involved with the *prevention* of illness and misfortune (Freeman and Motsei 1992).

As diagnosed and suspected AIDS patients increasingly seek out traditional healers for therapeutic and psycho-social support, healers are in a position to have a significant impact in terms of secondary prevention, by educating and counselling patients. The invasive nature of many of their healing practices, however, place traditional healers and their patients at risk of HIV infection. For example, traditional healers use razor blades or other cutting instruments to scarify patients. Tiny incisions or *nyora* are made on the body, usually the joints, and medicine is applied to the wounds. Risk of HIV transmission may occur when a single razor blade or cutting instrument is used to scarify a number of patients, when medicines are rubbed into the *nyora* with the bare hands, or care is not taken to avoid contaminating the contents of the *calabash*, or container in which the medicine is stored, with the patient's blood. Traditional healers are also called upon to 'clean' women's uteruses or to 'bite out'. In the case of 'biting out', an 'object' that has been induced into the patient's body by witchcraft is removed. The traditional healer 'traps' the object at some location on the body by making a series of *nyora*. Using her[1] teeth, she then bites the cuts where the object has been 'caught', and sucks out the object, taking the patient's blood into her mouth. Cleaning a woman's uterus requires the traditional healer to insert her fingers into the woman's vagina, bringing her into contact with the vaginal fluids and, in some cases, a bloody or STD-related discharge. Those traditional healers who practise midwifery unavoidably come into contact with blood and bodily fluids during the course of delivery and pre- and post-natal care. Circumcision and ear-piercing are sometimes performed on several individuals at one occasion with a family knife, in the former case, or needle, in the latter. The instrument may not be sterilized between individuals. At issue is not the appropriateness or invasiveness of the traditional healing practices, as many Western medical practices are equally, if not more, invasive, but how to modify existing practices to make them safer for patients and healers alike.

Designing a Culturally Compelling HIV/AIDS Educational Intervention for Traditional Healers

Concern over the risk of HIV transmission in the *matare* or 'surgery' of the traditional healer, coupled with a recognition of the healers' influential role in the community and experience and expertise in counselling and advising patients in personal and social matters, motivated the development of an AIDS educational workshop for traditional healers with the following goals:

1. to develop with the traditional healers a model of HIV/AIDS that helps them to assess risk of HIV transmission, including aspects of their practices that are risky to themselves and to their patients;
2. to increase the traditional healers' awareness of the significant impact they can have on the HIV/AIDS problem in terms of primary and secondary prevention, both in the *matare* and the community, by educating and counselling their patients, providing psycho-social support and moving towards greater collaboration with Western-trained medical practitioners; and
3. to develop new practice procedures that reduce the risk of HIV transmission in the *matare* as well as guidelines for patient education and counselling.

Our primary goal was to identify and change risky healing practices. Change of any kind, however, is inherently threatening to people who are dependent on, and are protectors of, tradition, as are the traditional healers. There are many reasons for important HIV/AIDS risk reduction messages to be either rejected or subtly ignored, as they have been in previous AIDS education programmes for traditional healers. Not the least of these is the underlying suggestion to the healers that their healing practices are potentially dangerous. Such messages are disempowering rather than enabling.

By explicitly concentrating on the second intervention goal, it was felt that the other two would be more easily accomplished. To focus on the positive contribution traditional healers can make in terms of providing compelling information and advice is inherently empowering. It was posited that in the context of learning how to educate their patients, the traditional healers would more readily accept the idea of changing the risky aspects of their practice.

The principal challenges of the workshop thus lay in engaging the traditional healers in a participatory learning process and negotiating a merged model of AIDS that was satisfactory from both the indigenous and biomedical perspectives – that is, one that was acceptable and understandable to the traditional healers and resulted in an appreciation of risk events and how they could be eliminated. From our prior ethnographic study, we gained insight into indigenous understandings of AIDS, from which a preliminary version of a merged model was developed. Through the dialectical structure of the workshops, the preliminary version of the model was refined and elaborated.

The participatory intervention strategy that we adopted (Smith et al. 1997) evolved over time. From the outset, it was evident that the traditional didactic approach often employed in HIV/AIDS educational interventions was unworkable. In the past, the Zimbabwean National AIDS Control Program (NACP) would emphasize 'what traditional healers should not do' in educational sessions. These sessions tended not to be tailored to the life world of traditional healers, but rather 'targeted' a generic audience. Traditional healers invited to these meetings would be told about how HIV is transmitted and how the use of razor blades put them and their patients at risk of contracting HIV/AIDS. Not surprisingly, lecturing to traditional healers that what they were doing in their surgeries put them at risk had limited impact. They could 'parrot' messages taught, but were unprepared to change their therapeutic practices in ways that reduced or minimized risk of HIV transmission. It was noted, in fact, that when traditional healers attended these kinds of educational sessions, they would leave saying, 'This is not my problem ... my *mudzimu* [ancestral spirits] protect me from getting AIDS.'

The critical question we then faced was: 'What educational strategy would cause traditional healers to "own" the problem, engage them in a process of problem-solving, and safely permit them to confront and navigate both scientific and indigenous understandings of HIV/AIDS?' A second, equally important, question was: 'How would we get traditional healers to talk comfortably about HIV/AIDS concerns in a safe yet critical manner?'

An answer was to build on the natural process of a traditional healing ceremony, which involves not only the healer and the patient, but also the ancestral spirits. A conversation is encouraged between these three 'interested parties'. A moral imperative governs the entire session. There is, in short, a 'moral calculus' (Farmer 1992) that guides how the health problem should be resolved in a traditional healing ceremony. It was clear to us that the educational intervention must work within processes and structures that were familiar to, and respected by, the healers themselves. Thus the elements of the traditional healing ceremony became guiding principles for our partnership with healers.

More specifically, the design of the three-and-a-half-day event was guided by the following notions.

Traditional healers should be respected as autonomous professionals Traditional healers were not regarded as 'extra bodies' to be recruited as trusted, accessible and inexpensive community health workers who would hand out condoms or, to paraphrase Nzimande (1988), 'make their clients available to Western interventions' by recognizing symptoms and referring to Western medical practitioners. Many projects involving traditional healers in community health programmes (see Hoff 1992 for an overview) have developed strategies based on an 'incorporation' rather than 'collaboration' model of linkages between traditional healers and Western medical practitioners.

The traditional healers' unequal relationship with Western medical practitioners, and their political struggle for power in relationship to this group, were carefully considered. It would have been futile, and possibly damaging to the purpose of the workshop, to fail to recognize healers as private practitioners and suggest that they refer all suspected AIDS patients to the hospital or clinic for testing, or to have had Western medical practitioners alone facilitate the workshop.

The importance of the spirits in the healing process must be recognized and respected Most traditional healers claim to be possessed by a spirit that is called upon when diagnosing and treating patients (Arkovitz and Manley 1990). As it is the healing spirit that makes decisions and conducts therapeutic events in the opinion of both healers and patients, the spirits must be accorded a proper place in the process of the workshop. It would be inappropriate, therefore, to deny that traditional healers are protected from getting AIDS because there are no *mudzimi* (ancestral spirits) protecting them. Instead, facilitators needed to help traditional healers convince each other that the spirits may not be able to protect them because this is a new disease that the spirits have not yet mastered. Moreover, the healers themselves needed to arrive at the possibility of negotiating change in practice with the spirits in the same manner that they have, in the past, negotiated such things as wearing modern clothes and using modern transportation.

In order to make the traditional healers feel comfortable with the workshop process and demonstrate acceptance of their belief system and the reality of their spirits, the healers' own process of initiating an event ceremonially was adopted. Each morning, the local spiritual leaders led the group in a private prayer asking the spirits to open the way for them to learn.

Ceremony, including prayer, songs, beating of drums and dancing, was an important part of the structure of the entire workshop. The first half of the morning sessions consisted of ceremonial activities and discussions of the previous day's events. The traditional healers were encouraged to consult their spirits in the evening on the day's activities, through prayer and dreams, so that on the following morning the spirits' opinions could be presented and discussed in a public forum. In this way, information was shared by all three types of participants. On the evening of the third day, the traditional healers and facilitators sometimes jointly planned and participated in a *bira* – a traditional ceremony to honour the spirits.

The facilitators and traditional healers should be equal partners in the learning process Everyone had something to learn from or teach each other. Communication was as evenly two-way (actually three-way, including the spirits) as possible, and an equal power relationship was established. Establishing a successful working relationship between the facilitators and the participants was a key factor in the success of the workshop. Seven workshops were conducted – one workshop per randomly selected district in seven of the eight provinces in Zimbabwe – over a four-month period from December 1994 to April 1995. On average, each of the workshops was attended by thirty healers. One workshop, however, was attended by only ten healers. The majority of the traditional healers who attended were those who had been randomly selected from the district to participate and who had completed a pre-intervention programme survey in the intervention districts. Usually, two or three traditional healers who had not completed the survey would arrive at a workshop wishing to attend and would be asked to complete the survey prior to participating. Generally, two district and two provincial health personnel attended each workshop and shared their perspective on the AIDS problem. The participation of chiefs and *kraal* heads was also encouraged.

The same team of facilitators led each of the workshops. Initially, there were five facilitators. One was a traditional healer and a research assistant on the project, T. Mark Musara. An additional one or two research assistants, Thoko Fuyane and Gertrude Khumalo-Sakutukwa, guided by one or both of the research investigators from the University of Zimbabwe, Alfred Chingono and Maureen Wellington, also acted as facilitators. The traditional healer facilitator provided an intimate knowledge of the language, culture and practice of traditional healing. He was able to identify with the needs and aspirations of the participants. The other facilitators provided an objective, 'outside' perspective. Their team facilitation actively demonstrated the possiblities of cooperation and sharing across health disciplines (clinical epidemiology, clinical and health psychology, social work and medical anthropology) and between different systems of thought.

The facilitators were required to conduct themselves in a respectful (see Hoff 1992) and friendly manner and be good, responsive listeners. At the outset of the workshop, roles, working procedure and expected outcomes were discussed to allay participants' fears of hidden motives and exploitation and to convince them that the facilitators had something of benefit to offer. Every attempt was made to address the healers' concerns. In some instances, the workshop programme was modified slightly to suit their expectations.

The form as well as the content of the workshop should be sensitive to social, cultural, political and economic barriers to acceptance of information In order that the workshop would seem relevant and authentic to the

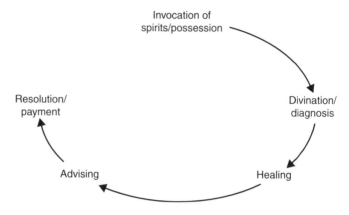

FIGURE 8.1 Stages in a traditional *matare* healing

participants, oral and performed messages were favoured over the written word, ancestral spirits were systematically included (by making references to them during the day and asking that they be consulted at night), and the entire learning process was explicitly structured after a traditional healing in a *matare*.[2] Ideally, this process follows the path represented in Figure 8.1.

Materials and items used in the practice of traditional healing, such as *gona* (medicine containers), *hakata* (bones thrown for diagnosing patients) and scarification instruments, were brought to the workshops to help make the traditional healers feel more at home and the demonstrations and role plays more authentic.

People need to 'own' a problem – that is, they must be 'disturbed' by the problem and feel compelled and capable of doing something about it – in order to participate actively in its solution We suspected that many traditional healers had had direct, disturbing experience of AIDS, including the deaths of their own family members. However, comments made by traditional healers to the effect that the AIDS epidemic is decreasing, that fewer and fewer AIDS patients are showing up every year for treatment and that the AIDS epidemic is overblown for some political end, necessitated an initial stage in the workshop whereby the traditional healers were 'disturbed' about the magnitude of the problem and the need to take action. Traditional healers were asked to share their personal experiences of AIDS. They talked about how AIDS had affected their families, neighbours, friends and community. The facilitators directed the focus away from the healers' failure or success in treating AIDS and the healers

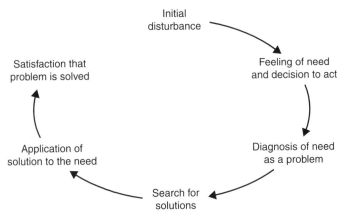

FIGURE 8.2 Innovation acceptance model

exposed their own vulnerability in the stories they related of the deaths of family members and acquaintances. It was only after these realizations that the traditional healers could make a decision to do something about the problem and actively participate in the workshop.

Active participation by the traditional healers was crucial. People must own not only the problem but the solution as well. They need to participate fully in defining the problem, searching for solutions and applying them. Figure 8.2, adapted from Havelock (1973), illustrates the process through which the workshop needed to take the traditional healers both individually and collectively in order for them to feel bound to the solutions and for the workshop to be successful.

An initial objective, then, was to develop a feeling of need – for the traditional healers to ask themselves what could be done about the AIDS problem. It was the facilitators' task to help them realize that they were the ones who could do something. This was the focus of Day 1.

The next step was to diagnose the problem. Through a morning of discussion that attempted to merge indigenous and biomedical under-standings of what HIV is, how it affects the body, and how it is passed from one individual to another, the facilitators helped the traditional healers to define the problem and move towards the idea that the solution is two-pronged and involves changing their own practices as well as providing information to patients and community influentials. This was the focus of the first half of Day 2.

The second half of Day 2, all of Day 3 and the early part of Day 4 were devoted to discussion, negotiation and rehearsal of changes in traditional healers' practices and guidelines for educating and counselling patients.

The remainder of Day 4 focused on consolidation of what had been learned and consideration of what steps the traditional healers needed to take to further their own knowledge, share their knowledge with other traditional healers and take AIDS prevention into their communities.

There is a remarkable similarity of structure between the stages of a traditional *matare* healing and the stages suggested by the innovation acceptance model. This might be expected considering the generality of the model and the healers' goal of themselves creating change (healing). However, it also demonstrates the appropriateness of adopting the *matare* healing structure as an explicit model for the workshop.

People learn best when they actively 'work' with new information in problem-solving or role-playing exercises Each segment of the workshop began with discussion that laid a foundation of existing indigenous knowledge. These traditional constructs and 'ways of knowing' were fused with biomedical understandings through further discourse employing analogies, metaphors and parables from traditional therapeutic practice. The healers were then given the opportunity to apply the results of the discussion to a concrete and practical problem. They were divided into small groups, often on the basis of their type of practice, and asked to role-play different risk scenarios and patient–healer interactions or to decide how they might deal with certain moral and professional dilemmas. The focus was on traditional healers teaching and learning from each other.

A facilitators' manual was produced in order to standardize the educational intervention. It contains a schedule of activities and a theoretical and background section that describes much of the thought behind the crafting of the workshop (Willms et al. 1996). The schedule is laid out so as to provide the facilitators, at a glance, with a description of the goals, rationale and activities for each segment. Also included in the schedule of activities are summaries of the kinds of things that traditional healers were saying with respect to the topic at hand.[3]

Workshop Content: Using Ethnographic Findings to Create Culturally Compelling Interventions

An ethnographic study involving participant observation, in-depth interviews and focus groups with 30 traditional healers in both urban (Harare) and rural (Gutu) districts was conducted over a two-year period. Analysis and interpretation of the ethnographic data produced case studies of traditional healers, illness narratives documenting the health-seeking behaviours of AIDS patients, texts describing risk scenarios in the *matare* of the healers, and interpretive summaries of emergent issues and themes with respect to indigenous understandings of HIV/AIDS.

The following sections describe traditional healers' understandings of AIDS as they emerged in the texts generated from the ethnographic research, and demonstrate both the richness of the data that can be obtained through such an approach and how such information was used to develop a preliminary version of a merged model of AIDS.

Traditional healers' explanatory models of AIDS   Substantial variation occurs in what traditional healers say, publicly and privately, about AIDS. There are, however, areas of consensus from which two indigenous base models of AIDS can be discerned.

A great deal of debate exists among healers around whether AIDS is a new disease or a new name for the traditional diseases known as *runyoka* and *rukombe* (see also Green et al. 1993). *Runyoka* and *rukombe* are diseases that an individual acquires as punishment for engaging in culturally inappropriate sexual behaviour – that is, sexual behaviour that violates cultural taboos (taboos around extramarital sex in the case of *runyoka* and around premarital sex with *rukombe*). Publicly at least, most traditional healers, while acknowledging that the symptoms of AIDS closely resemble those of *runyoka* and *rukombe*, state that AIDS is a new disease. There is good cause to suspect, however, that many are privately of the opinion that AIDS is, in fact, *runyoka/rukombe*, or at minimum, feel that there is some kind of relationship between AIDS and these traditional diseases, but are uncertain what it is.

On the one hand, it is argued that AIDS is not *runyoka/rukombe* because: (1) *runyoka* attacks only men, while both sexes can get AIDS; (2) *runyoka* and *rukombe* are curable, whereas AIDS is not; (3) infants and young children can get AIDS but not *runyoka* or *rukombe*; (4) AIDS is found all over the world, but *runyoka* and *rukombe* are illnesses that can be found only in some African countries; and (5) people die from *runyoka* and *rukombe* much more quickly than they do of AIDS. In essence what is being argued is that 'guilty' people (people who have violated a cultural taboo) get *runyoka* and *rukombe*. This does not fit with the observational reality that 'less guilty' (spouses) and 'innocent' (children) people also get AIDS.

It became apparent during the ethnographic research that traditional healers are struggling with the notion of *transmission*. They use *runyoka/rukombe* as the base model for understanding AIDS, but have modified it to accommodate the observational evidence about who does or does not get AIDS (for instance the fact that children can get this new disease). How is this new disease 'passed'? What is being 'passed'? Does the 'something' that is passed start the disease, or is the disease created because of a wrongful act?

For those traditional healers who understand or suspect AIDS to be a new name for *runyoka/rukombe* or a new type of *runyoka/rukombe*, the disease has always existed. It was not as prevalent in the past because people used to be 'decent' – that is, they used to respect their culture and did not engage in 'promiscuous' behaviour. *Runyoka* and *rukombe* have become more prevalent, as well as difficult to treat, because now, 'men sleep with so many women [that] when they get *runyoka* they do not know which woman they got it from', and therefore cannot make the appropriate restitution and affect their cure.

Those traditional healers who understand AIDS to be a new disease often state that it came from outside Zimbabwe and was brought by Europeans. That AIDS was 'brought by Europeans' appears to be understood in several different ways. Traditional healers observe that many people fled the country during the independence war and later returned, guerrillas went overseas for military training, and after independence there was an influx of tourists and business travellers from Europe and elsewhere. They argue that visiting 'outsiders' or Zimbabweans who left the country and later returned brought AIDS to Zimbabwe. Alternatively, some traditional healers state that AIDS was brought to Zimbabwe by Italian soldiers during the Second World War. 'Brought' may mean that AIDS existed among Europeans and was introduced to Zimbabwe, or it may mean that AIDS arose out of the 'mixing' of the races, in the sense that this mixing 'breeds something evil', or the adoption of European/Western ways and the loss of traditional culture.

Whether AIDS is understood to be a new disease or a new name for an old disease, traditional healers agree that an increase in prostitution and promiscuity has led to the spread of AIDS. The term 'promiscuity', as it is used by the healers, connotes sexual behaviour that violates a cultural taboo. Being promiscuous does not simply mean, as it generally does in Western use, 'having many partners'. Traditionally, culturally inappropriate sexual behaviour includes premarital sex, extramarital sex, extra-racial/tribal sex, sex with someone outside one's own age set, and sex with a woman who has recently aborted or given birth or who is menstruating. Those who engage in such behaviour are understood to be *guilty* or *unclean*.

That the loss of traditional culture and the adoption of Western ways are at the root of the increase in promiscuity/prostitution is universally accepted by traditional healers. It is for this reason that they advocate a return to traditional culture as the primary means of controlling the spread of AIDS. It is here, at the level of ultimate causation, that biomedical and indigenous explanatory models of AIDS converge. Both knowledge systems hold that:

- AIDS is spread primarily through sexual intercourse (non-sexual spread of the disease is de-emphasized in indigenous understandings);
- it is people's sexual behaviour that puts them at risk of getting AIDS; and
- the way to stop the spread of AIDS is for people to change their sexual behaviour.

The two understandings diverge in the knowledge of *how* various sexual behaviours put people in danger of getting AIDS – that is, in how AIDS 'gets started' in the body and how it 'gets passed' from one person to another.

How AIDS 'gets started': a traditional healing perspective   Much of what traditional healers understand about how AIDS 'works' is bound up in how they understand AIDS 'gets started'. Those traditional healers who argue that AIDS is a new disease offer a variety of explanations for how AIDS starts. AIDS starts when, during sexual intercourse:

- young (hot) blood mixes with old (cold) blood;
- white (European) blood mixes with black (Zimbabwean) blood;
- the blood of one tribe mixes with the blood of another tribe;
- 'dirty' blood mixes with 'clean' blood (where 'dirty' blood is that of a woman who is 'dirty' – that is, one who is menstruating or has recently given birth or aborted);
- many kinds of blood mix;
- local diseases mix with foreign diseases; or
- various STDs mix together to start AIDS.

These explanations may be thought of as attempts to link a particular manifestation of the loss of traditional culture and inappropriate sexual behaviour with one of two notions about how AIDS starts – the 'mixing of blood' or the 'mixing of diseases' (see Table 8.1).

According to the 'mixing of blood' explanations, the blood of the partners 'mixes' or 'meets' during sexual intercourse. Presumably, the mixing would be two-way and the disease would start in both partners. Instead, the focus is on the 'guilty' partner with his or her blood becoming 'diluted', 'weakened' or 'spoilt' during the mixing. The 'diluted' or 'spoilt' blood 'weakens' the body so that it becomes vulnerable to the many illnesses that together constitute AIDS (weight loss, diarrhoea, vomiting, etc.).

The base model for understanding AIDS appears to be that of *runyoka/ rukombe*:

Table 8.1 Loss of traditional culture and notions about how AIDS 'starts'

Indigenous explanations of how AIDS starts	Culturally inappropriate sexual behaviour
Mixing of blood	Violation of proscriptions about appropriate partners
Young (hot) blood + old (cold) blood	Wrong partner = someone outside own age set
White (European) blood + black (Zimbabwean) blood	Wrong partner = someone outside own race
Blood of different tribes	Wrong partner = someone outside own tribe
'Dirty' blood + 'clean' blood	Violation of taboos concerning time of intercourse
	Wrong time = during menstruation, soon after childbirth or aborting
Blood of many different persons	Violation of proscriptions about number of partners
	Too many partners = no partners outside of marriage (premarital or extramarital)
Mixing of diseases	
Local diseases + foreign diseases	Sex with 'outsiders'
STD + STD + STD	Too many partners

- the disease starts when a man and woman engage in immoral sex;
- it is the guilty person in whom the disease starts; and
- one act of immoral sex is sufficient to start the disease in someone.

According to the 'mixing of diseases' explanations, AIDS starts with the accumulation of disease, foreign and local or various STDs, as a result of which, when some unspecified threshold is reached, one of two things may happen:

- the body becomes so weak that many illnesses begin to attack it; or
- a new disease (AIDS) arises from the combination of diseases.

The base model here may be that of syphilis and gonorrhoea – other diseases *caused by sex* (although not necessarily immoral sex). Alternatively, some of the things that traditional healers say may be novel integrations of what they have heard about AIDS with their own way of thinking. The 'mixing of diseases' explanations may not be indigenous. Western bio-medical discourse such as 'AIDS is a complex of diseases' – meaning 'HIV can result in a complex of diseases' – may have been understood by traditional healers as 'AIDS is caused by mixing a complex of diseases'. Some traditional healers' understandings that AIDS is caused by a mixing of diseases may be about the different manifestations AIDS can have.

STDs are said to be caused by an accumulation of 'dirt' (*tsvina*) in the stomach, the bladder or the sex organs. The 'dirt' forms an 'egg', which 'hatches', sprouting worms that invade the whole body via the blood. These worms kill the body and make the person vulnerable to all sorts of diseases. 'Dirt' is not well defined (see also Green et al. 1993). Sometimes it is described as dead sperm, menstrual blood, or 'leftovers' of STDs. What is pertinent is that this 'dirt' is 'passed' or transmitted during sexual intercourse and that it accumulates to produce an illness state. The 'mixing of diseases' explanations entail:

- something (diseases) being passed during sexual intercourse (moral and immoral); and
- something (diseases) accumulating to produce a new illness state – AIDS.

Towards a Merged Model of AIDS

Given that traditional healers are unlikely to dispense entirely with their base explanatory models, a merged model must incorporate indigenous understandings, highlighting where they converge with biomedical ones. Where understandings diverge, the gaps must be bridged in a language or idiom that is familiar, acceptable and understandable to traditional healers. A merged model of how AIDS starts in the body would need to predict that:

- people may be dangerous without having symptoms of AIDS (i.e., while HIV+);
- one exposure may be enough to contract the disease;
- AIDS can be passed by non-immoral sex (sex with a spouse or spouses);
- AIDS can be passed by non-sexual blood contact;
- only a very small amount of contact is necessary;
- having an active STD increases the risk of getting AIDS; and
- healers are not protected by their *mudzimus*.

The biomedical understanding that predicts or explains these things is that of 'infection', which is not currently an important part of disease or illness understandings among traditional healers. *The challenge of creating a culturally compelling intervention requires, in this instance, that we take pieces of each of the indigenous base models, which fit with the biomedical notion of infection or disease causation by means of a transmissible agent, and put them together in a new way, phrased in a suitable idiom.* The problem with the *runyoka* model is that it predicts that only those who engage in immoral sex will get AIDS. The difficulty with the STD model is that an accumulation of dirt, resulting from many sexual encounters, rather than a very small amount of the transmissible agent from just one sexual encounter, starts the disease. We therefore borrowed the notion from the *runyoka* model that one sexual act, moral or immoral, is enough to start the disease, taking also from the STD model the idea that there is something, 'dirt' or *tsvina*, that resides in the body and is passed from one individual to another during sexual intercourse. The strength, in biomedical terms, of one indigenous base model is at the heart of the problem with the other one. Our challenge was to combine the strengths of each model to create a new model which avoids the pitfalls of the others. According to this new merged model, disease formation is the result of the *moral and immoral acquisition of 'dirt'* (tsvina) *or virus in any amount rather than its accumulation.*

Moving from Sexual Transmission to Non-sexual Transmission: Learning to Assess Risk in the *Matare*

Only with this new merged model in place can we begin to consider, along with the traditional healers, non-sexual transmission in the context of the *matare* and their various healing practices. Our ethnographic research revealed that AIDS is categorized along with other diseases *caused by sex* such as gonorrhoea and syphilis. The danger of getting AIDS is in the act of sexual intercourse, and as such, non-sexual means of HIV transmission through therapeutic practices such as scarification are, by definition, not recognized or experienced as risky.

Rather than supply the traditional healers with ready-made solutions to perceived problems in their practices, we helped them identify risky practices and develop their own solutions. In the course of the workshops, facilitators asked traditional healers their sense of when and how particular therapeutic situations become risky, as well as specific aspects of their practices in which they or their patients came into contact with blood or other bodily fluids. Facilitators also asked the traditional healers to think about their practice settings and the types of patients they had and their expectations, and to identify problems and solutions.

The final step in the workshop develops the traditional healers' abilities to communicate new understandings to a wider audience. It is felt that generally patients probably need to go through a learning process similar to that undergone by the traditional healers. That is, they need to be disturbed by the seriousness of the disease and convinced that prevention is the answer so that they will have an interest in understanding, in a new way, how AIDS works.

The workshops provide a context in which the traditional healers develop ideas about the kinds of things that are important to say to particular types of patients and methods for saying them. Traditional healers also need to reason through the moral dilemmas with which they are faced. Many of these dilemmas have to do with their patients' welfare versus the welfare of the patients' contacts. These dilemmas are discussed as a first step in moving from concern for the patient to a concern for the larger community.

Evaluation of the Impact of the Workshops

During the three-and-a-half-day workshop, there was a noticeable change in the way in which the facilitators and healers related to each other. Traditional healers remembered the original National AIDS Control Program (NACP) strategy for HIV/AIDS education – didactic in format and accusatory in tone. Despite initial suspicion, this experience proved to be different.

On the first workshop day, each of the parties staked out their claim, searching to find a common ground. The traditional healers talked about their successes with HIV/AIDS patients, and, reluctantly, their failures and concerns about treatment. The facilitators talked about their understandings and highlighted what they had in common with the traditional healers – specifically, that no one had a cure for HIV/AIDS (see also Berger et al. 1994).

The second day, both parties were more relaxed in their deliberations and eventually dropped their guard. Traditional healers and the facilitation team began to talk about the reality of HIV/AIDS in Zimbabwe and problems associated with prevention and the absence of a cure. Eventually, they came to recognize the need to work together.

On the third and fourth days, the traditional healers acknowledged that they needed to safeguard themselves in their therapeutic practices and find ways to protect their clients. In addition, they began to see themselves as catalysts for change in their own communities. They recognized the importance of networking (with chiefs and *kraal* heads) and the significance of community-based strategies for addressing the problem of HIV/AIDS. The traditional healers feel that they own the educational process and are inviting chiefs, headmen, and *kraal* heads to HIV/AIDS educational events.

Moreover, traditional healers are asking for these workshops as a way to address problems of HIV/AIDS in their practices (see also Karim 1993).

Conclusions

The development of culturally compelling HIV/AIDS interventions can be a formidable task, involving the navigation of diverse cultural worlds. At the outset, these worlds may appear more competitive than complementary, with stakeholders holding claim to truths, principles or even cures that they vigorously defend. Yet, if a common ground is established early on in the process, through trust, respect, mutual support and agreements to remain morally accountable to each other, an opportunity is afforded for healers and researchers to expose illness and disease to new avenues of conceptualization, healing and support.

Like our traditional healer counterparts, we, as Western-trained researchers, have a tendency to find solace in fixed, culturally constructed explanations. Our propensity to advance primary prevention strategies in languages and idioms often ill-suited to the life world of those most affected by HIV/AIDS may result in the collision of personalistic, spiritual and moral explanatories with scientific explanatories.

What is required, therefore, is a more dynamic and transcultural approach to addressing the problems and solutions to HIV/AIDS. A social science perspective is fundamental in achieving this aim. Without the insights gleaned into how AIDS is understood by healers and their patients, the importance of the ancestral spirits in the healers' practice and the healers' political struggle for power in relationship to Western medical practitioners, the intervention would have been unlikely to succeed. Equally crucial to its success was the respect accorded the traditional healers as autonomous professionals and collaborators in the project. Evaluation results, indeed, confirm the worthwhile nature of this participatory approach: traditional healers are talking to chiefs, *kraal* heads and other healers. Perhaps most importantly, traditional healers are urging their ancestral spirits to renegotiate with them the meaning of this disease and how to treat it. They are seeking a new way to understand the relationship between human behaviour and AIDS.

Acknowledgements

Financial support for this research was generously provided by the following donors and foundations: the World AIDS Foundation (WAF), the Southern African AIDS Training Programme (SAT), the J. F. Kapnek Charitable Trust, the International Clinical Epidemiology Network (INCLEN, Inc.) and the Royal Norwegian Embassy – Agency for Development Cooperation (NORAD). These donors are committed to ameliorating priority health concerns, and their investment in locally relevant action-oriented intervention research is respectfully acknowledged.

Notes

1. Chavanduka estimates that the majority (54.8 per cent) of traditional healers in Zimbabwe are women (1994: 43). Traditional birth attendants are, of course, usually women. In this chapter, we switch between the male and female case when referring to traditional healers, except in instances where the text obviously refers to one sex over the other.

2. The _matare_ is the equivalent of a physician's surgery or clinic. It is the place or site of therapeutic work for the traditional healer or _n'anga_.

3. Supported by funds from UNICEF, a resource manual for traditional healers has been written in Ndbele and Shona to complement the training strategy. It is entitled _AIDS Mumatare Nemumaruwa Edu_ and is available from Dr Alfred Chingono, Department of Psychiatry, PO Box A178, Avondale, Harare, Zimbabwe.

References

Arkovitz, M. S. and M. Manley (1990) 'Specialization and referral among the _n'anga_ (traditional healers) of Zimbabwe', _Tropical Doctor_ 20: 109–10.

Baleta, A. (1988) 'South Africa to bring traditional healers into mainstream medicine', _The Lancet_ 352 (15 August): 554.

Berger, R. A., L. Porter, G. Mekisini and P. Courtright (1994) 'Traditional healers and AIDS control', _AIDS_ 8(10): 1511–12.

Bischoff, P. and M. Ostergaard (1994) 'Zimbabwean healers help in the fight against AIDS', _Choices_ (The Human Development Magazine), UNDP, 27–28 March.

Chavunduka, G. L. (1986) 'ZINATHA: the organization of traditional medicine in Zimbabwe', in M. Last and G. L. Chavunduka (eds) _The Professionalisation of African Medicine_, Manchester: Manchester University Press, pp. 29–51.

— (1994) _Traditional Medicine in Modern Zimbabwe_, Harare: University of Zimbabwe Publications.

Courtright, P., S. Lewallen and S. Kanjaloti (1996) 'Changing patterns of corneal disease and associated vision loss at a rural African hospital following a training programme for traditional healers', _British Journal of Ophthalmology_ 80(8): 694–7.

Farmer, P. (1992) _AIDS and Accusation: Haiti and the Geography of Blame_, Berkeley: University of California Press.

Freeman, M. and M. Motsei (1992) 'Planning health care in South Africa – is there a role for traditional healers?', _Social Science and Medicine_ 34(11): 1183–90.

Green, E. C. (1988) 'Can collaborative programs between biomedical and African indigenous health practitioners succeed?', _Social Science and Medicine_ 27(11): 1125–30.

— (1997) 'The participation of African traditional healers in AIDS/STD prevention programmes', _Tropical Doctor_ 27 (Supplement 1): 56–9.

— (1999) 'Engaging indigenous African healers in the prevention of AIDS and STDs', in R. A. Hahn (ed.), _Anthropology in Public Health: Bridging Difference in Culture and Society_, New York and Oxford: Oxford University Press, pp. 63–83.

Green, E. C., A. Jurg and A. Dgedge (1993) 'Sexually-transmitted diseases, AIDS and traditional healers in Mozambique', *Medical Anthropology* 15: 261–81.

Green, E. C., B. Zokwe and J. D. Zokwe (1995) 'The experience of an AIDS prevention program focused on South African traditional healers', *Social Science and Medicine* 40(4): 503–15.

Groce, N. E. and M. E. Reeve (1996) 'Traditional healers and global surveillance strategies for emerging diseases: closing the gap', *Emerging Infectious Diseases* 2(4): 351–3.

Havelock, R. G. (1973) *The Change Agents Guide to Innovation in Education*, Englewood Cliffs, NJ: Education Technology Publications.

Hewson, M. G. (1998) 'Traditional healers in Southern Africa', *Annals of Internal Medicine* 128(12): 1029–34.

Hoff, W. (1992) 'Traditional healers and community health', *World Health Forum* 13: 182–7.

Karim, S. S. A. (1993) 'Traditional healers and AIDS prevention', *South African Medical Journal* 83 (June): 423–4.

King, R. and J. Homsy (1997) 'Involving traditional healers in AIDS education and counseling in Sub-Saharan Africa: a review', *AIDS* 11 (Supplement A): S217–25.

Neumann, A. K. and P. Lauro (1982) 'Ethnomedicine and biomedicine linking', *Social Science and Medicine* 16: 1817-24.

Nichter, M. and M. Nichter (1996) 'Education by appropriate analogy', in *Anthropology and International Health*, Amsterdam: Gordon and Breach, pp. 287–305.

Nzimande, B. (1988) 'African life and the "hidden abode" of mental health: some unmasked questions about "tradition" and progressive social services in South Africa', in *Mental Health: Struggle and Transformation, OASSSA*, 3rd National Conference, Durban.

Smith, S. E., D. G. Willms and N. A. Johnson (1997) *Nurtured by Knowledge: Learning to Do Participatory Action-Research*, New York and Ottawa: Apex Press and the International Development Research Centre.

Tessendorf, K. E. and P. W. Cunningham (1997) 'One person, two roles: nurse and traditional healer', *World Health Forum* 18: 59–62.

VanBuren, M. P. (n.d.) 'Zimbabwe's herbal secrets: modern medicine taps into a healing tradition', *WKKF International Journal* 5(1): 14–17.

Van Der Geest, S. (1997) 'Is there a role for traditional medicine in basic health services in Africa? A plea for a community perspective', *Tropical Medicine and International Health* 2(9): 903–11.

Were, M. K. (1992) 'The community as focus of development in Africa', in *Proceedings of the First International Conference of the Social Science and Medicine Africa Network*, Nairobi: 6–16.

Willms, D. G. and N. K. Sewankambo (1995) 'The risk reality model: an ethnographically-derived model for eliciting and explaining social-cultural determinants of risk for HIV/AIDS', oral presentation to the IXth International Conference on AIDS and STDs in Africa, Kampala, Uganda, 13 December.

Willms, D. G., A. Chingono, M. Wellington et al. (1996) *AIDS Prevention in the Matare and the Community: A Training Strategy for Traditional Healers in Zimbabwe*, Hamilton, Ontario, Canada: Department of Anthropology, McMaster University.

Part IV

Latin America

Introduction

Roberto Briceño-León

In Latin America, the presence of social science in health has been remarkably brief in contrast with the long-felt appreciation of social issues shown by a number of the region's physicians and public health specialists. Many highly trained doctors, who devoted years to the study of disease, stressed in their writings and actions the importance of society, the environment and people's ways of living towards understanding health. The explanation for this attention to the broader determinants of health may lie in the way medicine was taught and practised at the beginning of the twentieth century. Social aspects of health were given more weight than the scarce medications and meagre technology available at the time. In keeping with the language of the period, physicians wrote 'social-sanitary' reports, and many showed a keen social sensitivity, though they had few theoretical or conceptual tools with which to work. As the development of the social sciences in Latin America is very recent, what little social science existed in the early twentieth century could not easily reach practising physicians.

One is struck, however, by how outstanding medical figures took social factors into account in their work. This was true of Oswaldo Cruz, with his environmental sanitation campaign in Rio de Janeiro, and of Carlos Chagas, who not only discovered Chagas' disease in Minas Gerais, Brazil, but also described the environmental and social components of its transmission. It was also true of Arnoldo Gabaldón in Venezuela, who, in his anti-malaria campaign (the first broadly successful one in the world), analysed the relevant aspects of social organization and the economic impact of the disease. All were well-respected scientists, whose humanistic concern spurred them to approach social conditions as determinants of disease with great enthusiasm and curiosity.

When the social sciences became institutionalized, technical training programmes were created (at the junior college level) for social workers or assistants, and a number of sociologists were trained to work in public health agencies. Their basic task was to assist individuals and families in adapting to the rapid urbanization process that accompanied 'modern-ization'. The social sciences were also called upon to help improve environmental sanitation conditions in the countryside. No one asked why the peasants, both rural and newly urbanized, lived as they did; rather, there was a will to change their behaviour and to adapt them to a new 'social-sanitary' way of living.

At the same time, in the academy, the social sciences began to study what could be called the sociology or anthropology of medicine, through sociologists who focused on the doctor–patient relationship or hospital organization, and anthropologists who specialized in traditional or 'folk' medicine. This trend continued into the 1960s, when a major change of orientation took place, and social and preventive medicine courses were created at the region's Schools of Medicine with support from the Pan American Health Organization (PAHO).

Two events, in particular, influenced the relationship between the social sciences and health in Latin America after the 1960s. The first was a change in the orientation of medicine. The humanist perspective, with its emphasis on preventive medicine and public health, was replaced by medicine focused on individuals, with a basically curative and biotechnological approach. The second event concerned the influence of Marxism and the triumph of the Cuban revolution. In the context of the Cold War and the geopolitical changes that occurred in the 1950s and 1960s, Marxist thought swiftly gained broad acceptance in Latin American social science, and soon spread to the medical profession as well. Doctors with social sensitivity, who had generously devoted themselves to charity work or had viewed changes in micro-social conditions as the road to health improvement during the first half of the century, took up Marxism, as did their successors. The focus of attention shifted away from the changes that should be made in housing or use of latrines, to the demand for comprehensive social change. A revolution was thought to be the prerequisite to improving health con-ditions; the need was for a great social transformation that would change society as a whole. Then, and only then, would it become possible to improve the population's health. The focus moved from micro-social change to macro-social change.

In this context, a movement took shape in Brazil that rejected the United States public health approach with its emphasis on individual behavioural and small-scale social change. Instead, it was asserted that change should come about among the entire collectivity of persons, at the level of society and social organization, rather than at that of the individual. This move-ment took the name 'collective health' as opposed to public health, and the Brazilian Collective Health Association (ABRASCO) was formed. It intro-duced a radical change in the way health problems were approached.

Another organization, known as the Latin American Association for Social Medicine (ALAMES), was created under the influence of PAHO physician Juan César García. It organized courses and meetings, and tracked the changes taking place in Cuban medical care. It also brought together physicians imbued with social sensitivity and a Marxist ideological perspective.

This movement, which went so far as to sponsor a master's programme in Mexico, was lead chiefly by doctors who rebelled against repressed and unhealthy living conditions, attributing them to an unjust society and exploitation of workers, which could be overcome only by radical social transformation. Accordingly, the social sciences' fundamental contribution to health was the assertion of a theory of social change, with Marxism as its highest form of expression.

Little by little, motivated by the crisis in 'real socialism' and the never-ending divisions in the Marxist movement from the Soviet invasion of Czechoslovakia to the appearance of Eurocommunism, the doors were opened to new theoretical visions of the social dimensions of health, accompanied by more participation of social scientists and reflecting a different political perspective.

It was in this context that a new school of thought emerged, oriented towards working in a less ideological fashion and towards analysis and micro-social intervention. In general, its adepts do not deny the need for major social change in the region, but they do not believe they have to wait for a comprehensive social transformation in order to be in a position to take action. Rather, they believe small-scale work and actions can generate micro-social changes that have or may soon have a significant influence on greater social change. This line of thinking coincides with the movement to strengthen civil society, the emergence of grassroots organizations, and the creation of thousands of NGOs throughout the region. The political atomization provoked first by military dictatorships and then by the crisis of Marxism favours these grassroots movements, which work in social and community development and have made enormous efforts in the health field. These groups require a different sort of theoretical support, since the macro-social theories do not serve them. In general, they do not reject such theories, but they need social sciences capable of helping them in organization and participation processes.

Parallel to this, though in a very unequal fashion, universities have been shedding their ideological and highly politicized character and, above all, adopting a 'pluriparadigmatic' perspective. No longer does a single theory dominate and rule; now multiple theories compete for acceptance among professors and students.

It is in this context that the International Forum for Social Sciences in

Health (IFSSH) has emerged in Latin America, as a non-exclusive alternative with a more academic, scientific and ideologically pluralistic orientation. The Latin America Network of the IFSSH initially sprang from a group linked to the journal *Social Sciences & Medicine*, which organized the first meeting in the region. An attempt was then made to repeat the International Social Science and Medicine conference experience regionally, but cost, linguistic and capacity restrictions made it impossible to include as many participants. Still, it was an alternative to the ALAMES meetings, which had hardened in ideological orthodoxy and had ceased to be a viable alternative for many.

By the time the IFSSH appeared on the scene, a different scientific community working in the social science and health fields in the region had come into being. The academic groups from the universities, the NGO research groups and the base communities had undergone major changes and had done important work, with the support of philanthropic institutions such as the Ford Foundation, the Kellogg Foundation and Canada's IDRC. Significantly, the Special Programme for Research and Training in Tropical Diseases (TDR) provided considerable support for groups working on social and economic aspects of tropical diseases.

The Latin America Network of the IFSSH has brought many people together, and in the process it has revived the Social Science and Medicine meetings and integrated them with other initiatives to advance in terms of both knowledge and organization. Five Latin American meetings were held in the last decade of the twentieth century, at two-year intervals, in Chile, Argentina, Brazil, Mexico and Venezuela. In addition, national social science and health meetings have begun to be held in Brazil and Venezuela.

At the beginning of the new century, the landscape is completely different, and the potential areas of work and encounter have multiplied. The relationship between the social sciences and health is now very diverse, but also characterized by enormous theoretical wealth and reflection. As is the case in all processes of change and innovation, there are more questions to ask in Latin America than answers to give.

9

Lay Beliefs and Gender Stereotypes: Unacknowledged Dimensions of STD Prevention Strategies

Mónica Gogna and Silvina Ramos

In contrast to the previous insensitivity of STD/HIV health education and promotion programmes to psycho-social and cultural dimensions of health behaviour (Campbell 1995; Cleary 1988; Parker 1991), there is a growing consensus regarding the need for culturally appropriate interventions. That is, in order for a sexual health educational intervention to be effective in changing behaviour, there is increasing recognition that it has to be based upon an understanding of 'context' and 'meaning' (how people perceive, conceptualize and find meaning in their social and physical worlds). It must also take into account the social and cultural norms and expectations regarding sexuality and gender (de Zalduondo and Bernard 1993; Dixon-Mueller 1993; Gupta and Weiss 1993; WHO 1993).

There has been scant research, however, seeking to uncover lay understandings of STDs on the part of Argentinean adults. The few KAP surveys carried out in Buenos Aires City addressed people's knowledge and attitudes regarding HIV/AIDS. One KAP survey administered to students from secondary public schools included a question about the way in which syphilis is transmitted (Kornblit and Méndez Diz 1993). The only anthropological study on STDs we could identify focused on public health services and how social stigma was constructed in the doctor–patient relationship (Domínguez Mon 1991).

We therefore undertook a study focused on the cultural and psycho-social dimensions of STDs among men and women from a low-income neighbourhood in Greater Buenos Aires. We wanted to describe and understand people's ideas and behaviour regarding STDs in order to develop interventions aimed at enhancing their ability to prevent and seek treatment for these diseases. To do so, we adopted an 'emic' perspective in which we attempted to understand and define the problem from the people's point of view (Pelto and Pelto 1978). The research focused on knowledge about

STDs, meanings attached to them, and the way in which sexual norms and gender stereotypes affect prevention and treatment.

Study Design

The study used qualitative data collection techniques: focus groups and in-depth interviews in which free lists and pile sorts were applied. Free listing is a deceptively simple but powerful data-gathering technique generally used to study a cultural domain. Pile sorting is an efficient method for eliciting shared cultural beliefs (Bernard 1994). The multi-method approach arose out of our concern about engaging people in discussions about private or taboo issues. This concern was exacerbated by the fact that participants were likely to know one another.

Research participants were men and women between the ages of 18 and 50, presumably heterosexual, who live in a low-income neighbourhood in Greater Buenos Aires. The neighbourhood was chosen on the basis of convenience and its typicality: our previous relationship with a female community leader granted us access to both the health centre and community. The neighbourhood was not atypical, extreme or deviant (Patton 1990).

We considered age a key dimension of the sampling design, since one can reasonably expect that differences in the socialization of younger and older adults have led to differences in the way in which sexuality is conceived and/or in the amount and quality of information they have received about STDs. More specifically, we presumed differences in the attitudes and concerns of those who became sexually active in the time of HIV/AIDS and those who initiated their sexual lives without the constraints posed by this threat. We decided not to include teenagers (under 18), assuming that their chances of having been exposed to STDs would be smaller than those of young adults (18–25).

We chose to focus on low-income individuals because of their social vulnerability and the comparatively greater negative impact that the absence of public policies regarding reproductive and sexual health has on this population *vis-à-vis* the middle and upper classes. In addition, key informants indicated that prevalence of STDs was higher among men who applied for a commercial licence (the majority of whom belong to the low-income population) than among couples applying for a pre-nuptial health certificate (a group that includes a proportionately higher number of middle-class individuals). Sexual orientation was assumed, given the fact that heterosexuality is predominant and that it was not feasible to use this variable as a recruitment criterion.

Participants were recruited by a female community leader who invited them to take part in a study 'about people's opinions regarding health and sexual life'. This person was given precise instructions regarding sex, age and number of participants to be recruited for focus groups and individual interviews.

We conducted ten focus groups and 20 in-depth interviews. In total, 112 people participated in the study. Even though the original idea had been to select interviewees from among focus group participants, some ethical concerns raised by World Health Organization (WHO) reviewers made us change the strategy. Thus participants attending the focus groups were not eligible for the subsequent interviews.

Individual interviews and group sessions took place at the health centre outside office hours and were conducted by same-sex interviewers. Male group and individual interviews were carried out by Dr Marcelo Giterman, a physician and psychoanalyst with experience in AIDS prevention. Focus groups and interviews with women were conducted by the authors.

Three focus groups were held with young men aged 18 to 25; another three with young women; two with adult men aged 35 to 50 and two with adult women. Female focus groups had an average of eight participants and male focus groups an average of nine participants. Interviewees and focus group participants received a small sum of money as compensation for their time.

Defining the opening question for both the focus groups and the interviews was a demanding task since, in the local context, lay notions of STDs among low-income individuals had not been explored before. The question we used was a slightly revised version of one of the alternatives suggested in the Helitzer-Allen and Allen (1994) ethnographic protocol for the study of STDs. Thus the opening question was framed as follows: 'What are the health problems or discomforts people may have related to their sexual life?' From our point of view, this framing would better elicit the emic perspective than a question containing the words 'illness' and 'sexual intercourse'. We considered the former to be a more loaded and narrower term than the vaguer 'problems or discomforts'; regarding the latter, we did not know how it would be interpreted in the local context and thus preferred 'sexual life' as a more unequivocal term.

The interviews and group sessions were audio-taped and transcripts coded by more than one of the researchers to ensure consistency in the use of the coding scheme. Data were analysed by the principal researchers using qualitative data management software programmes.

Given the ethical and methodological implications of recruiting participants from a single neighbourhood, some safeguards were taken to promote confidentiality. In the introduction to focus group discussions, moderators emphasized that we were interested not in personal experiences but rather in what participants thought were the opinions of people of their same age and gender regarding the research topics. In addition, participants were requested to make a 'confidentiality contract' that also included respect for all the opinions voiced. Despite these guidelines, as group discussions evolved some male and female participants provided examples from their personal experience. A few others, in turn, did not participate actively in the group sessions even when the moderator (and sometimes group members) tried to include them in the discussion. In almost every group there were a few 'silent participants'. This lack of participation was regarded positively by researchers as a sign that people were not feeling 'pressed' either by moderators or by the fact that monetary compensation was offered.

Triangulating data-gathering techniques proved to be a fruitful strategy for two reasons. First, it allowed us to obtain data we might otherwise have missed. For instance, the pile sorting revealed that women knew some popular names for STDs that they had not mentioned spontaneously in the focus group discussions or in the responses to the open-ended interview questions.

Second, the combination of techniques allowed the differential ability of both genders to address our research topics to emerge. Generally speaking, women seemed to be more comfortable in the face-to-face interviews while men did better in the focus group discussions. Unlike the women, the men were less tentative and more explicit in discussing research issues with their peers, frequently resorting to jokes, scoffing and coarse expressions. These differences were conspicuously evident in the focus groups.

Men's greater familiarity and comfort with the topic of discussion seemed to be related both to personal experiences with STDs and gender socialization. In contrast, the women proved to be more reluctant to speak about these subjects. In fact, it is worth noting that seven of the ten women interviewed individually wanted to make it clear that they had never had an STD. Expressions such as 'It didn't happen to me' or 'I never had it' were repeatedly used. Women also stated that they had no friends, acquaintances or relatives who had STDs. The same reactions hold true for the focus groups. In comparison, only two of the ten men in the in-depth interviews stated that they had never had diseases of this kind and the majority of the participants in the focus groups admitted to having had experiences and to knowing of friends or acquaintances with the problem.

Women's greater reluctance to discuss STDs may be explained by the particular way in which STDs affect them in social and cultural terms. Women found it more difficult to anchor the conversation around STDs and frequently tended to shift the discussion to other topics, such as partner relationships, infidelity and contraception. If, as our experience suggests, the power of focus groups and interviews to elicit information regarding STDs varies according to the participants' gender, a multi-method approach was not just a good choice but *the* appropriate one.

Last, but not least, combining data-gathering techniques reminded us of the way in which contextual or individual dimensions might influence research findings. Such was the case with respect to women's perceptions of vulnerability to STDs/HIV. While data collected in semi-structured interviews gave the impression that perception of vulnerability was weak, focus group discussions suggested the contrary. Peer interaction allowed for the emergence of women's fears about their partners bringing 'the plague' home.

Theoretical Underpinnings

Several social science constructs oriented our approach. Applied qualitative research on sexuality and reproductive health confronts a variety of complexities in health behaviour that theoretical social sciences approaches and medical research have often side-stepped in the past. The reproductive health and sexuality (RHS) field is at the intersection of three complex domains: sexuality, gender and health. Theory and research heretofore have addressed one or sometimes two domains at a time. Yet most crucial RHS problems involve all three domains simultaneously (De Zalduondo 1994). Therefore, we argue that research on STD/HIV prevention and health-seeking behaviour needs to be informed by *all* three, if it is to address the issue effectively.

Our approach was shaped, in part, by the 'lay notions of health and illness' perspective (Fitzpatrick 1984; Freidson 1978; Helman 1994), which recognizes the fact that popular beliefs regarding health and illness are seldom formalized or integrated, and are frequently expressed tentatively and hesitantly. They are syncretic in origin, respond to experience in a flexible manner, and do so according to the current concerns of the individual (Helman 1994). Furthermore, lay concepts not only define an alternative set of entities (diseases, body parts and physiological processes) and causes to those of medicine, but also act as condensed symbols that refer to a wider variety of experiences contained in a culture. As Fitzpatrick indicates, 'lay concepts of illness do not merely name entities in the body but are powerful images associated with other realms of life' (1984: 21). In our research, the fact that women used the 'plague' metaphor to conceptualize STDs clearly exemplifies that they were concerned not only with the health consequences of these diseases but also with the devastating emotional conflicts that STDs bring to the partner relationship and the family.

In addition, we were interested in exploring some of the 'classic' determinants of individual health-seeking behaviour, posited in the Health Belief Model (Becker and Maiman 1983; Hochbaum 1981; Mechanic 1978; Rosenstock 1960, 1966; Rosenstock and Becker 1974; Rosenstock and Kirscht 1974; Suchman 1965), since these categories have oriented the vast majority of social science research on health behaviour related to HIV/AIDS. In particular, we focused on the following categories: perceived susceptibility, severity of the disease, perceived costs of different preventive and treatment measures, availability and quality of the information about STDs, and evaluation of the efficacy of available treatments. The purpose was to elicit the emic perspective on some variables that are frequently used without knowing their actual meaning in the local context.

Moreover, we assumed that the health belief approach would be insufficient for several reasons. First, it has already been acknowledged that this model is weak in understanding and predicting behaviour regarding HIV/ AIDS. Much has been written about the gap between knowledge and practice and between intentions and behaviour (Aggleton 1996; Pollak 1992): 'It has long been observed that excellent AIDS knowledge, while it may lessen stigmatizing attitudes is not enough to change behaviour' (Haour-Knipe 1996: 20).

Second, as an individual-focused approach, the HBM has not proved to be a good tool for addressing behaviours related to sexuality. As Gagnon observes, 'sexuality is a form of conduct that is complexly related to pleasure, sin, reproduction, getting old, growing up, enduring loss' (1988: 600), and thus has little to do with rationality and cost-benefit analysis. In addition, the sexual bond implies a relation between two people. The prevention and treatment of STDs is subject to the nature and dynamic of the relationship, inevitably engaging (by action or omission) both partners.

Drawing on feminist theory (Benería and Roldán 1992; Giele 1988; Rubin 1992), and the social constructivist approach to sexuality (Gagnon 1988, 1990; Giddens 1992; Laumann et al. 1994; Vance 1991), we considered sexuality and gender as 'interlocking domains' (Dixon-Mueller 1993). More specifically, we explored the influence of gender and sexuality stereotypes, norms and values on people's ability to protect themselves and others from STDs. Special attention was given to the 'double sexual standard' (which sanctions the exercise of sexuality of men and women differently), the dual female stereotype (bad girl/whore; good girl/ madonna) and the norms that label inter-partner communication about sex as taboo (especially when initiated by women) or associate condoms with 'illicit sex'.

We also took into account the fact that STDs affect men and women in a different way, both biologically and culturally. As Dixon-Mueller and

Wasserheit state, 'It is not only more likely that a noninfected woman acquire an STD from an infected partner than vice versa, but it is also more probable that she will suffer more serious consequences in the long run, such as inflammatory pelvic disease, ectopic pregnancy, cancer of the cervix, chronic pelvic pain, and infertility' (1991: 10). It must also be pointed out that STDs are more frequently asymptomatic in women than in men. In addition to this 'biological sexism', we considered cultural sexism: women are often blamed for the spread of STDs (McCormack 1982) and the stigma attached to STDs does not affect both genders equally.

In summary, a heterodox approach was developed to try to capture the links between the three multilayered and dynamic domains of health/ illness, sexuality and gender. In so doing, we have tried to follow the advice of Denzin and Lincoln: 'the (qualitative) researcher-as-*bricoleur*-theorist works between and within competing and overlapping perspectives and paradigms' (1994: 2). This enables the research 'to connect the parts to the whole, stressing the meaningful relationships that operate in the situations and social worlds studied' (Weinstein and Weinstein 1991, cited in Denzin and Lincoln 1994: 3).

Lay Beliefs and Gender Stereotypes Uncovered

Beliefs about STDs: a complex mix of information, meanings and emotions The study participants identified a wide and heterogeneous group of terms for 'health problems people may have related to their sexual life'. The list included three medical terms (syphilis, AIDS and HPV – human papilloma virus); some terms from common language (*purgación*/ 'purging', *pudrición*/'rotting' and 'fungus'); other terms referring to a generic affliction ('infections'); others that designate fluids ('discharge', 'women's internal problems' or 'strong menstruation'), or specific problems that may appear in the 'nether area' (such as haemorrhoids and urinary infections), and an old and well-known expression used in reference to STDs – 'venereal diseases'. Other studies have also confirmed that, in the popular imagination, the notion of sexually transmitted diseases differs greatly from the biomedical perspective. In relation to a similar opening question, a study in Haiti revealed that the interviewees included some diseases in the list that could be transmitted between couples living together by means other than through sexual intercourse. Some of the mentioned diseases, such as tuberculosis, were viewed as STDs because the close proximity of the partners during the sexual act could facilitate contagion (Désormeaux et al. 1992).

It is interesting to note that men and women did not recall identical sets of health problems related to sexual life. Men reported almost twice as many terms as women did (21 and 12, respectively), and only seven terms were named by both men and women (venereal diseases, flux, fungus, urinary infection, crab lice, syphilis and AIDS). AIDS was referred to most by both sexes. Excluding AIDS, the diseases most frequently cited by men were 'rotting', crab lice, and fungus. Women, in turn, mentioned syphilis, vaginal infections, venereal diseases and fungus. There is contradictory evidence, however, with respect to which STD the popular expression 'rotting' refers. On the one hand, some key informants contend that the term alludes to syphilis. On the other, the symptoms attributed to 'rotting', together with the short time in which the testimonies maintain that the symptoms appear, suggest that they might be referring to gonorrhoea or chlamydia (Helitzer-Allen and Allen 1994).

Men appeared to recognize a wider spectrum of sexual health problems than women and included male and female problems in their lists. They also exhibited a wider vocabulary to describe STDs, using different words for the same problem. In contrast, women had a narrower list of terms, the majority of which could be catalogued as women's problems (e.g., vaginal infections, sores, warts, flux), with the exception of AIDS, syphilis and venereal diseases. It seemed as if men were more knowledgeable about STDs and felt more comfortable talking about them.

Also uncovered were a variety of explanations about how different diseases are transmitted. In the case of AIDS, they varied from unspecific expressions such as 'AIDS is everywhere' or 'AIDS can be transmitted in manifold ways' to statements of more precise transmission processes such as sexual contact and blood transmission through injection drug use, wounds or cuts, and transfusions. In relation to sexual contact, there was evident confusion about the specific mechanism through which the contagion is produced: 'I don't know what it's about, maybe the blood gets it altogether in there [referring to the vagina]' (male, aged 28).

Although the sexual transmission of HIV/AIDS was recognized as the main source of contagion, the interviewees described other blood transmission situations: 'if you get stuck with the needle of someone who has AIDS'; 'if a drop of blood falls on you'. The greater ability to conceptualize blood transmission rather than sexual transmission was also reported in Loyola (1994). In that study, similar findings were associated with the fact that, in the local health culture, blood is a central element in explaining organic functioning and the health–illness process. We believe that a complementary explanation lies in the observation that our study participants found it difficult to imagine that semen can transmit a disease as it is deemed a symbol of vitality and thus cannot be associated with anything that damages or spoils. The idea of semen as a 'noble fluid' contrasts with the widely held notion about menstruation and *'strong flux'* as being vehicles of STD transmission. The latter are viewed by almost all men but few women as dangerous fluids, with special pollution powers that weaken men. The cultural significance of menses as a polluting or purifying agent has been explored in different cultures (e.g. Fachel 1995; Martin 1992; Ngubane 1977; Skultans 1970; Snow and Johnson 1977). Although we did not systematically explore the cultural meanings of menstruation in this study, other research conducted with the same population reveals a widespread belief among women that menstruation is a purification or cleansing process by which the body rids itself of all impurities (Balán and Ramos 1989).

As a means of transmission, sexual contact was frequently cited in the following ways: a casual sexual encounter, very frequent sexual contact, and a sexual encounter with a stranger. These types of sexual meetings inevitably imply an 'erroneous selection' of the sexual partner, thus further endangering the participants. This belief is reinforced by one that considers 'knowing the person' to be an efficacious way of protecting oneself from acquiring an STD: 'Know who you are with. Surround yourself with people you can trust' (female, aged 27).

The idea that STDs are transmitted by women was widely held among the male participants. Some interviewees went so far as to suggest that STDs originate in women. As indicated in the literature, women were often blamed for the spread of STDs. In some languages these diseases are described as 'women's diseases' or characterized as infections that 'good' men catch from 'bad' women (McCormack 1982). Some of the men in our study related STDs to a particular category of women ('women of the street', 'women of the night,' 'dirty women'), but the majority of them mentioned that friends or acquaintances had contracted STDs from women. Popular expressions convey the idea that women 'rot' men ('a woman rotted him'), do them wrong, or pass STDs on to men:

> The heavy menstruation that women have is what makes all these diseases, that's what they have. (male, aged 42, married)

> I know people who have been sick because they had sex with a woman. (male, aged 46, divorced)

> He had sex only with her and she was the one who rotted him. I don't know if it's because he was weak or she was very strong. Because she was a girl of the streets. I don't know. He was always rotting. (male, aged 35, married)

But it is worth highlighting that some women also blamed women for STD transmission: 'being with different women' ('different' meaning women unlike themselves) was sometimes referred to as a transmission route.

Another stated cause of STDs was weakness of the body owing to depression, poor nutrition, hard work, or low self-defences. This was stressed by men and derives from the belief that strong flux may carry 'bad things' that are particularly risky to a man if he is not healthy. This idea is clearly expressed in the following statement:

> Rotting is when you're sleeping with someone. The girl has this strong discharge and you're weak and you rot. From the strong discharge she has. (male, aged 20)

Finally, special attention was given to lack of personal care and unclean surroundings as means of STD transmission. Describing the absence of hygienic habits as causes of STDs, men were particularly concerned about the fact that some people (women or men) do not wash their genitals after sexual intercourse. The lack of hygiene argument was sometimes associated with promiscuous practices:

> They don't wash and they do it over and over and over again. The time comes when the girl rots. When you do it with her, you get it. (male, aged 28)

Both men and women described situations of contagion through unclean linen, exchanged underwear and dirty bathrooms. It is probably due to the fact that men are more frequent users of public bathrooms than women that they devoted quite a long time to talking about the possibility of acquiring an STD through this source. Key informant interviews with a small number of doctors indicated that physicians may reinforce many lay notions about 'environmental' transmission by providing vague answers to questions about STD transmission and referring only to the importance of hygiene in order to 'protect the family' from an admission of adultery.

In summary, both male and female study participants attributed STDs to a wide range of sources such as lack of personal hygiene, 'naturally strong flux', poor selection of sexual partners and unclean surroundings. This multiplicity of origins requiring different preventive strategies may explain people's difficulties in taking effective precautions against STD transmission.

The severity of various STDs was described in relation to their symptoms and consequences. The symptoms reported were diverse and varied widely between men and women, both in terms of their specificity and in relation to the magnitude of alarm to which they gave rise.

Only when discussing AIDS did interviewees give a shared set of specific and unmistakable symptoms: blemishes, hair loss and acute thinness. At the same time, references to the differences between the carrier and the person with AIDS demonstrate misperceptions such as: carriers are easier to identify; carriers do not transmit the virus; there are both healthy and unhealthy carriers; either only the man or only the woman can infect when they are carriers; and people with AIDS are less infectious than carriers since they are weaker. The notion of a 'healthy carrier' – that is, someone who has the virus but neither looks nor feels ill and yet is capable of transmitting it – is difficult to conceptualize (Vasconcelos et al. 1993). These confusions and the pre-eminence that the symptoms characterizing the terminal phase of the illness had in our interviewees' discourse may explain why people can fail to perceive certain sexual encounters as 'risky'. The emphasis given to the idea that 'knowing the person' is the best prevention against AIDS seems to fit with the idea that people with AIDS can be easily identified.

The symptoms associated with other STDs differed between male and female participants. Men were very precise and assertive in identifying a group of 'male symptoms', highlighting that they were unmistakable: burning, pain, suppuration, swelling, itching, physical weakness and an inability to penetrate. The intensity of discomfort and pain that characterize male symptoms seems to explain men's responsiveness to them as well as promptness in seeking treatment.

Men described the stench of bad flux as a clear sign a woman has an STD. One participant declared: 'You can smell it half a block away.' They also showed deep concern, however, about not being able to recognize that women are carriers of this kind of disease given the hidden or mysterious and threatening characteristic of their genitals:

> What happens is that in a man you can see what he has, but you can't tell what a girl has inside; outside she looks fine, everything is all right, and inside she's real rotten. You don't know what she's got inside; she's got a disease you can get but you can't see it; you realize after you've slept with her and you've got caught ... you can't tell what a woman has unless she tells you. (male, aged 32, married)

Women's references to symptoms were vaguer than men's both in the case of male and female symptoms. Coloured flux and strong-smelling flux were most often cited. Women's discourse, however, showed that flux was also associated with other vital but non-disturbing situations (such as the beginning of sexual life, the insertion of an IUD, or menopause). In other words, for women the most explicit male evidence is perceived both as an indication of a problem and as part of ordinary physiological processes. This perception may inhibit health-seeking behaviour. The fact that STDs are more frequently asymptomatic in women than in men is yet another obstacle.

With respect to the emotional consequences of STDs, both men and women stressed the emotional and conjugal problems that might arise between a couple if an STD appears. The breakdown of the marriage, violent reactions, disappointment ('it will never be the same') and the 'destruction of the family' were some of the catastrophic consequences imagined. People emphasized the interpersonal conflicts that might appear latently or manifestly when a partner acquires an STD. The fact that symptoms may be experienced by one partner but not the other is difficult to comprehend and can cause distrust or suspicion. Most participants feel it is better not to ask or talk about such sensitive issues. Only a few considered the need for dialogue, mutual understanding and compassion. The profound emotional consequences of STDs call for medical counsellors who have been trained to deal with such complex issues.

In contrast to the similarity of responses about 'emotional consequences', men and women differed greatly in their perception of the severity of STDs' physical consequences. Men feared losing their penis as a consequence of extreme disregard of their symptoms. Expressions such as 'a little more and they have to cut it off' and 'it's so rotten that it falls to pieces' surfaced in their discourse. Another negative consequence reported by men was the disruptive effect of STDs on sexual life. For women, few understood the negative physical outcomes. In fact, only one of them remarked about the eventual negative impact of STDs on a woman's fertility. No reference was made by women to the impact of STDs on their sexual life. Physical consequences appeared to be much more negative and 'concrete' for men than for women. Nevertheless, women expressed unspecified concern about the consequences of STDs in terms of 'men bringing the plague home'. It is our hypothesis that this expression refers more to the symbolic value of STDs as diseases that 'break up the family' than to feared 'physical' consequences – with the obvious exception of HIV/AIDS.

The reported strategy for avoiding STDs was the same for both genders: the use of the male condom. Implementing this strategy, however, was differently conceived. For women, it was a question of their partners using the condom in secondary relationships. For men, this strategy presupposed condom use only with selected women, who were easy to detect:

> If I haven't got a condom, I do it anyway. Depending on who the woman is. Some women are half crazy. But you can tell. From how they act, how they dress. Some women have tattoos on their arms. Then you really have to think about sleeping with her. I don't take risks often, not all of the time. (male, aged 21, married)

Men and women alike are confident that they can select partners that do not put them at risk. But this strategy works differently for each gender. For men, it is a matter of distinguishing between a housewife and another type of woman (a woman of the streets, a 'crazy', a woman with a very active sexual life). The first is dependable and the condom is unnecessary, whereas you have to take care with the second. Women, in contrast, make their selection by 'knowing the person well' – that is, by knowing what the man is like, where he lives, what he does, what his family is like, whom he has gone out with. These references and conditions of life make it possible to build up the necessary trust and feeling of self-protection to enter a sexual relationship.

A third strategy, reciprocal fidelity, was also mentioned. As one participant explained: 'have a safe woman that's yours and nobody else's, and don't wander around'. Women, however, expressed some doubts about the viability of this solution considering the 'natural infidelity drive' of men.

Treatment options were also differently perceived. For men, they seem to be efficacious and simple to implement. For women, in contrast, treatment always implies problems – emotional difficulties related to the need to have their partner's compliance and practical problems regarding the use of ovules (pessaries), which are perceived as having low efficacy. Two participants observed:

I know that with a couple of injections of antibiotics everything goes away. It's easy. I don't worry about it. (male, aged 32, separated)

This business with the ovules is a big complication; first they're difficult to put in and after, sooner or later, you get it again. (female, aged 27, married)

Last but not least, the symbolic connotations of these diseases need highlighting. In the local culture, STDs are charged with negative social and cultural values because they are diseases associated with promiscuity and lack of personal care. For men, and to a lesser extent women, they are diseases propagated through women. Thus STDs carry shame and humiliation for women, who are thought to be unclean or promiscuous. Fears of social, emotional and conjugal consequences often take priority over fears of health consequences, making women reluctant to inform their male partners of their symptoms or to inquire about the health status or sexual behaviour of their partners. For some women, the eventual risk of being beaten or abandoned or of losing a source of emotional or financial support far exceeds the perceived health risk of acquiring an STD. As has already been pointed out in the literature, 'In many cultures, women accept vaginal discharges, discomfort during intercourse, or even the chronic abdominal pain which accompanies some STDs as an inevitable part of their womanhood' (Dixon-Mueller and Wasserheit 1991: 11).

The set of sexual health problems identified by the study participants did not constitute a clearly defined (in terms of symptoms, causes and forms of transmission) or serious group of diseases. This observation does not strictly apply to AIDS, which seemed to be more appropriately conceptualized, although some misperceptions and lack of information were noted. Data also showed that men and women had significantly different views, experiences, awareness and information regarding STDs. The negative symbolic value and the perceived emotional consequences help us to understand the barriers people (and particularly women) face in acknowledging their infections – thereby labelling themselves as careless, dirty or promiscuous – and seeking treatment.

How cultural norms of sexuality and gender stereotypes affect STD prevention and treatment Lay notions about STDs are linked to, and reinforced by, cultural norms and proscriptions surrounding sexuality and gender. Like other 'master statuses' (age, race, education), gender organizes people's understanding of the social world around them and, particularly, their very understanding of sexuality. More specifically, ideas about what constitutes the essence of 'maleness' and 'femaleness' are expressed in sexual norms and ideologies such as the 'double sexual standard' or the dual female stereotype (bad girl/whore; good girl/madonna), as well as norms that label inter-partner communication about sex as taboo (especially when initiated by women) or that associate condoms with 'illicit sex'. Gender is also closely associated with the scripts to which people are exposed and the types of choices they perceive as viable and legitimate – as well as the costs and benefits that they associate with these choices (Laumann et al. 1994).

It is through these mechanisms that gender norms, power and stereotypes affect people's ability to conceive, propose and/or adopt effective practices to prevent and treat STDs. For example, Paiva notes that 'safer sex' practices such as male condom use confront the most basic notions of masculinity and femininity. She writes:

> Condom use confronts the most basic notions of male virility, that being a man means 'naturally' to have less control over sexual and aggressive impulses and to feel them more strongly than a woman. To wear a condom, to be rational, to control sexual drives or take a woman partner's needs into consideration, is to betray maleness. Being a woman is 'naturally' to be more fragile, less aggressive and to be able to control sexual drives. It means being ignorant about sex until marriage, and then to give in to her husband's impulses. (1993: 100)

As some authors have pointed out, by proposing or carrying condoms, a woman may be viewed as sexually active or looking for sex, a perception that may contradict socially-accepted norms of female passivity (Gupta and Weiss 1993; Martin et al. 1990). In addition, economic dependence on men may make it difficult for women to insist on mutual fidelity or condom use (WHO 1993). Clearly, gender stereotypes and power relations between men and women play a key role in people's ability to consider themselves at risk of STDs or HIV/AIDS and, therefore, to adopt 'safer sex' (among others, Carovano, 1995; De Zalduondo and Bernard, 1993; Gupta and Weiss 1993; Martin et al. 1990).

Essentially, these arguments hold true for the low-income population in our study even though fieldwork made evident a certain pluralism of values and norms regarding gender roles, as well as ambiguities and breakdowns in male and female discourses. There were men who tried to persuade peers that a woman who proposes or carries condoms is not a 'bad woman' or who stated they used condoms to prevent unwanted pregnancies. We also found women who talked openly about expecting their husbands to use condoms in secondary relationships and women who refused condoms, arguing that they interfere with pleasure. Last, but not least, a few young women stated they would not have sex without condoms and a small number of adult women challenged others to protect themselves, arguing that if husbands loved them they had to care for their health.

Gender norms and stereotypes, however, were found to impinge strongly on risk perception, along with the popular views about STDs (ideas of contagion, prevention, STD consequences) previously discussed. The idea that STDs are transmitted by 'street women' and, more vaguely, 'by women' was broadly conceived by male interviewees. Some even considered men more vulnerable than women regarding sexuality. Male participants' discourse evokes Petchesky's observation with respect to men's concerns about the undesirable side-effects that chemical contraceptives could cause in men: 'One senses that where sex is at issue, the male of the species is still regarded by a patriarchal culture and medicine as the delicate and vulnerable one' (1984: 173). In our study, the belief about male vulnerability stemmed from the idea that *la pudrición* (rotting) inhibits men from having sex (or makes it extremely painful) but does not affect women to the same extent, and that women's strong flux or menstrual blood are sources of contagion. Male suspiciousness about how 'clean' a woman is, as well as female suspiciousness regarding men's fidelity, are part of a sex/gender system characterized by ambivalence and hostility. For instance, the men in our study tended to blame women, describing them as dirty, over-demanding and too smart (*vivas*). Women, in turn, considered men irresponsible, cold and naturally unfaithful. Women lamented their share in the sexual division of labour and complained about not having the same freedom as men.

Going back to men's sense of vulnerability, testimonies seemed to suggest that risk awareness was high among men. Paradoxically, this was not the case. In the local culture, stereotypes about masculinity (men are fearless, horny and prisoners of a 'boy-scout sexuality') counterbalance male perceptions of vulnerability. The following quotations illustrate wide-spread notions among men that 'real men take risks' and never pass up an opportunity for a sexual encounter:

> You just have to do it (have sex) if the woman is willing. (male, aged 20)
>
> If you are too horny, you may make a mistake. (male, aged 26)
>
> A man goes ahead and does it anyway. 'I am a man, and I do it,' he says to himself. (male, aged 43)
>
> Hair was meant to be combed [a somewhat vulgar remark to the effect that wherever there's a woman, you have to do it]. (male, aged 33)

These beliefs and attitudes coexist with the STD prevention strategies described earlier: not having sex or using condoms with certain women (those with tattoos or 'street women').

Women, in turn, felt quite vulnerable. With a few exceptions, the majority considered men 'naturally' unfaithful and women consequently to be at risk of STDs/HIV. Some women explicitly described themselves as 'women of the home' or 'nice women' (*señora de su casa*) and believed that their status protected them from the risk of STDs. Others stated that they were more worried about the threat of 'the plague' than about being deceived. Despite their awareness of risk, they were reluctant to propose 'safer sex' to their partners. In fact, only three young women out of the 60 women interviewed declared that they would not have sex without a condom. Some women did not think condom use was necessary ('you know him') and others declared they would not dare propose it. Women expressed fears regarding male reaction, including the chance that men might feel mistrusted. It is worth mentioning that married women did conceive of some preventive strategies: expecting husbands to use condoms in secondary relationships and using female condoms themselves. The latter strategy, however, did not seem to be a very realistic option (they are expensive, men did not agree with their use, and women feared they would not be able to put them in correctly). Nevertheless, the fact that women took these alternatives into consideration may support our argument that they do feel at risk.

Borrowing Pollak's (1992: 97) categories, women in our study tended to think in terms of 'protection strategies' while men tended to think more in terms of 'selection (of partners) strategies'. Yet prevention of STDs entails changes in sexual behaviour and eroticism. Given that the only method of reducing the risk of STDs/HIV for sexually active persons is the male condom, prevention depends largely on its acceptance by men. The majority of our interviewees were reluctant to use condoms, even though many of them referred to having used them or using them to avoid unwanted pregnancies. Men complained about loss of pleasure and interference with the sexual dynamic. It is interesting to note that even men who eventually acknowledged never having used condoms repeated the 'loss of sensation' argument. Some men also indicated that they did not use condoms because it was very important for them to leave the semen inside the vagina.

Many of the women had little or no experience at all with condoms (particularly the older women), and placed little value on them. Female arguments against condoms varied depending on whether testimonies were gathered in interviews or in focus groups. In face-to-face interviews women used arguments similar to those of the men (e.g., interferes with pleasure, prevents their feeling the semen inside during intercourse, makes them feel 'distant'). Some women also mentioned that condoms were usually associated with 'illicit sex'. In the group discussions, barriers to condom use most commonly mentioned were fear that the condom would break during sexual intercourse or fear that it would cause itching and/or burning. The more intimate climate of the interview may have encouraged women to refer more openly to eroticism, thus explaining the difference from testimonies collected in group sessions.

Both in interviews and group sessions women indicated that negotiating condom use in stable relationships would be highly problematic. Some of them also indicated that teenagers of both sexes tend to accept condoms much more readily than adults, and envisaged that if they were younger or single they would request eventual partners to use condoms.

Finally, the research findings suggest that many women do not seek treatment for STDs because they are unaware of the signs and symptoms or because they accept vaginal discharge and itching as an inevitable part of womanhood and sexual life. The stigma STDs confer as well as the fear or shame of being classified as 'unfaithful' or 'deceived' may also affect their willingness to acknowledge symptoms and seek out proper care. The study also revealed that some women have difficulty in complying with treatment, particularly when given ovules for vaginal insertion. They are considered uncomfortable to insert and/or not very effective. Several women indicated that their partners would not comply with treatment (usually, pills, injections and sexual abstinence or protected intercourse) and only one woman referred to a successful negotiation episode. Men's failure to comply with STD treatment was also referred to by male interviewees. It is worth noting that although men do consult doctors and follow their instructions when they have *la pudrición* (rotting) they exhibit little compliance with their partners' treatment.

Some Final Reflections

We have attempted to analyse a complex set of social and cultural dimensions that have to be addressed in order to understand people's ideas and behaviour regarding STDs and thus design strategies to enhance their agency to prevent and treat these diseases. In discussing knowledge and beliefs, meanings, feelings, social norms, sexuality and gender stereotypes, we hope we have convinced our readers of the value of a comprehensive approach: one that takes into consideration lay notions of health and illness, but also cultural scenarios of gender and sexuality and interpersonal relations.

Only recently acknowledged by family planning and reproductive health programmes, gender and sexuality dynamics are of key importance in improving our understanding of lay notions of reproductive health and the way in which risk and prevention strategies are conceived by the population. The latter have received comparatively less attention in the number of studies conducted in the last decade on factors affecting repro-ductive health (Barbosa and Uziel 1996; Bronfman et al. 1995; George 1996; Langer et al. 1996; Paiva 1993; Rivera et al. 1995). Conversely, in other studies, emphasis on lay notions may have overshadowed the impact of gender and sexuality norms on reproductive health behaviours (Fachel 1995; Nichter 1997).

Turning now to the principal findings of the study, it is evident that people do have ideas about STD transmission, consequences and pre-vention, and that these ideas differ greatly from the biomedical perspective. Lay beliefs about STDs proved to be coloured by deeply rooted ideas about body fluids (discharge, menstrual blood, semen) and complexly related to ideas about gender identities and relations and sexual matters. Lay strategies of STD prevention, resembling the partner-centred strat-egies frequently described in the HIV/AIDS prevention literature (Paiva 1993; Wight 1993), were identified.

A great diversity in the level of knowledge about STDs was observed, with men in general being better informed about the variety of STDs and the types and efficacy of treatments. Even though there were differences in the amount and quality of information on HIV/AIDS that people pos-sessed, this information seemed to be more homogeneous *vis-à-vis* STDs.

Lay prevention strategies included having sexual relationships with someone 'you know' and using condoms, particularly with occasional or new partners. Condom use in secondary relations was a strategy that some men claimed to practise and married women expected their husbands to adopt. Married women were in favour of using female condoms themselves even though they are not perceived as a feasible strategy.

Both 'protection strategies' and 'selection of partners strategies' were envisaged by the study participants. As studies in very different contexts have shown, the majority of males in our study believed they could discern the type of woman who is likely to have an STD or AIDS (Waldy et al. 1993; Wight 1993). The best means of discriminating between 'clean' and 'unclean women' was considered to be a personal acquaintanceship with the woman over a period of time, allowing for 'observation'. If this was not possible, most of the men decided on the basis of how a woman dressed and other external signs such as tattoos whether or not she was 'clean'. This links with our second major finding.

Gender relations and norms concerning appropriate sexual and non-sexual behaviour proved to affect people's willingness and ability to conceive, propose and adopt effective practices to prevent and treat STDs. The dual female image (good woman/bad woman) and the stereotypes about masculinity (men are fearless, horny and prisoners of a 'boy-scout sexuality') counterbalance male and female perceptions of vulnerability and affect people's willingness and ability to adopt 'safer sex'. These images and norms inhibit men from protecting themselves and others since 'a real man takes risks' and has to take advantage of any opportunity for a sexual encounter. In turn, norms, stereotypes and gender relations affect women by providing 'good women' (housewives) an imagined protection or by preventing them from proposing 'safer sex' to their stable partners. This was the dominant scenario, even though fieldwork made evident a certain pluralism of values and norms regarding gender roles and sexuality as well as ambiguities and nuances in male and female discourses.

While reconstructing lay ideas about STDs it became clear to us that our initial assumption about the importance of addressing the interface between health/illness, sexuality and gender had been correct. Research participants' testimonies showed that people's attitudes towards STD prevention and treatment are the product of several and sometimes conflicting logics (for example not hurting one's partner or potential partner, avoiding emotional conflicts and protecting oneself and/or one's partner from what are perceived as dangerous situations).

In other words, the research illustrates that lay concepts of STDs are indeed 'powerful images associated with other realms of life' (Fitzpatrick 1984: 21). It has also uncovered the tradeoffs people face when making decisions that involve sexuality, where such complex issues as pleasure, power, love, trust or self-esteem are at stake. Finally, to a lesser extent, the findings gave a hint of the 'identity work' required of people as they respond to fears of contagion and/or stigma and make decisions about their sexuality: protecting or reformulating self boundaries, reinforcing images or reimagining the other, and protecting themselves from implication (i.e., symbolic connection to 'infected' others and the negative characteristics ascribed to them) (Crawford 1994).

In revealing these complexities, the findings of the study provide certain cues for the design of culturally appropriate health promotion and education strategies that enable people to construct the knowledge required to adopt preventive and treatment behaviours regarding STDs/HIV. As De Koning and Martin (1996) note, knowledge construction is based on the development of a critical awareness of circumstances influencing one's life. Health interventions aimed at producing change by fostering such awareness should encourage people to reflect on internalized images and norm and value systems that are often taken for granted.

This study has produced rich information about the internalized images of STDs as well as gender norms and values, and thus can illuminate the design of sexual health educational interventions. Regarding communication of information, the findings suggest that it is necessary to provide young people and adults, of both sexes, with basic knowledge about the reproductive system, including the characteristics and functions of genital fluids. Sexual health educational efforts should aim to clarify that although some STDs may be caused by overgrowth of vaginal organisms or are associated with unhygienic personal practices, most of them are sexually transmitted. In addition, the message should emphasize that condom use is crucial for STD prevention and treatment efficacy.

Another message to communicate is that women are more susceptible to infection than men because of biological and cultural factors and are more likely to suffer from complications of untreated STDs. Awareness of infertility or abdominal pain as middle-term consequences of untreated STDs needs to be raised. Building on existing knowledge, the notion that vaginal discharge may be a symptom of an STD must be conveyed.

The frequently asymptomatic nature of some STDs, particularly in women, must also be acknowledged. The basic message here is that even though symptoms may be present in only one of the partners, treatment should be undergone by both.

Finally, the population needs to understand that having an STD greatly increases the risk of contracting HIV. Regarding beliefs about HIV/AIDS, the distinction between being HIV-positive and having AIDS also needs to be addressed and misunderstandings and doubts about transmission and prevention clarified. In particular, the fact that someone can be asymptomatic but still transmit the virus is an essential issue.

The transmission of messages about the aetiology, modes of transmission and consequences of STDs must also be part of an intervention in which sexual norms and gender stereotypes are addressed and discussed, as they have proved to be powerful barriers to the adoption of 'safer sex' practices. Also crucial is the ability to negotiate sexual practices that are safer, pleasurable, consensual and acceptable to the partner, along with access to the material conditions to make reproductive and safer sex choices (Paiva 1996). Fostering this 'sexual subject' – an individual capable of being the regulating agent of his or her own sexual life – is a complex process. The insights and experience provided by Freire's pedagogy and feminist theory and practice (Boston Women's Health Book Collective 1984; Freire 1972) are useful tools to enhance this process.

Workshop methodology lends itself well to a sexual health intervention with these aims as it allows for the emergence of differing perspectives, emotions and prejudices, and strengthens participants' confidence to explore alternative behaviours. Given the dual sexual standard of Latin American culture, providing men and women with the opportunity for separate group interactions to discuss sexuality, gender and reproductive health issues seems to be a necessary first step towards the deconstruction of internalized images, the development of negotiation skills and the promotion of communication on sexual matters among partners. We agree with Campbell that 'men should be targeted directly as a group of male sex partners, rather than through women (e.g. at the workplace, in the community)' (1995: 198). This seems to be a better strategy, from both a practical and a strategic point of view, than putting the emphasis on improving women's negotiation skills, particularly in the case of married women.

Successful health education programmes using male peer counsellors have frequently been described in the literature (Campbell 1995; Carovano 1995; Weiss et al. 1996). In the focus groups we conducted, both younger and older adult men observed that the presence of an 'outsider' working as a group coordinator had enabled them to talk candidly by neutralizing the atmosphere of competition and exhibitionism that characterizes male interaction when talking about sexual matters. In fact, group discussions turned out to be a stimulating experience for both genders, particularly for women. There was consensus among group participants on the importance of sharing experiences with peers about the research issues and on the positive effect of this 'learning process'.

In addition, interventions targeting men may take advantage of the fact that they do seek out the advice of doctors and/or pharmacists when they suspect that they have an STD. The doctor–patient visit can be turned into an opportunity to sensitize men about their responsibility in the prevention of unwanted pregnancies and STDs/HIV.

Face-to-face work with women needs to address women's concerns about sexuality, reproduction and contraception and to promote self-esteem as well as critical consciousness regarding their gender condition. In addition, promoting the accessibility of the female condom seems to be a strategy worth exploring given the positive attitude that women spontaneously showed towards it in focus group discussions.

For both men and women, the promotion of condom use can rely heavily on its advantages as a contraceptive since negative opinions about the pill were frequently voiced by both sexes. Moreover, condom use to avoid unwanted pregnancies is seen as legitimate by men both in stable and casual relationships. The research findings, however, also showed that condom use is still associated with illicit sex by both men and women. Thus, as Gupta and Weiss (1993) indicate, face-to-face education and mass media campaigns that destigmatize the condom are greatly needed.

Finally, given the evidence that physicians and pharmacists play a central role in men's strategies to treat STDs, interventions should also target health professionals. The small number of interviews conducted with doctors in our study suggest that gender stereotypes also affect physicians' willingness and ability to give clear and effective instructions for prevention and treatment. We therefore suggest developing interventions aimed at helping health professionals to become familiar with lay notions of STDs and aware of the way in which gender stereotypes shape their professional practices (i.e., asking men but not women about secondary relationships or emphasizing the association between STDs and lack of hygiene to avoid provoking a conflict between husband and wife).

To conclude, the results of this study make clear that in order to enhance people's agency in sexual and health behaviour, the nature and dynamic of the interlocking domains of sexuality, gender and health need to be addressed. Lay notions of these diseases as well as gender and sexual norms and values constitute a complex set of 'resources' that shape and guide men's and women's perceptions, choices, decisions and actions regarding the prevention and treatment of STDs. We hope this insight contributes to the design of culturally appropriate responses to what has been described as the 'silent epidemic'.

Acknowledgements

This chapter is based on the results of the project 'Psychosocial and cultural factors in the prevention and treatment of STDs. Power, love and pleasure in the negotiations between genders', conducted by the authors and Edith A. Pantelides (CENEP, Argentina), and supported by WHO, Task Force for Social Science Research on Human Reproduction.

An earlier version of this chapter, 'Gender Stereotypes and Power Relations: Unacknowledged Risks for STDs in Argentina', by Monica Gogna and Silvina Ramos, appeared in Richard Parker, Regina Maria Barbosa and Peter Aggleton (eds), *Framing the Sexual Subject: The Politics of Gender, Sexuality and Power*, Berkeley, CA: University of California Press, 1999. Copyright permission to use this material has been granted by The Regents of the University of California.

References

Aggleton, P. (1996) '(Is there) method in the madness? Methodology and interpretation in socio-sexual research on HIV and AIDS', paper presented at Conference on Reconceiving Sexuality. International Perspectives on Gender, Sexuality and Sexual Health, organized by the IMS/Universidade Estadual do Rio de Janeiro, Río de Janeiro, 14–17 April.

Balán, J. and S. Ramos (1989) 'La medicalización del comportamiento reproductivo. Un estudio de los sectores populares urbanos', *Documentos CEDES 29*, Buenos Aires.

Barbosa, R. and A. P. Uziel (1996) 'Gender and power: sexual negotiation in the time of AIDS', paper presented at Conference on Reconceiving Sexuality. International Perspectives on Gender, Sexuality and Sexual Health, organized by the IMS/Universidade Estadual do Rio de Janeiro, Río de Janeiro, 14–17 April.

Becker, M. and L. Maiman (1983) 'Models of health-related behavior', in D. Mechanic (ed.), *Handbook of Health, Health Care and the Health Professions*, New York: The Free Press.

Benería, L. and M. Roldán (1992) *Las encrucijadas de clase y género: trabajo a domicilio, subcontratación y dinámica de la unidad doméstica en la ciudad de México*, México, D.F.: El Colegio de México-FCE.

Bernard, R. H. (1994) *Research Methods in Anthropology, Qualitative and Quantitative Approaches*, 2nd edn, Thousand Oaks, CA: Sage.

Boston Women's Health Book Collective (1984) *The New Our Bodies, Ourselves*, New York, NY: Simon & Schuster.

Bronfman, M., H. Gómez Dantés and C. Magis Rodríguez (1995) 'SIDA, enfermedades de transmisión sexual y salud reproductiva', *Reflexiones*, Año I, No. 7, Programa Salud Reproductiva y Sociedad, El Colegio de México.

Campbell, C. (1995) 'Male gender roles and sexuality: implications for women's AIDS risk and prevention', *Social Science and Medicine* 41(2): 197–210.

Carovano, K. (1995) 'VIH/SIDA y los desafíos que enfrentan los hombres. Implicaciones para un cambio de conducta', *DESIDAMOS* 3(1): 17–18.

Cleary, P. (1988) 'Education and the prevention of AIDS', *Law, Medicine and Health Care* 16(3–4): 267–73.

Crawford, R. (1994) 'The boundaries of self and the unhealthy other: reflections on health, culture and AIDS', *Social Science and Medicine* 38(10): 1347–65.

De Koning, K. and M. Martin (1996) 'Participatory research in health: setting the context', in K. de Koning and M. Martin (eds), *Participatory Research in Health: Issues and Experiences*, London: Zed Books.

Denzin, N. and Y. Lincoln (1994) *Handbook of Qualitative Research*, Thousand Oaks, CA: Sage.

Désormeaux, J., B. de Zalduondo, M. C. Flambert, J. M. Bernard and D. A. Celentano (1992) 'The importance of local concepts of contagion and sexual conduct for AIDS education: a case from urban Haiti' (mimeo).

De Zalduondo, B. (1994) 'Strengthening capacity for systematic qualitative research on sexuality and reproductive health: modules and materials for short-term training in Latin America' (mimeo), Baltimore, MD: Johns Hopkins University.

De Zalduondo, B. and J. M. Bernard (1993) 'Sexual-economic exchange in urban Haiti: culture, gender and sexual risk behavior' (mimeo), paper presented at Conference on International Perspectives in Sex Research, Rio de Janeiro, 22–25 April 1993.

Dixon-Mueller, R. (1993) 'The sexuality connection in reproductive health', *Studies in Family Planning* 24(5): 269–82.

Dixon-Mueller, R. and J. Wasserheit (1991) *The Culture of Silence. Reproductive Tract Infection Among Women in the Third World*, New York: IWHC.

Domínguez Mon, A. (1991) 'La construcción social de estigmas: el caso de las ETS en la atención hospitalaria' (mimeo).

Fachel, O. (1995) 'Sangue, fertilidade e práticas contraceptivas', in O. Fachel (ed.), *Corpo e significado. Ensaios de Antropologia Social*, Porto Alegre: Editora da Universidade.

Fitzpatrick, R. (1984) 'Lay concepts of illness', in R. Fitzpatrick et al. (eds), *The Experience of Illness*, London: Tavistock.

Freidson, E. (1978) *La profesión médica. Un estudio de sociología del conocimiento aplicado*, Barcelona: Península.

Freire, P. (1972) *Pedagogy of the Oppressed*, Harmondsworth: Penguin.

Gagnon, J. (1988) 'Sex research and sexual conduct in the era of AIDS', *Journal of Acquired Immune Deficiency Syndromes* 1: 593–601.

— (1990) 'The explicit and implicit use of the scripting perspective in sex research', *Annual Review of Sex Research* 1: 1–43.

George, A. (1996) 'Gender relations in urban households in Bombay. Challenges for HIV/AIDS prevention', paper presented at Conference on Reconceiving Sexuality. International Perspectives on Gender, Sexuality and Sexual Health, organized by the IMS/Universidade Estadual do Rio de Janeiro, Río de Janeiro, 14–17 April.

Giddens, A. (1992) *The Transformation of Intimacy: Sexuality, Love and Eroticism in Modern Societies*, Stanford, CA: Stanford University Press.

Giele, J. (1988) *Gender and Sex Roles*, London: Sage.

Gupta, G. R. and E. Weiss (1993) *Women and Aids: Developing a New Health Strategy*, Washington, DC: ICRW.

Haour-Knipe, M. (1996) 'From crisis to chronicity: issues in ETS related research', paper presented at the XIV International Conference on the Social Sciences and Medicine, Peebles, Scotland, 2–6 September 1996.

Helitzer-Allen, D. and H. Allen (1994) T*he Manual for Targeted Intervention Research on Sexually Transmitted Illnesses with Community Members*, Baltimore, MD: AIDSCAP.

Helman, C. G. (1994) *Culture, Health and Illness* (2nd edn), London: Butterworth, Heinemann.

Hochbaum, G. M. (1981) 'Behavior change as the goal of health education', keynote address presented at the Eta Sigma Gamma annual meeting, Washington, DC, 16 October 1981.

Kornblit, A. and A. Méndez Diz (1993) 'Modelos sexuales en jóvenes y adultos', Instituto de Investigaciones de la Facultad de Ciencias Sociales de la UBA (mimeo).

Langer, A., K. Tolbert and M. Romero (1996) 'Las enfermedades de transmisión sexual como problema de salud pública: situación actual y prioridades de investigación', in A. Langer and T. Tolbert (eds), *Mujer: Sexualidad y Salud Reproductiva en México*, México: The Population Council, EDAMEX.

Laumann, E., J. Gagnon, R. Michael and S. Michaels (1994) *The Social Organization of Sexuality. Sexual Practices in the United States*, Part I, Theoretical Background, Chicago: University of Chicago Press, pp. 3–73.

Loyola, A. (1994) 'AIDS e prevençao da AIDS no Rio de Janeiro', in A. Loyola (ed.), *AIDS e Sexualidade. O Punto de Vista das Ciencias Humanas*, Rio de Janeiro: Dumará.

McCormack, W. (1982) 'Sexually transmitted diseases: women as victims', *Journal of the American Medical Association* 248(2): 177–8.

Martin, D., R. Barbosa and W. Villela (1990) 'Mulher, sexualidade e prevençao da AIDS' (mimeo).

Martin, E. (1992) *The Women in the Body: A Cultural Analysis of Reproduction*, Boston, MA: Beacon Press.

Mechanic, D. (1978) *Medical Sociology: A Comprehensive Text*, New York, NY: The Free Press.

Ngubane, H. (1977) *Body and Mind in Zulu Medicine*, London: Academic Press.

Nichter, M. (1997) 'Prophylactic antibiotic use as a barometer of vulnerability and misguided appropriation of medical resources: the case of STDs in S.E. Asia', paper presented at the Seminar on Cultural Perspectives on Reproductive Health, organized by the IUSSP Committee on Reproductive Health and the University of Witwatersrand, Rustenburg, South Africa, 16–19 June.

Paiva, V. (1993) 'Sexuality, condom use and gender norms among Brazilian teenagers', *Reproductive Health Matters* 2: 98–109.

— (1996) 'Fostering the sexual subject. Gender and class in the sexual scene', paper presented at Conference on Reconceiving Sexuality. International Perspectives on Gender, Sexuality and Sexual Health, organized by the IMS/Universidade Estadual do Rio de Janeiro, Río de Janeiro, 14–17 April.

Parker, R. (1991) 'Sexual diversity, cultural analysis and AIDS education in Brazil', in G. Herdt and S. Lindembaum (eds), *The Times of AIDS: Social Analysis, Theory and Method*, Newbury Park, CA: Sage, pp. 225–42.

Patton, M. (1990) *Qualitative Evaluation and Research Methods*, Newbury Park, CA: Sage.

Pelto, P. and G. Pelto (1978) 'Units of observation: emic and etic approaches', in *Anthropological Research: The Structure of Inquiry*, Cambridge and New York: Cambridge University Press, pp. 54–66.

Petchesky, R. (1984) *Abortion and Woman's Choice. The State, Sexuality and Reproductive Freedom*, Boston, MA: Northeastern University Press.

Pollak, M. (1992) 'Attitudes, beliefs and opinions', in 'Understanding sexual behaviour and its change', in M. Pollak, G. Paicheler and J. Pierret (eds), 'A problem for sociological research', *Current Sociology* 40(3): 24–35, 85–102.

Rivera, D., A. Rodó, D. Sharim and U. Silva (1995) *Relaciones de Género y Sexualidad*, Documento de Trabajo No. 153, Santiago de Chile: SUR, Centro de Estudios Sociales y Educación.

Rosenstock, I. M. (1960) 'What research in motivation suggests for public health', *American Journal of Public Health*, 50: 295–301.

— (1966) 'Why people use health services', *Milbank Memorial Fund Quarterly*, 44: 94–124.

Rosenstock, I. M. and M. H. Becker (1974) 'Social learning theory and the health belief model', *Health Education Quarterly* 15: 175–83.

Rosenstock, I. M. and J. P. Kirscht (1974) 'The health belief model and personal health behavior', *Health Education Monographs* 2: 470–3.

Rubin, G. (1992) 'El placer y el peligro: hacia una política de la sexualidad', in C. Vance (ed.), *Placer y peligro. Explorando la sexualidad femenina*, Madrid: Revolución, pp. 113–90.

Skultans, V. (1970) 'The symbolic significance of menstruation and menopause', *Man* 5: 639–51.

Snow, L. F. and S. M. Johnson (1977) 'Modern day menstrual folklore', *Journal of the American Medical Association* 237: 2736–9.

Suchman, E. A. (1965) 'Stages of illness and medical care', *Journal of Health and Social Behavior* 6: 114–28.

Vance, C. (1991) 'Anthropology rediscovers sexuality: a theoretical comment', *Social Science and Medicine* 33(8): 875–84.

Vasconcelos, A., A. Neto and A. Valença (1993) *AIDS and Sexuality Among Low-income Adolescent Women in Recife, Brazil*, Washington, DC: ICRW.

Waldby, C., S. Kippax and J. Crawford (1993) '"Clean" and "unclean" women in the AIDS discourse of young heterosexual men', in P. Aggleton, P. Davies and G. Hart (eds), *AIDS: Facing the Second Decade*, Lewes: Falmer Press.

Weinstein, D. and M. Weinstein (1991) 'George Simmel: sociological flâneur bricoleur', *Theory Culture and Society* 8: 151–68.

Weiss, E., D. Whelan and G. R. Gupta (1996) *Vulnerability and Opportunity: Adolescents and HIV/AIDS in the Developing World*, Washington, DC: ICRW.

WHO, Global Programme on AIDS (1993) 'Sexual negotiation, the empowerment of women and the female condom', general protocol (mimeo).

Wight, D. (1993) 'Constraints or cognition? Young men and safer heterosexual sex', in P. Aggleton, P. Davies and D. Hart (eds), *AIDS: Facing the Second Decade*, Lewes: Falmer Press.

10

From 'Milk Bread' to Control of Visceral Leishmaniasis among the Zenú Indians of the Caribbean Coast of Colombia

Iván D. Vélez, Susana Jaramillo, Sonia del Pilar Agudelo, Gloria Palma, Jorge Gallego and Bruno Travi

Leishmaniasis is a disease that affects both humans and animals. Produced by parasites belonging to the *Leishmania* genus, it is transmitted by a small insect, commonly known as a sandfly. In humans, the disease results in skin lesions (cutaneous leishmaniasis), lesions in the nasal and throat mucous membranes (mucous leishmaniasis), or in the internal organs such as the liver and the spleen (visceral leishmaniasis, WHO 1995). The disease is prevalent in 88 countries of the world, located in tropical and subtropical regions. The World Health Organization (WHO) estimates that two million new cases appear every year worldwide. Visceral leishmaniasis (VL) is the cause of 50,000 to 200,000 deaths annually. For this reason, it is considered by WHO to be one of those diseases whose study and control have high priority. In Latin America, it occurs from Mexico to northern Argentina (Desjeux 1992; WHO 1995).

Clinically, VL is characterized by fever, pallor, enlargement of the liver and spleen, and anaemia. Diagnosis is confirmed through visual observation of the isolated parasite in samples obtained from the patient's spleen or bone marrow. Ninety per cent of VL cases diagnosed in Latin America occur in children under five years of age, who are typically undernourished, live in the disease transmission zones, and are exposed to the sting of the sandfly. The disease may be fatal if a specific and timely treatment with pentavalent antimonials (meglumine antimoniate or sodium stibogluconate) is not received (WHO 1995).

Most cases of VL in Colombia have been reported from two large geographical zones (foci) – those of the Magdalena River Valley and the Caribbean Coast area (Corredor et al. 1989). The University of Antioquia has been studying VL in the Caribbean Coast since 1987. These investigations have focused on the Zenú Indian community in San Andrés de Sotavento, Córdoba (Vélez et al. 1988; Vélez et al. 1995).

The Study Area

The municipality of San Andrés de Sotavento spans an area of approximately 336 square kilometres. This region has an altitude of 100 m above sea level, with an average temperature of 24°C and an average annual rainfall of 1,500 mm. Vegetation is primarily tropical dry forest. The community is inhabited by direct descendants of the old Zenúes, who lived in this territory in the sixteenth century when the Spanish arrived. As a result of cultural contact, which began with the conquest, the Zenú community has suffered marked changes, including the loss of their language and mythology.

The community's main source of income comes from the weaving of hats and baskets. Diet consists mainly of rice, yucca and corn with little animal protein. Consequently, the population suffers from a high level of malnutrition.

San Andrés de Sotavento is considered one of the ten poorest municipalities in Colombia. There is no aqueduct or sewerage system and water for human consumption is taken from rainfall lagoons, artificially built for livestock. Water is transported to houses by donkeys; this work is done mainly by women and children. The houses have walls made of plaited cane and mud. The roofs are made of thatched palm and the floors of dirt. The people live with domestic animals (dogs, pigs and chickens) and defecate outdoors.

At the political level, the community is organized into town councils (*cabildos*). Each council has a main representative, known as a *cacique* (chief), as well as several minor captains who are appointed by the community to defend its cultural and territorial interests.

There is a medical centre in the town of San Andrés de Sotavento, staffed by two permanent physicians and assistant personnel. For specialized attention, patients are referred to a regional hospital, located 37 km from the town. According to the medical visit registries in the San Andrés de Sotavento Health Centre, the Zenú population seeks medical attention primarily for respiratory diseases, acute diarrhoea, malnutrition and intestinal parasites.

Discovery of the Visceral Leishmaniasis Focus

In 1987, Zenú community leaders in the San Andrés de Sotavento municipality requested, through a community leader who travelled to the city of Medellín, assistance from the University of Antioquia (PECET) for the diagnosis and treatment of members of their community who showed lesions similar to those of cutaneous leishmaniosis (CL). A multi-disciplinary team travelled to the Indian community and found, in addition to CL cases, several children who presented symptoms compatible with those of VL (Vélez et al. 1988).

No cases of VL had been reported previously in this region. The children and their parents were taken to the hospital, and the disease was confirmed. This discovery prompted studies related to the transmission of VL in the region. In meetings held with parents, indigenous healers and health promoters, it was learned that in previous years many children had died from an illness with symptoms similar to those suffered by the children diagnosed with VL.

Evaluation of the VL Focus

In successive studies, applying the eco-epidemiologic method (Rioux et al. 1986), the different elements of disease transmission were studied. A population census, together with a household epidemiological survey, was carried out in rural hamlets of the municipality. The survey included an active search for cases of VL and a physical examination of the residents of each house, which included a cutaneous test to determine previous infection with *Leishmania* (Montenegro Test). Cutaneous tests showed that 47 per cent of the children under seven had been in contact with the parasite. The parents of 24 of the children who showed clinical characteristics compatible with VL eventually gave consent for their children to receive the diagnostic test and subsequent treatment. Some of the parents were initially reluctant. The improved health of those children who had received treatment, plus the primary health education activities carried out by the team, were helpful in persuading the community, little by little, to accept the procedures.

Clinical and laboratory exams carried out on 573 dogs showed that 15 per cent of them were infected with *Leishmania*. Some of the dogs showed characteristic clinical symptoms of the disease, such as emaciation, loss of hair, growth of ganglions and an exaggerated increase of the length of their claws. Samples taken from wild animals that might host this species of *Leishmania* showed 23 per cent of opossums to be infected (Travi et al. 1994). Thus dogs and oppposums were found to be the principal animal hosts of the parasite. It is from these animals that sandflies acquire the parasite and transmit it to humans.

The capture and identification of nearly 12,000 specimens of possible insect transmitters showed that, of the ten species found, only *Lutzomyia evansi* could be the transmitter of VL in the region (Travi et al. 1990; Travi et al. 1996; Vélez et al. 1995). The study of the behaviour of this species made it possible to determine some fundamental aspects of transmission:

- The highest population density of *Lu. evansi* occurs during the rainy season, mainly between the months of October and December. It is during this period of time that transmission of the parasite is most frequent.
- The greatest number of VL cases occur in rural areas, where there is abundant vegetation around the houses and rural electrification exists. The insects enter houses, drawn by the light.
- Intradomiciliary biting activity by *Lu. evansi* is primarily nocturnal, beginning at approximately 18.00 hours and lasting throughout the night until 06.00 hours. Two peaks in biting activity were observed, the first occurring from 23.00 to 01.00 hours and the second just before dawn.
- Based on those areas in which *Lu. evansi* was found, maps were prepared indicating areas where there is risk of transmission.

To summarize, the eco-epidemiologic study showed that VL is endemic in the region. It is children under four years of age who are developing the disease. It is the interior of houses where children come in contact with *Lu. evansi* and are infected. Moreover, it is during the rainy season and mainly at the end of the year that most of the transmissions occur. Biting happens during the night hours, primarily around midnight and dawn.

Ethnographic Study

The task of the social science team members was to provide a description of the health knowledge and practices of the Indian community, with special reference to VL. They also wished to gain a better understanding of why parents who see their children's health seriously deteriorate with VL symptoms do not take them to the local hospital. A third objective was to advise the group on how to interact with the Indian community and achieve an honest and respectful communication with them.

Several initial hypotheses were entertained as to why parents would be reluctant to take children suffering from VL to the local hospital. Among these were hypotheses related to lack of economic resources, the distance between the hospital and the Indian reservation, concern about racial discrimination by medical practitioners, fear of leaving their small children in the hospital and lack of confidence in the competence of Western medicine-trained physicians to treat the disease.

The main objective of the ethnographic investigation was to describe Zenú Indian beliefs regarding the nature of health, the causes of illness, treatment practices and the social resources (family, medical centres, hospitals, etc.) that surround the sick person. Structured and informal interviews were carried out with six specialists in traditional medicine as well as 17 mothers whose children were diagnosed with VL and received treatment at the hospital, two mothers of children diagnosed with VL but who did not go to the hospital to receive treatment, and four mothers of children with symptoms compatible with VL but who were not diagnosed and died as a consequence of the disease. Doctors and nurses at the hospital were also interviewed. Workshops were held with community members to get feedback about the project.

The Zenúes, it was revealed, distinguish between 'bush' or 'Indian' diseases for which treatment is sought from 'the curious one', or indigenous healer, and diseases cured by Western doctors and medicine (Jaramillo and Turbay 1998; Turbay and Jaramillo 1986). 'Bush' or 'Indian' diseases fall into three classes, according to their aetiology: diseases brought about by supernatural beings, diseases brought about by witchcraft, and diseases resulting from natural causes.

Diseases brought about by supernatural beings The Zenúes believe in the existence of underground and aquatic supernatural beings that take on human or animal form. These beings, called 'charms', inhabit the waters, winds, thunder and lightning. They can grab the spirit of a person and take it to their caves or underground labyrinths, where such animals as rabbits, armadillos, *ñeques* (*Dasyprocta sp.*) and *guatinaja* (*Agouti paca*) abound. According to the myths, charms take possession of the animal and occasionally try to lure humans into their realm. Many men claim to have seen female charms – beautiful, tall, white, blonde women. Women, on the other hand, have seen male charms – black, naked men who whistle at them from the banks of the lagoons.

Zenúes believe that thorny shrubs are a sort of threshold that simultaneously communicates with, and separates the world of humans from, the world of charms. When female charms leave their caves and lagoons, their hair gets entangled in the thorns. When the spirit of a child goes away with the charms, its relatives find its body on one of these thorny bushes.

The charm called Chimpín is particularly dangerous. He is a short man who leaves 'backwards' (the heel at the front and the tips of the toes to the rear) on the banks of creeks. It is he who exercises justice in the world of the charms and takes revenge on those families whose ancestors, years ago, took possession of his daughter, a female charm. The Chimpín chases women and makes them sick so he can carry them, once dead, to his territory.

The spirits of ancestors, though inhabiting 'the other world', typically stalk though the towns and visit their relatives. They are said to cause diseases among their loved ones in order to take them to the world of the dead, thus sparing their relatives the sufferings of this world, while, at the same time, enjoying their company. These wicked spirits have negative traits, although the female charms have both positive and negative qualities.

Another disease brought about by supernatural beings is called the 'zed' or 'wicked wind.' The symptoms by which it is identified are fever, pain in the body, pain in the head and possible swooning or madness. The family visits 'the curious one' with a sample of the sick person's urine, in order to receive the diagnosis. The treatment is based on plants, nutritious diet and prohibition of visits for a period of time. In children, the disease occurs because the soul leaves the body, the spirit wanders about aimlessly and the boy or girl gets sick and may die. The soul is thought to abandon the body if the mother does not observe the following practices:

- When the mother goes out with the child, in particular at dawn or dusk, she must carry along lighted tobacco in order to prevent the 'wicked wind' wandering in the bush from taking possession of the child's soul.
- The mother should never carry a sleeping child from one dwelling to another, thus leaving the child's soul in the first dwelling. The loss of the spirit produces fever, crying, lack of appetite, loss of hair, diarrhoea and sometimes swelling of the body, accompanied by the presence of a swelling or what is described as a 'loaf of bread' on the left side of the abdomen. The mother takes a urine sample to the 'the curious one'. If he diagnoses the disease, the child will be treated with plants, baths, aromatic smokes or potions.

Among the 16 families interviewed who had children suffering from VL, all the mothers had gone to the 'the curious one' as a first medical recourse and in all cases the diagnosis had been the 'wicked wind'.

Diseases brought about by witchcraft The Zenúes believe that witches live in the villages disguised as normal women. They are recognized because they dress in rags and their hair is uncombed. Some fly but others never leave the ground; they spy through windows and tell the whole town the intimacies of families. They also go whistling around houses where there are newborn children, avid to drink their blood. In such cases, the Zenúes protect the walls with paper, to deter witches from entering through holes. Some witches know how to prepare poisons to kill people and can change their appearance and assume that of animals, such as monkeys, dogs, vixens and donkeys.

Madness is another disease treated by the 'the curious ones'. It is interpreted as an effect of toxic substances, nervous stress, or witchcraft. The 'curious ones' classify mad patients as 'calm' or 'violent'. They believe that madness caused by witchcraft occurs when someone sends a spirit to the patient by means of a current of air, a drink, a conversation, or with the help of an animal. By examining the patient's urine 'the curious one' diagnoses the type of madness and decides if the sick person can be cured or not.

Another disease brought about by witchcraft is the 'evil eye', which occurs when a person has 'a very fixed glance' and stops to stare at a child. A short time later, the child will suffer from diarrhoea, fever and permanent crying. This disease can be prevented by putting a 'mate' (the seed of a certain tree) on the neck, hand or foot of newborn babies.

Diseases brought about by natural causes The Zenúes describe the symptoms of diseases in this category by saying, for example, that they have a 'bad wind' in the body (colic), that they feel a 'stab' in the heart (acute pain), that they have a 'bad humour' (wounds that do not heal), that they are 'drying off' (becoming thin), etc. These diseases are almost always the result of the abrupt contact between heat and coldness. For example, indigestion can be produced by walking barefoot or taking a bath when the day is hot.

Medicinal plants are classified as 'hot' and 'cool'. 'Hot' diseases are treated with 'cool' plants and vice versa. Some of the hot plants are cinnamon (*Cinamomum zeilanicum*), poleo (*Bistrogon mollis*), coriander (*Coriandrum sativum*), balsamina (*Momordica charantia*) and the venturosa (*Lantana sp.*). Those considered 'cool' are basil (*Ocimun basilicum*), linseed (*Linum usitatis simum*), corn (*Zea mays*) and guanábano leaf (*Anona muricata*). Some of these plants grow in the reservation, while others are bought in the marketplaces of nearby cities. The leaves are prepared as an infusion or a potion is made by cooking leaves, stems and roots, to be used in baths or compresses.

Another of the diseases brought about by natural causes is 'milk bread', which occurs when a pregnant mother breastfeeds an older sibling. Maternal milk spoils and the nursing child suffers from constant fever, loss of appetite, swelling of the abdomen, and from a 'bread' (spleen) that starts to grow until it reaches the navel and the child dies. The elders say that this disease is very ancient and many children have died with fevers that did not subside and a swollen abdomen. Some 'curious ones' recognized VL as 'milk bread'.

Zenú indigenous healers attend all three classes of disease. 'The curious ones' may be men or women, but when it comes to assisting cases of madness, specialists belong only to the masculine sex. 'The curious one' knows medicinal plants well enough to treat diseases of a natural origin. He or she, however, is also a medium between men and spirits, communicating with them, travelling to their underground labyrinths to rescue those who have been captured by the charms, expelling charms with the help of aromatic smokes, and combating the wicked spirits who have made patients go mad. Their main instrument of power is the spoken word, followed by botanical knowledge. They never use hallucinogens and going into a trance is not a part of how they communicate with spirits. According to popular imagination, 'the curious ones' are also sorcerers and can turn into animals, but they oppose practising magic in order to harm others.

The name 'the curious one' indicates that this is a person who loves to know and to learn, and that his or her power comes from study alongside a master – the father, in most cases. 'The curious one' assumes the role of shaman when the disease has a supernatural origin.

In summary, VL is thought, by the Zenú, to belong to the 'bush' diseases, but is explained as originating in two different ways. According to the first explanation, it is brought about by supernatural causes ('disease of the wind') and according to the second, it is the result of natural causes ('milk bread'). In both cases, the first medical recourse sought by all mothers was the indigenous healer or 'the curious one', with disastrous consequences, since traditional medicine cannot cure the disease.

Design and Implementation of a VL Control Programme

Given our findings and commitment to improved public health, in 1993 the PECET started a VL control programme for the Colombian Caribbean Coast. We proposed that a VL control programme should be integrated into existing health services and involve traditional sources of health care – that is, healers and mothers. A primary objective was to reshape, along biomedical lines, understandings of the origin and control of VL in the Indian community. This was carried out through the cooperation of biological and social science professionals.

The programme has three central components. The first is a basic health education programme at the community level, covering a total of 63 hamlets. A multidisciplinary team comprising a doctor, a medical technologist, a biologist and an anthropologist travelled to each of the hamlets, where they stayed for three to four days. The team gave the community, through one-to-one discussions, workshops and talks, a description of the important clinical and epidemiological aspects of VL. Healers actively took part in these activities. The anthropologist's work was fundamental since she had won the respect of the indigenous healers, town council and the community.

The second component of the programme entailed a thorough search for children showing clinical manifestations of VL. Through dialogue with parents and explanation of disease prognosis if treatment was not administered, parents were, in some cases, persuaded to allow their children be diagnosed and treated at the health centre. If their condition was not critical, children positive for VL were treated at home under daily medical supervision. Community and healers participated in the management of these cases, and improved health had a positive effect on the community's perception of the programme and of the benefits of Western medicine.

The third component involved training community health workers, including physicians, medical technologists, nurses, health promoters, teachers and community leaders. Training included recognition of the clinical characteristics of the disease; means of transmission; diagnostic procedures; case management; community beliefs, attitudes and practices related to VL; and the strategies for timely diagnosis. Continued education activities included reviews, in workshops, of the clinical and epidemiological findings regarding the medical management of cases.

A better understanding of VL by health personnel, an active search for cases, and recognition by parents of the symptoms and signs of the disease resulted in an 80 per cent increase in the number of verified VL cases, compared to previous years. This increase in the number of demonstrated cases may be attributed to a decrease in the number of cases previously attended by healers and therefore not officially recorded in the past.

In view of the increased number of diagnosed cases, the Health Service financed the purchase of mosquito nets impregnated with insecticides, for the population at greatest risk. Instructions were given on their use and care; they were only to be used for children under five years of age. Six months later, the mosquito nets were once again impregnated with insecticide and basic health concepts were revisited.

An evaluation of the programme was made in August 1996 by visiting some of the rural areas where the programme had been carried out. Interviews were held with residents from 46 houses in nine hamlets. Interviews with the people were held in their homes and it was observed if the bed net was being used. The most important findings may be summarized as follows:

- Mosquito nets have been well accepted by the population and are being used every night.
- The population associate sick dogs with VL in children.
- On their own initiative, the Indians are killing dogs that look sick and in some houses where there have been VL cases the Indians are not getting new dogs.

- The number of dogs per house decreased from 1.6 in 1993 to 0.9 in 1996.
- From January to August 1996, no cases of VL were diagnosed in the municipality of San Andrés de Sotavento. In the same period, in 1995, 14 VL cases were diagnosed.

The basic health education programme focused on the community's recognition of 'milk bread' as a frequent cause of child mortality and on traditional Zenú treatment practices. Its success hinged on the community witnessing the improved health of children treated with Western medicine. Anthropological knowledge helped in understanding the disease in the context of the Zenú belief system, and in carrying out culturally appropriate primary health education activities in the community. Additionally, the anthropologist trained the research team in the language and behaviour they should adopt in their relationship with the community, in order to achieve a respectful dialogue and exchange of knowledge.

References

Corredor, A., J. F. Gallego, R. B. Tesh et al. (1989) 'Epidemiology of visceral leishmaniasis in Colombia', *American Journal of Tropical Medicine and Hygiene* 40(5): 480–5.

Desjeux, P. (1992) *Information on the Epidemiology and Control of the Leishmaniasis by Country or Territory*, WHO/LEISH/91.30, pp. 38–9.

Jaramillo, S. and S. Turbay (1998) *Los indígenas Zenúes. Geografía humana de Colombia. Región andina central*, Tomo 4, vol. 3, Santa Instituto Colombiano de Cultura Hispánica.

Rioux, J. A., G. Lannotte, F. Petter et al. (1986) 'Les leishmanioses cutanées du bassin Méditerranéen occidental. De l'identification enzymatique à l'analyse écoépidémiologique. L'example de trois "foyers", Tunisien, Marocain et Français', in J. A. Rioux (ed.), *Leishmania: Taxonomie et Phylogenèse*, Montpellier: IMEEE.

Travi, B., C. Jaramillo, J. Montoya et al. (1994) '*Didelphis marsupialis*, an important reservoir of *Trypanosoma (Schizotrypanum) cruzi* and *Leishmania (Leishmania) chagasi* in Colombia', *American Journal of Tropical Medicine and Hygiene* 50: 557–65.

Travi, B., I. D. Vélez, L. Brutus et al. (1990) '*Lutzomyia evansi*: an alternate vector of *Leishmania chagasi* in a Colombian focus of visceral leishmaniasis', *Transaction of the Royal Society of Tropical Medicine and Hygiene* 84: 676–7.

Travi, B., I. D. Vélez et al. (1996) 'Bionomics of *Lutzomyia evansi (Diptera: Psychodidae)* vector of visceral leishmaniasis in northern Colombia', *Journal of Medical Entomology* 33: 278–85.

Turbay, S. and S. Jaramillo (1986) 'Identidad cultural entre los indígenas de San Andrés de Sotavento, Cordoba', monografía de grado en antropología, Universidad de Antioquia.

Vélez, I. D., J. I. Gallego, J. C. Adarve et al. (1995) 'Eco-epidemiological delimitation of visceral leishmaniosis in the Colombian Caribbean coast', *Boletií de la Dirección de Malariología y Saneamiento Ambiental de Venezuela* 35: 359–69.

Vélez, I. D., G. Ghysais, J. Marulanda et al. (1988) 'Leishmaniasis tegumentaria americana: encuesta epidemiológica en una comunidad indígena', *IATREIA* 1: 29–33.

Vélez I. D., B. L. Travi, J. I. Gallego et al. (1995) 'Evaluación ecoepidemiologica de la leishmaniosis visceral en la comunidad indígena Zenú de san Andrés de Sotavento, Córdoba: primer paso para su control', *Revista Colombiana de Entomología* 21: 111–21.

World Health Organization (1995) *Control of Leishmaniasis*, Technical Report series 793, Geneva: WHO.

11

Mud, Bugs and Community Participation: Remodelling Village Houses to Eradicate Vector-borne Disease

Roberto Briceño-León

Inhabitants of rural areas of Latin America have traditionally built their houses from materials that can be obtained directly and easily from nature. With mud walls and straw or palm-leaf roofs, the living quarters are climatically more pleasant. These dwellings, however, can house a small biting bug, a haematophagous insect, which transmits a disease without cure.

It is estimated that there are between 16 and 18 million people infected with Chagas' disease and that some 90 million additional people in 21 countries who live in zones where the disease is endemic are at risk of contracting the disease (WHO 1998). The insect found to carry the Chagas' disease parasite has been described by various chroniclers since colonization of the Americas. Fernández de Oviedo, as early as 1535, referred to them. Priest Bernardo Cobo, in his 1653 New World History, describes how the *Panstrongylus megistus* lives in the roofs of houses and from there dives into the beds where people sleep. Gumilla, in a travel narrative of Venezuela published in 1741, says the insects bite and suck blood with such 'touch and gentleness that they are not felt' (Gumilla 1975). Charles Darwin describes in detail their feeding habits in his *Diary of Voyages*. Ironically, it is believed that Darwin acquired Chagas' during his voyage on *The Beagle*, suffering the chronic form for 40 years before dying from the disease in 1882 (Havard 1987).

It was not until the beginning of this century that the link between the insect and the disease was identified by Carlos Chagas, while working in the anti-malaria campaign that accompanied the construction of a railway in Brazil (Lewinsohn 1981). He was able to reproduce the disease experimentally, to isolate the parasite and describe it as a new illness associated with the insect and housing (Chagas 1909).

Chagas' Disease

Chagas' disease or American trypanosomiasis is caused by a parasite called *Trypanosoma cruzi*. This parasite is transmitted to people by an insect vector, a member of the *Reduviidae* family (Schofield 1994). The insect, which looks like a cockroach, bites and sucks blood, but does not inoculate the human host with the parasite. Instead, it deposits the parasite on the skin through its faeces, defecating while it feeds. Later, the individual scratches himself and introduces the parasite through the wound left by the biting or through other injuries caused to the skin by scratching.

Once the parasite is in the blood, the disease goes through an acute phase that occurs soon after the transmission of the parasite. In adults, this can be very mild and may pass undetected or be mistaken for other diseases. In children under two years of age it can be very serious and lead to death. If the person does not die, the disease progresses to a chronic and asymptomatic phase that can last from ten to 20 years, after which approximately 30 per cent of those infected suffer from cardiac, digestive or neuralgic damage and even sudden death (Acquatella et al. 1987; Bastien 1998; Maguirre et al. 1987).

Means of Transmission

Chagas' disease can also be acquired through blood transfusion and by congenital transmission where the mother passes on the parasite to her child causing spontaneous abortion, premature birth or hepatosplenomegaly (enlarged spleen and liver) (Schmuñis 1985). Blood transfusion is an important means of transmission in urban areas, where the disease is associated with migrations from the fields to the city or from endemic countries to non-endemic areas (Brisseau et al. 1988; Goldbaum 1982). The most common means of transmission is vectorial and is associated with living and population conditions. The disease is considered a zoonosis that was transferred to humans with the domestication of certain animals during the pre-Columbian era. In the north of Chile, mummies with enlarged viscera, an obvious symptom of the disease, have been found (Rothhammer et al. 1984).

The jungle is the insect's natural habitat. With the deforestation that has accompanied agriculture, it has lost animal sources of nourishment and has moved into houses seeking a human food source (Gamboa 1962, 1970). Since the vector lives in palm trees, its eggs may be brought into dwellings on the leaves of palms cut to roof houses (Rabinovich 1985).

In the house, the insect hides during the day from its predators, which include people, hens, cats and other domestic animals, and appears at night to bite. Straw, palm or crevices in cracked dried-mud walls are ideal for colonization. Piled firewood and clay bricks, stored crops and earthen floors also make good hiding places (Minter 1978; Schofield 1988).

It is interesting, however, to note that although disease vectors are distributed throughout the Americas, from Salt Lake City to Patagonia, the disease does not appear in indigenous populations of the Amazon. The same materials are used to construct houses, but the mobility of these almost nomadic people and the existence of alternative food sources may account for the absence of the disease (Coimbra 1988, 1992), indicating that a sedentary subsistence pattern is as significant as the type of housing (Silva 1999).

For a long time, the mud construction was blamed for the transmission of the disease. Diverse studies demonstrated, however, that what was important was not the material itself but the crevices found in a house, regardless of whether the walls were built of mud or cement (De Raadt 1976; Dias and Dias 1982; Gamboa 1973; Gamboa and Pérez Ríos 1965; OPS 1998; Schofield and Mardsen 1982).

Control Policies

The predominant means of controlling Chagas' disease transmission is by spraying houses with an insecticide that exterminates, at least temporarily, the vectors. During the 1950s and 1960s hydrocarbon chlorinated-type insecticides were used. These had to be applied several times – first to kill adult insects and then the nymphs that hatch from eggs not eliminated during the first spraying. Organophosphate insecticides were also used during the 1960s. These were more effective but their bad smell made people reject their use. In the 1980s, synthetic pyrethroids that could keep a house vector-free for up to two years were introduced (Marsden et al. 1998).

Every one or two years, however, the house must be sprayed again with the insecticide, meaning repetitive costs to the programme and a nuisance for the population, who see it as a never-ending battle. Because the houses maintain the same conditions that allow for new vector infestation from other buildings, henhouses or the neighbouring jungle, the benefits of chemical control are short-lived. This is of particular importance in Venezuela, Colombia and Ecuador as well as countries in Central America, where the wild *Rhodnius prolixus* vector invades susceptible houses.

Previous Housing Programmes

A number of studies recognize housing improvement as the most adequate strategy to control Chagas' disease permanently (Arias et al. 1999;

Gamboa and Pérez Ríos 1965; Garcia-Zapata and Marsden 1993; Pessoa 1962; Primio 1952; Romaña 1952). Improving existing living quarters or constructing new ones less conducive to vector infestation, however, is not simple for health ministries or governments. Building new housing is costly and is not given much consideration since the people suffering from the disease are poor and isolated, with little political power.

Even when a massive programme for rural housing is launched, such as that undertaken by the Venezuelan government at the beginning of the 1960s, problems arise. Buoyed by its success in achieving the first and largest zone of malaria eradication in the tropics, and driven by a political need to benefit the peasant population and diminish support for an incipient guerrilla movement, Venezuela introduced an agrarian reform programme, funded by abundant fiscal resources from oil exportation, to give land and healthy housing to peasants. Resources and personnel were seconded from the malaria programme (Briceño-León 1996).

Programme planners, however, had difficulty in culturally adapting the house to families used to lodgings that were larger and allowed cooking with firewood. In many cases, people used the new house for storage and continued to live in the old one. As a result, the project began to demand demolition of the former house as part of the contract to deliver the new one. This achieved relative acceptance of the new lodgings but iron and cement construction remained alien to people used to wood and mud. When an enlargement was required to accommodate additional children or a mother-in-law who had joined the family, the walls of the new room or kitchen were built with mud and the roof with palm leafs, creating conditions for infestation by Chagas' disease vectors.

These circumstances gave rise to several questions. Why did peasants maintain this type of house knowing the possible health risks? How could an economical house be built that also prevented colonization by the disease vector? How could such a house be culturally adapted so that people could build it with easily obtainable materials? How could people be encouraged to participate in building their own house?

Social Determinants of Chagas' Disease

The importance of the social determinants of Chagas' disease are frequently acknowledged in statements at the beginning or at the end of papers, but never delved into deeply (Dias 1958; Gabaldón 1965). Some studies argue that the disease is a product of individual circumstances that create a fatal cycle of poverty–disease–poverty (Silveira 1985), or of an economic means of production that engenders poverty (Dias 1985). Others view the problem as resulting not from poverty or an unjust society, but from ignorance, lack of education (Petana 1976) or traditionalism and unwillingness to change (Carcavallo 1979).

Poverty, education, traditionalism and cultural values have many expressions in the disease's prevalence and therefore their role has always been evident but elusive. It is for this reason, when referring to the social determinants of Chagas' disease, that authors point to different and sometimes opposite socio-economic factors and interpretative theories of society (Briceño-León 1993). In some cases, interpretation is at the macro-social level; pointing out social inequalities that arise from both national and international power differentials. The explanation may correspond to situational or materialistic theories which explain social reality and individual behaviour in terms of the objective circumstances in which people find themselves (Boudon 1985; Marx 1970; Popper 1981). In other cases, use of subjectivist or cultural theories are adopted, providing an interpretation based on conditions internal to the individual, be these psychological, educational or cultural (Freud 1973; Weber 1969).

Why are Some Houses Better Maintained Than Others?

Visiting areas in Latin America where the disease is endemic, it is possible to see houses in good repair, with plastered walls and metal-plate roofs. Close by are others with palm roofs and unplastered walls. All seem to be inhabited by families of similar social-economic status. Why this difference?

To investigate the social determinants of the lodging conditions that allow transmission of the disease, Laboratorio de Ciencias Sociales (LACSO) undertook a study aimed at examining associations between certain social variables and housing characteristics. We first constructed a scale to allow us to classify the houses according to their susceptibility to vector colonization. The scale was based on previous entomological studies, which found the most important aspects of the house for the presence of the *Rhodnius prolixus* insect to be roof condition, wall friezing, separation of bedroom and remainder of house by walls, crop storage, storage of clothes and objects, and 'peri-domicile' conditions, such as storage sheds, chicken houses and fences (Dias 1985; Gamboa and Pérez Ríos 1965; Whitlaw and Chaniotis 1978; Zeledon and Vargas 1984). Using these criteria, all dwellings were classified as low, medium or high in promoting vector colonization.

Drawing on situational and subjectivist (i.e., social psychological) theories, we postulated six other variables. Situational variables included land ownership, marketability of houses, and occupation-income. It was hypothesized that peasants who owned their houses would be more willing to improve their lodgings than those who were tenants or squatters. If the house was marketable, the individual could rationalize that by investing to improve it, he could recover his investment, but otherwise not. With respect to occupation-income, occupation categories were assigned on the basis of the regularity with which monetary income was received. All of the peasants were poor, but some received income in cash once a year when they sold their crops. Some received income monthly for working two or three days per week, and others, working in the fields, were paid weekly salaries. It was assumed that the larger the income the better a family's capacity to purchase materials and modify the house.

Among the variables derived from subjectivist/psychological theories is one that captures cultural notions of the fatalism among Latin American peasants. We chose to use the locus of control scale developed by Rotter (1966) and applied to health by Wallston (1992). With it we were able to measure the expectations peasants have concerning whether it is up to them what happens in their future (internal control) or whether it is in the hands of God, luck or simply chance (external control). For greater precision, we decided to differentiate external control when it depends on chance and when it depends on the intervention of powerful others, according to Levenson's classification (1981). In addition, we modified Rotter's instrument so that it could be administered to illiterate peasants. The hypothesis was that higher internality would be associated with better housing.

A second related variable pertains to expectations of control of the disease. Since the vector is wild and can reach the lodging through phototropism, and some vectors can carry the parasite and others not, we were interested in learning whether people thought they could do something to control the disease or if they believed that it was by chance that someone got sick, in which case they might do nothing to protect themselves. A third subjectivist variable measures anticipated permanency in place of residence. If a person expected to remain for a long time, it was hypothesized they would be more willing to improve their living quarters. Which of these were actually important for the peasants and which were simply the researchers' ideological impositions?

The Study Area

The research was conducted in Tinaquillo Municipality, Cojedes State, Venezuela – a traditionally endemic Chagas' disease zone. Located in the centre of the country, at the foot of the mount that connects the mountain range with the central plain, it has a mean altitude of 630 metres above sea level and a mean temperature of 25.5 °C. There are two annual seasons: a dry one from October to March and a rainy one the rest of the year.

Vegetation is tropical jungle or savannah where the royal palm, the disease vector's natural habitat, is abundant.

In 1961, before the insecticide campaign was launched, disease vectors were found in 91 per cent of the villages and in half the houses (51 per cent). These figures began to decrease as the zone became urbanized. At the time of the research, vectors were found in 34 per cent of the villages and in 2.3 per cent of houses, all of them in the poor and isolated rural areas (MSAS 1986). The study zone had the second highest rate of vector infestation in the country (Sequeda et al. 1986) and the second highest national rate of seropositive detection in blood bank samples.

Methods

The LACSO research team carried out the investigation in the rural area where housing is dispersed. An oral questionnaire was completed by the family head and a detailed examination of the houses and a ground survey plan of each was completed. Of the 572 homes included in our study sample, 556 households participated. The refusal rate was 2.7 per cent. Eighty-nine per cent of family heads were men and the same percentage had been born in the municipality. Forty-five per cent were illiterate and 30 per cent had completed three years of schooling, leading us to calculate functional illiteracy at around 75 per cent. The population is primarily sedentary: 28 per cent of family heads had never changed jobs and probably not even employer. Thirty per cent had changed jobs once and 22 per cent twice. Statistical analyses were performed to test study hypotheses using Pearson's Chi square coefficients to evaluate association between categorical and ordinal variables as well as Mann's predictive statistic for determining direction of the association.

Results

More than half of the 556 houses studied displayed conditions conducive to vector colonization. Nearly 22 per cent offered ideal conditions (high vector promotion): palm-leaf roofs, non-plastered wattle and mud walls, and crops stored in the house. Another 34.3 per cent demonstrated some of these characteristics (medium promotion): for example, plastered walls, but a palm-leaf roof. Forty-four per cent showed few or none of those conditions and could be considered resistant to vector infestation (low promotion). Overall results of association between situational and subjective variables and house susceptibility to vector colonization are shown in Table 11.1.

As hypothesized, certain social conditions were correlated with house

TABLE 11.1 Relationship between situational/subjective variables and level of house susceptibility to vector colonization (N=556)

Theoretical variable	Pearson's Chi square		Mann's predictors	
	Statistic	Significance	Statistic	Significance
Land ownership	15.972	0.0140	-0.692	0.2440
House property and marketability	18.558	0.0170	-1.210	0.1130
Occupation-income	50.506	0.0000	-6.414	0.0000
Locus of control	31.390	0.0000	-5.526	0.0000
Expectation about disease control	39.911	0.0000	-6.240	0.0000
Anticipated permanency	14.858	0.0620	-2.460	0.0700

characteristics, although two important indicators were not. Land ownership did not predict dwelling structure at a statistically significant level using the Mann's test. This finding can be explained in terms of the Venezuelan legal context where, after an agrarian reform, land occupants gained a great deal of rights, making it impossible to evict them. Hence land ownership in the rural areas is no longer a critical predictor of land residency and family material resources. Only 2.7 per cent of the 556 peasants interviewed 'legally' owned the land, and a still smaller percentage (1.6 per cent) occupied government lands. The remainder occupied legally owned private lands for which only 23.4 per cent paid rent in the form of money or produce, while 72.3 per cent did not pay any type of rent, either because the landowners did not charge it or because the owners existed only legally. Such is the case where an old landowner bequeathed his land to Saint Anthony (to the saint, not to the church). As expected, the saint could not claim the inheritance and therefore the land remained without an owner and is community property.

The Mann's test showed no statistically significant association between marketability of house and the condition of the dwelling in terms of vector colonization. This is surprising. Although 90 per cent of the housing was built on land not owned by the proprietor of the house, 67 per cent thought that they could readily sell their house if they wished. Thus inability to sell one's house was not an obstacle to improving its structure. The majority of peasant households (58.3 per cent) had built their own house and were well acquainted with building techniques. Slightly more than 22 per cent had bought their home already built, and 7 per cent had contracted other people to build it. Rent was almost non-existent (only

0.2 per cent paid rent). The remaining 11.3 per cent of respondents lived in houses provided by their employer or on loan from a relative.

Table 11.2 expands the detail shown in Table 11.1 by giving the percentages of people with low, medium or high vector-promoting houses according to their level of income and locus of control. Importantly, occupation-income was highly associated with type of dwelling structure. Houses of individuals with unskilled occupations and more irregular incomes displayed conditions conducive for colonization by disease vector insects. Agriculturist peasants obtain food from their harvest but get very little cash and this must go to purchase goods they do not produce, such as salt, oil and sugar as well as transportation, clothing, medicines or radio batteries. Therefore, it is difficult for those with lower cash incomes to set aside money for house improvements. Although many housing materials are obtainable from nature, metal plates for the roof, nails and cement must be purchased.

Locus of control was also found to be a highly significant predictor. Individuals who thought they controlled their destiny through their actions tended to have a house less conducive to vector colonization than those who thought their destiny was controlled by God, luck or powerful others. Of the 556 family heads studied, 63.5 per cent had an external locus of control. They thought their destiny was controlled by 'powerful others' (33 per cent) or by chance (30.5 per cent). Results clearly suggest that a general expectation of the future drives actions in the present and leads those who have an internal locus of control to act to improve their houses themselves, and induces those who have an external locus of control to leave houses incomplete. Caution needs to be exercised, however, in the case of powerless peasants, in interpreting the attribution of control to 'powerful others'. The danger lies in confusing fatalism with realistic knowledge of the political, social and economic conditions faced by illiterate and landless peasants.

Expectations about the control of the disease varied in the same direction as locus of control and dwelling structure as seen in Table 11.1. Those who believed they could do very little or nothing to prevent the disease had houses with some or many conditions enhancing disease vector colonization. The percentage of those who thought they could control the disease is higher than the percentage of those who expressed general feelings of being in control of their destiny, but the variation resulted in the same directionality.

Finally, the degree of anticipated permanency in the house proved to be only a moderately significant predictor of dwelling structure. Individuals who thought they would remain for only a short period of time in a place and house tended to have houses that promoted disease vector colonization.

In summary, the research showed that two of the variables were highly

TABLE 11.2 Association between level of house susceptibility to vector colonization and occupation-income and locus of control

Conditions promoting vector colonization	Occupation-income				Locus of control		
	Farmers (owners)	Farmers without property	Workers, small-scale retailers	Peasants, seasonal workers	Internality	Powerful others	Externality luck
Low	3.30%	9.40%	17.2%	14.0%	22.8%	14.6%	10.1%
Medium	0.70	2.70	12.9	18.0	10.6	11.6	11.3
High	0.00	2.70	5.6	13.4	3.1	7.0	9.1
Total	4.00	14.90	35.8	45.4	36.5	33.1	30.5

significant, while others, such as land or house ownership, previously thought to play an important role, were not significant.

Social Intervention

The LACSO team decided to engage in a research-action process in which we would attempt to address the three variables found to hamper construction of healthy living quarters: income, locus of control, and beliefs about the disease. We wished to intervene in a community at the same time as we investigated it. From a classical research design perspective, we were proposing a quasi-experimental before-and-after study, with no control group.

A small village in Cojedes's mountains in Venezuela was chosen. The village had been studied in the previous research and the Ministry of Health's entomological inspections had shown it was infested by vectors of the disease. It is located between smooth hills and a dry river bed, from which it takes its name: Caño Muerto (Dead Stream).

Twenty-three families inhabited the village in dispersed houses along the hillsides; they were without drinkable water, electricity or sewerage. Some had latrines. Villagers worked on state-owned land, harvesting corn, beans and casaba. A few also worked on cattle or chicken farms close by. A wagon road reached the village, but since there was no public transportation, they had to walk for an hour to a crossroad where they could board a transport to the closest village and market.

Our intervention efforts occurred at three different levels: situational, psycho-social and symbolic-normative. At the situational level, we tried to overcome the financial constraints families faced in acquiring materials needed to improve their homes. It was necessary to offer a type of house that minimized purchases of manufactured materials and maximized the use of those materials the peasant could take directly from nature. Hence traditional wattle and daub construction, for years blamed for the disease transmission, was proposed, since new entomological studies had shown it could be healthy. This method of construction was accessible in terms not only of families' financial situations but also of their knowledge system. These were the houses used for centuries by their parents, grandparents and great-grandparents. The intervention entailed granting a credit in materials that they could not get from nature: metal plates for the roof, cement, lime and paint. Although joining could be done with vegetable products, nails and wire were purchased since the cost was minimal and the savings in labour considerable.

At the psycho-social level, we tried to reinforce self-confidence and perception of a positive relationship between effort and achievement, and to increase notions of individual responsibility. Building self-confidence consisted of communicating simple messages such as: 'You can do it' and 'What a nice kitchen'. Reinforcement of the effort–achievement relationship was accomplished by setting goals difficult enough to represent a challenge, but simple enough to reach without becoming frustrated. The peasant had to fix a goal to improve part of his house and was given part of the credit in material needed for that job. If he accomplished the goal, he was congratulated and allowed to set up another goal and get more material. If he did not reach the goal, he would not get additional material. The LACSO team monitored the feasibility of goals, but in the end the decision was always made by the peasant himself. If he could not achieve his goal, a dialogue about what had happened and goal feasibility was established. Finally, work was always completed individually in order to stimulate personal responsibility. Collective meetings were held at the beginning and at the end of the project, but otherwise work was always with families in their houses. Participation in the programme was voluntary and on an individual basis. Successes and failures were personal ones. We did nothing to encourage meetings, cooperation or group work, although this happened on people's own initiative and according to rules of reciprocity. We hold that community participation is not necessarily collective participation. When the end product is one for collective consumption, such as a school, strategies for collective action should be set up, but with goods for family consumption such as housing they are not necessary. Furthermore, trying to undertake collective action means complicating the process and altering the effort–achievement relationship that can be established at the family level.

At the symbolic-normative level, we tried to counterpoise social resistance to earthen architecture houses that symbolize a backward past, poverty and illness. Called 'huts', mud and waddle dwellings were viewed as not deserving the status of house. We conveyed affirming messages about earthen houses, portraying them as beautiful and holding social prestige. Establishment of clear and valid norms for all participants reinforced the effort–achievement relationship. There were rewards and penalties. The important aspect was compliance with goals and rules, not friendship or political party affiliation, influential in the world of political patronage.

Research Techniques

While the intervention was designed to be carried out by health promoters or sanitary inspectors, the research had to be done by qualified personnel. The intervention was therefore executed by professionals hired by LACSO, making it possible to collect information at the same time.

Data collection involved participant observation of the roles of children (above 15 years of age) and women in the household, social group pressure, world vision and experience, attitudes towards mud construction techniques, and family income, which were recorded in a field diary. Pre- and post-intervention assessments of locus of control and housing conditions susceptible to colonization by the vector of the disease were also carried out. The validity of qualitative data was ensured through researcher and data source triangulation. Later, numerical values were assigned to the observations systematically in order to enable quantitative data analysis.

From 'Caño Muerto' to 'Caño Nuevo'

A collective meeting was held to launch the intervention. The disease was explained, together with ways of transmission and how a housing programme such as the one being proposed could prevent them or their children from getting sick. In the days that followed, each of the families was visited to explain the programme's conditions and rules. The agreement was simple: nothing was free. Everything, from materials to work, had a value. The project contributed construction materials and technical support and the family contributed labour. As a demonstration of a family's will to participate, a letter of agreement was signed, with more symbolic than legal value, and a first task was fixed to be undertaken by the family.

The programme was carried out in partnership with the state government, LACSO and WHO's Tropical Disease Research (TDR) programme. The government, through its housing agency, contributed the funds for materials and LACSO designed and executed the work with the community, with support for research received from the TDR programme.

Of the 23 families in the village, 16 decided to participate in the programme, five were against it, and two neither participated in nor opposed it. The five families that opposed the initiative thought the proposed houses were not real houses and demanded cement houses built under the Ministry of Health's traditional programme – that is, without beneficiary participation. These families were linked to the governing party and therefore were the most influential. A political decision allowed the project to proceed and the opposing families were left out altogether, thus invigorating the remaining families' work. During the five months that followed, ten visits were made to each of the families. Construction plans were made, materials supplied and evaluations conducted.

All decisions pertaining to options concerning personal taste, comfort or costs were left to the peasants. They had to decide on the size of their house, space distribution and paint colours. The programme personnel showed families the existing possibilities and the costs these entailed, but the family made the decision.

Of the 16 participating families, twelve finished their house improvement with a high-rated performance, and four with a medium-rated performance since at the time the programme ended some details were missing. In six months, the peasants were able to improve or reconstruct their living quarters, which in some cases had gone up to twelve years unfinished. In a short time, they were able to build a healthy house that would protect them against Chagas' disease.

During the last visit, a summary of the improvements made by each family was made, accounts were set for credits granted, and a deadline for payment was fixed. Shortly afterwards, the families were revisited and shown photographs of their houses before improvement. The opinions given by the peasants at the beginning of the project, which had been recorded in the field diaries, were discussed. Once the houses were finished, it was decided to hold a closing ceremony. The peasants organized a traditional feast attended by peasant leaders, the state governor and the bishop. A representative of the Ministry of Health was also present, together with middle-level local government officials who had not wanted to learn about the experience or who had been against it. That day, the peasants decided that the process had been so valuable for them that they would change the name of their village from 'Caño Muerto' (Dead Stream) to 'Caño Nuevo' (New Stream).

Changing Houses and Behaviours

The programme experience demonstrates that houses can be changed not through paternalistic or authoritarian action, but by establishing conditions that nudge individual action in the direction desired from the social and epidemiological points of view. However, changes did not happen independently of the social micro-changes that occurred in the community brought about by external agents, but were a consequence of new inter-actions generated between a variety of local factors.

An analysis of the association between occupation-income and non-participation in the project, as well as moderate or high performance in house improvement, revealed an inverse relationship between better income and participation. It was the peasants without income, and thus also without power, who took advantage of the exceptional opportunity afforded by the programme. This was not the case for those with better incomes, who could make improvements of their own accord, without needing the credit offered and, because of their political connections, thought they could get government assistance at another time.

Using procedures developed by Romero Garcia (1981) to analyse locus of control data, we found that this variable was not a significant predictor of participation or performance. Participation appeared to be independent of individual or general expectations of the future as measured prior to the intervention. These findings underscore the need to undertake interventions that offer credit to remove financial barriers and increase self-confidence to overcome feelings of helplessness. People can, in fact, improve their houses and protect themselves against disease.

Equally impressive is the finding that those individuals who participated in the house improvement programme, on average, showed an increase in internality on pre- and post-intervention measures of locus of control. That is, they increased self-confidence and their capacity to control their destiny. Those who had a moderate-rated performance in house improvement increased their internality moderately. Finally, even those peasants who decided not to participate or opposed the programme also increased their internality, although to a lesser degree. What is evident is that while working to change their houses, the people changed. Although the desired outcome was healthy housing that did not permit transmission of Chagas' disease, the people showed themselves that they could do things to change their everyday lives. They became more confident and gained greater control of their destinies and health.

Caño Nuevo's experience showed that a housing initiative for the poorest peasants excluded from other rural housing programmes by the Ministry of Health was possible. It showed that an activity with appropriate technology and an appropriate social intervention was immediately feasible. Yet public officials still resisted the programme. A visit by the minister of health to the community provided support for a national initiative. A few weeks later, the minister ordered the establishment of a peasant housing programme, adopting as its motto the success of Caño Nuevo. In essence, the insights of university social researchers combined with the ingenuity of a group of rural peasants were transformed into public health policy.

Actors and Institutions

Five institutions played a role in the process: the state government, the Ministry of Health, LACSO backed by TDR/WHO, the Pan American Health Organization (PAHO) and the governing political party. Wishing to undertake a housing and Chagas' disease control project, the governor sought out the assistance of LACSO, which had been carrying out research in this area with financial backing from TDR's Social and Economic Research Scientific Working Group. LACSO contributed knowledge and legitimacy to carry out the wattle and mud housing programme – something the state government would never have dared, much less within a Chagas' disease control policy. But since the governor had recently founded the Housing Institute and wished to raise its national profile, he was compelled to be innovative.

The Ministry of Health's participation was, at times, contradictory. At the national level it provided information and technical support. The talk about the disease, organized at the beginning of the intervention, was given by the chief physician of the Chagas' Disease Control Office. At the regional level, however, the ministry office did not offer any support and precipitated conflict with LACSO and the local government. It is possible that regional officials felt their territory was being encroached upon. Another interpretation, offered by several people, is that a low-cost community participation programme of this sort was unattractive to many public officials since housing projects have always been a source of corruption. This undertaking made it impossible for them to collect commissions.

PAHO performed an important role bridging the university and the Ministry of Health. Traditionally, both parties have felt tremendous mutual jealousy and prejudice. PAHO's activities, although productive among central-level officials, did not carry much influence with regional administrators.

Finally, the regional leader of the governing party endeavoured to torpedo the programme in the community and at the local Ministry of Health office.

LACSO was diligent in demonstrating the importance of the results, while remaining politically impartial and showing a constant will to work cooperatively with other institutions. Politically LACSO was the weakest, but institutionally it held the prestige granted by science and expertise. It sought the permanent support of Dr Arnoldo Gabaldón, who had founded the malaria eradication programme in Venezuela and who was a former minister of health with immense prestige among sanitary and political groups in the country. His mediation managed to attract the attention of the acting minister to learn about the Caño Nuevo experience and later implement the programme nationally. Another ally of great importance was a peasant woman leader who had directed a land rights movement years ago and knew the disease. A woman with great charisma and peasant knowledge, she provided insight into the peasants' sagacity and gave us legitimacy in the face of their suspicion of outsiders such as ourselves.

Some philosophers and sociologists interpret history as a need: the things that occur do so as a product of structures or of inevitable processes. The LACSO team interprets history more as a product of randomness and opportunity – as the confluence of multiple circumstances where the will of actors plays a fundamental role and good intentions can produce adverse, unwanted or undesirable consequences for the actors themselves (Boudon 1979; Briceño-León 1990; Popper 1981).

The Caño Nuevo experience shows some of the structures, institutions and actors as well as the social, financial and cultural limitations involved in producing healthy housing. The will and ingenuity that these multiple actors contribute to overcome such limitations are also evident.

The Importance of a Social Science Perspective

This was not the first time housing programmes for Chagas' disease control had been implemented. What contributed to the success of this project perhaps lies in the perspective provided by the social sciences – a holistic perspective integrating the objective and the subjective, the macro-social and the micro-social. It is a perspective that can be shaped by others' suffering, but one that is, at the same time, capable of detachment and looking at the other with cultural distance. Moreover, it offers the opportunity to act, but at the same time to reflect on the process that it is trying to understand and change. Social sciences can translate common knowledge, some of it well-founded, some of it not, into scientific hypotheses to be tested and verified.

There are many admirable goals in health policy that are difficult to operationalize – such as health for all, community participation and patient empowerment. Social sciences have the possibility and the obligation to endeavour to realize these ideals, as each requires interventions involving institutions, power and individual or collective behaviours.

Acknowledgements

This research received financial support from the Special Programme for Research and Training in Tropical Diseases TDR, UNDP/World Bank/WHO. The author wishes to thank Nancy Johnson and Nick Higginbotham for the revision and corrections of the draft of this chapter.

References

Acquatella, H., F. Catalioti, J. R. Gómez-Mancebo, V. Davalos and L. Villalobos (1987) 'Long term-control of Chagas' Disease in Venezuela: effects on serology findings, electrocardiographic abnormalities, and clinical outcome', *Circulation* 76(3): 556–62.

Arias, A. R., E. A. Ferro, M. E. Ferreira and L. C. Simancas (1999) 'Chagas disease vector control through different intervention modalities in endemic localities of Paraguay', *Bulletin of the World Health Organization* 77(4): 331–9.

Bastien, J. W. (1998) *The Kiss of Death: Chagas' Disease in the Americas*, Salt Lake City: University of Utah Press.

Boudon, R. (1979) *Effets pervers et ordre social*, Paris: Presses Universitaires de France.

— (1985) *La Place du désordre*, France: Presses Universitaires de France.

Briceño-León, R. (1990) 'Los efectos perversos del petróleo', Caracas: Fondo Editorial Acta Científica Venezolana y Consorcio de Ediciones Capriles CA.

— (1993) 'Social aspects of Chagas disease', in S. Linderbaum and M. Lock (eds), *Knowledge, Power and Practice of Medicine and Everyday Life*, Berkeley, CA: University of California Press, pp. 287–302.

— (1996) 'El DDT y la modernización de Venezuela', *Boletín de Malariología y Saneamiento Ambiental* XXXVI(1–2): 44–50.

Brisseau, J. M., J. P. Lebron, T. Petit, M. Marjolet, P. Cuilliere, J. Godin and J. Y. Grolleau (1988) 'Chagas disease imported into France', *The Lancet* 1 May, 7(8593): 1046.

Carcavallo, R. (1979) 'A social disease', *Panamerican Health* 11(1–4): 15–17.

Chagas, C. (1909) 'Nova entidade morbida do homen. Resumo de mes studos etiologicos e clinicos', *Memorias do Instituto Oswaldo Cruz*, Vol. 3.

Coimbra, C.E.A. (1988) 'Human settlements, demographic patterns and epidemiology in Lowland Amazonia: the case of Chagas disease', *American Anthropologist* 90: 82–97.

— (1992) 'Environmental changes and human disease: a view from Amazonia', in L. Hansson and B. Jungen (eds), *Human Responsibility and Global Change*, Göterborg: University of Göterborg.

De Raadt, P. (1976) 'Improvement of rural housing as a means of control of Chagas' disease', in *American Trypanosomiasis Research*, Proceedings of the International Symposium of the Pan American Health Organization. Scientific Publication No. 318, pp. 323–5.

Dias, E. (1958) 'Doenca de Chagas: un problema americano', *Proceedings of the VI International Congress in Tropical Medicine and Malaria*, Lisbon, pp. 78–86.

Dias, J. C. P. (1985) 'Aspectos socioculturais e economicos na expansao e no controle da doenca de Chagas humana', *Annales de la Société Belge de Médicine Tropicale*, supplement 1: 120.

Dias, J. C. P. and R. B. Dias (1982) 'Las viviendas y la lucha contra los vectores de la enfermedad de Chagas en el hombre, en el estado de Minas Gerais, Brasil', *Boletín de la Oficina Sanitaria Panamericana* 93(5): 453–67.

Freud, S. (1973) 'Recuerdo, repetición y elaboración', *Obras Completas*, Tomo II, Madrid: Biblioteca Nueva, pp. 1683–8.

Gabaldón, A. (1965) *Una Política Sanitaria*, Caracas: Ministerio de Sanidad y Asistencia Social, pp. 435–500.

Gamboa, J. (1962) 'Dispersión de *Rhodnius prolixus* en Venezuela', *Boletín Informativo de la Dirección de Malriología y Saneamiento Ambiental* 3: 262–72.

— (1970) 'La población silvestre de *Rhodnius prolixus* en Venezuela', *Boletín Informativo de la Dirección de Malriología y Saneamiento Ambiental* 10: 186–207.

— (1973) 'El proceso modificador de la vivienda en el medio rural del estado Miranda (Venezuela), su relación con la infestación por *R. Prolixus*', *Archivos Venezolanos de Medicina Tropical y Parasitologia Médica* 5(2): 353–64.

Gamboa, J. and L. J. Pérez Ríos (1965) 'El rancho venezolano, su influencia en la prevalencia triatomina doméstica', *Archivos Venezolanos de Medicina Tropical y Parasitología Médica* 5: 305–28.

Garcia-Zapata, M. T. A. and P. D. Marsden (1993) 'Chagas' disease control and surveillance through use of insecticides and community participation in Mambaí, Goiás, Brazil', *Bulletin of the Pan American Health Organization* 27(3): 265–79.

Goldbaum, M. (1982) 'O problema das doenças tropicais e os movimentos migratorios no Brasil: situaçao en São Paulo', in *Doenças e Migraçao Humana*, Brasilia: Centro de Documentaçao do Ministerio de Saude, pp. 33–8.

Gumilla, J. (1975) 'El Orinoco ilustrado, historia natural, civil y geográfica de este gran río y de sus caudalosas vertientes', *Ediciones de la Acedemia Nacional de la Historia*, Caracas.

Havard, C. W. H. (ed.) (1987) *Black's Medical Dictionary*, London: A & C Black.

Levenson, H. (1981) 'Differentiating among internality, powerful others and chance', in H. M. Lefcourt (ed.), *Research with the Locus of Control Construct*, Vol. 1, New York, NY: Academic Press, pp. 15–61.

Lewinsohn, R. (1981) 'Carlos Chagas and the discovery of Chagas Disease', *Journal of the Royal Society of Medicine* 74: 451–5.

Maguirre, J. (1987) 'Cardiac morbidity and mortality due to Chagas disease: prospective electrocardiographic study of a Brazilian community', *Circulation* 75(6): 1140–5.

Marsden, P. D., F. C. Costa, R. W. A. Vitor, C. M. F. Antunes and M. Carneiro (1998) 'Chagas disease control programme in Brazil: a study of the effectiveness of 13 years of intervention', *Bulletin of the World Health Organization* 76(4): 385–91.

Marx, K. (1970) *Obras Escogidas*, Moscow: Editorial Progreso.

Minter, D. M. (1978) 'Triatomine bugs and household ecology of Chagas' diseases', Medical Entomology Centenary Symposium Proceedings (1977) *Proceedings of the Royal Society of Tropical Medicine and Hygiene* 72: 85–93.

MSAS (Ministerio de Sanidad y Asistencia Social, Venezuela) (1986) Archivos de Endemias Rurales de la Zona XXII, 1961–1986, San Carlos: Estado Cojedes.

OPS (Organización Panamericana de la Salud) (1998) *Control de la Enfermedad de Chagas a través del Mejoramiento de la Vivienda Rural. Proyecto Realizado en Trujillo, Venezuela, 1977–1985*, Washington, DC: OPS/HCP/HCT/98/97.

Pessoa, S. B. (1962) 'Domiciliacao dos triatomíneos e epidemiologia da doenca de Chagas', *Arquivos de Higiene e Saude Publica* 27: 161–71.

Petana, W. (1976) 'Educación para el Control de la Enfermedad de Chagas', *Boletín de la Oficina Sanitaria Panamericana*, July: 56.

Popper, K. (1981) *Conjectures and Refutations. The Growth of Scientific Knowledge*, London: Routledge and Kegan Paul.

Primio, R. (1952) 'Rural house proof against triatomids', *Revista Medica do Rio Grande do Sul* 8: 120–6.

Rabinovich, J. (1985) 'Ecología poblacional de triatominos, factores biológicos y ecológicos en la enfermedad de Chagas', in R. Carcavallo (ed.), *Servicio Nacional de Chagas*, Buenos Aires, I: 121–47.

Romaña, C. (1952) 'Cómo puede construirse un rancho higiénico antivinchuca', Instituto de Medicina Regional, Universidad de Tucumán, Folleto de divulgación No. 4.

Romero Garcia, O. (1981) 'Internalidad como motivación, valor incentivo de los estudios y ejecución intelectual esperada', Laboratorio de Psicología, Publicación 34, Universidad de los Andes, Mérida.

Rothhammer, F., V. Standen, L. Nuñez, M. Allison and B. Arriaza (1984) 'Origen y desarrollo de la tripanosomiasis en el área Centro-Sur Andina', *Revista Chungara* No. 12, August: 155–60.

Rotter, J. B. (1966) 'Generalized expectancies for internal versus external control of reinforcement', in G. Kimbley (ed.), *Psychological Monographs: General and Applied*, Washington, DC: American Psychological Association, 80(609): 1–28.

Schmuñis, G. (1985) 'Chagas' disease and Blood Transfussion', in R. Y. Dodd and L. E. Barker (eds), *Infection, Immunity and Blood Transfusion*, New York: Alan R. Liss, pp. 127–45.

Schofield, C. J. (1988) 'Biosystematics of the triatominae', *Biosystematics of Haematophagous Insects*, Oxford: Clarendon Press, pp. 285–312.

— (1994) *Triatominae: Biología y Control*, West Sussex: Eurocomunica Publications.

Schofield, C. J. and P. D. Marsden (1982) 'Efecto de del revoque de las paredes sobre una población doméstica de *Triatoma infestans*', *Boletín de la Oficina Sanitaria Panamericana* 93(1): 3–8.

Sequeda, M. L., L. Villalobos, G. A. Maekelt, H. Acquatella, J. Velasco, J. R. González and G. Anselmi (1986) 'Enfermedad de Chagas', VII Congreso Venezolano de Salud Pública, Caracas, Ministerio de Sanidad y Asistencia Social, Venezuela.

Silva, L. J. (1999) *A Evolucao da Doença de Chagas no Estado de São Paulo*, São Paulo: Editora Hucitec.

Silveira, A. C. (1985) 'O programa de controle da Doenca de Chagas no Brasil', *Annales de la Société Belge de Medicine Tropical* supplement 1: 140.

Tejera, E. (1919) 'Primer caso de Tripanosomiasis americana en el Estado Miranda', Caracas: *Gaceta Médica* 26: 113.

Torrealba, J. F. (1943) *Investigaciones sobre la Enfermedad de Chagas en Zaraza*, Caracas: Tipografía Garrido.

Wallston, K. A. (1992) 'Hocus-pocus, the focus isn't strictly on locus: Rotter's social learning theory modified for health', *Cognitive Therapy and Research* 16: 183–99.

Weber, M. (1969) *La Etica Protestante y el Espíritu del Capitalismo*, Barcelona: Península.

Whitlaw, J. T. Y. and B. N. Chaniotis (1978) 'Palm trees and Chagas' disease in Panamá', *American Journal of Tropical Medicine and Hygiene* 27: 873–81.

WHO (1998) *World Health Report 1998: Life in the 21st Century. A Vision for All*, Geneva: WHO.

Zeledon, R. and L. Vargas (1984) 'The role of dirt floors and of firewood in rural dwellings in the epidemiology of Chagas disease in Costa Rica', *American Journal of Tropical Medicine and Hygiene* 33(2): 232–5.

Part V

Lessons and Directions

12

Best Practice and Future Innovations in Applying Social Science to Advancing the Health of Populations

Nancy A. Johnson, Nick Higginbotham and
Roberto Briceño-León

The case studies from Asia Pacific, Africa and Latin America clearly show that in recent years the social and behavioural sciences have created effective partnerships with the biological and clinical sciences to address some of the world's most compelling human health concerns – mental illness, HIV/ AIDS, tropical diseases and chronic disease, as well as rational use of medicines and access to care. Health social science has become a vibrant and valued domain of research and practice by encouraging transdisciplinary approaches to health problems; fostering collective action in communities in defining and achieving health needs; underscoring the importance of the broader social, cultural, economic and political determinants of health; and discovering how to reach individuals and communities in a meaningful way so that they adopt health-promoting behaviours.

In this concluding chapter, we look across the case studies to distil what might be considered the essence of best practice in applying social science to health. The themes and principles that emerge suggest, first of all, that situational realities are deeply important to our understanding of how people explain and act in relation to health and illness. Second, revaluation of traditional or local knowledge is vital for framing intervention strategies. Third, health social scientists have moved from concern with culturally appropriate interventions to those offering culturally compelling elements for encouraging health protection. Fourth, effective programmes are those that can bridge the knowledge–behaviour gap and enhance people's con-struction of knowledge for themselves rather than strive to transfer knowledge. Fifth, community co-learning and collective action underpin research that can embody action towards health improvement. Sixth, health social science becomes most effective when the group engaged with the problem adopts transdisciplinary thinking. That is, they transcend disciplinary boundaries to synthesize knowledge about the problem in the quest to understand it fully as a complex, dynamic system.

In the second part of the chapter, we highlight new research directions and methodological developments that have captured the attention of health social scientists. Complexity theory has begun to have a profound impact on the imagination of scientists in all fields. Applied to health social science, it advocates analysing health problems as emergent properties of open, dynamic systems, and offers a common conceptual framework for uniting the work of transdisciplinary teams. Translational research is a second innovation that seeks to bridge the knowledge–action gap by translating scientific and experiential evidence into culturally compelling health interventions at the local level. Third, cybermedicine, which applies global networking technologies to preventive medicine and public health, is emerging as a force for transforming the relationship between health care consumers and health care providers. Also arising in the dynamic information technology context are new 'cybermethods'. The practice of health social science itself is changed as virtual communities are formed 'on-line' and researchers move onto the web to interact with geographically dispersed 'communities of interest'.

Current Best Practice in Applying Health Social Science: Themes and Principles from the Regional Case Studies

Context counts Central to all of the case studies is an effort to find workable solutions to health problems – solutions that are sensitive to the local and diverse social, cultural, economic and political contexts in which the problems manifest themselves and to the ways in which people understand and explain their world, in particular health and illness. The importance of *situational* realities – that is, circumstances external to the individual – in governing health and illness are highlighted, for example, in Chapters 2 and 11.

A broad perspective is offered by Briceño-León in Chapter 11 on the factors contributing to the vectorial transmission of Chagas' disease, including deforestation and destruction of the insect's natural habitat, the population's sedentary subsistence pattern, the peasants' geographical and political isolation, and preferred methods and materials of housing construction. It is the latter, however, that form the focus of the research-action study. Survey methods are used to investigate the social, cultural, political and economic context of housing construction and maintenance by rural peasants in Venezuela. Specifically, the relationship of three situational variables (land tenure, property marketability and occupation-income) to dwelling structure is examined along with variables related to the peasants' anticipated permanency in the community and their perception of the extent to which they control their own fate and can expect to prevent the disease. Strategies to overcome the situational constraints families face in acquiring materials needed to improve their homes – in particular, poverty – are a primary component of the resulting intervention programme.

Chapter 2 offers another example of how context counts – in this case, with respect to the day-to-day employment experiences of people diagnosed with schizophrenia in Hong Kong. The author integrates and then adapts two existing, and generic, models of social and interpersonal problem-solving skills to address the 'relevant concrete social situations' encountered in the Hong Kong workplace – specifically, in the sorts of jobs in which people with schizophrenia are likely to find employment. The result is what Tsang refers to as an 'indigenous model of work-related social skills'.

The chapter stands out against the others in the book in two respects. First, the model's construction is largely theory-driven, though grounded in the author's professional experience as an occupational therapist working with people with schizophrenia and validated through survey and interview data. Second is the notion of 'indigenous model'. Tsang is concerned with modelling the situation- or context-specific skills required by the study population. Indigenous models referred to elsewhere in the book describe traditional or lay explanatory models of illnesses. They are concerned with people's perceptual or cognitive realities – that is, how they apprehend their world. Moreover, the word 'indigenous' is used by Tsang to connote models that are 'targeted' or tailored to a defined population or group, as compared to models that describe traditional or local knowledge.

Revaluation of traditional/local knowledge As Devisch and his colleagues write in Chapter 6, 'a revaluation of culture-specific knowledge systems within social science discourse is fundamental to researching and working with communities'. Different shades of this respect for, and revaluing of, local or traditional knowledge can be found in the case studies. Chapters 11 and 6, respectively, by Briceño-León and by Devisch, Lapika Dimomfu, Le Roy and Crossman accentuate rediscovery of the functionality of traditional knowledge, which has been devalued or lost with social change. The housing programme developed by Briceño-León and the project team from the Laboratorio Ciencias Sociales encouraged traditional wattle and daub construction of homes – a method used for centuries, but in recent years blamed by health officials for transmission of Chagas' disease. In so doing, the programme also strove to overcome social resistance to earthen architecture houses that had come to symbolize 'a backward past, poverty and illness' among the peasants. Similarly, Devisch and his colleagues describe what they refer to as the current process of 'villagization of town' in Kinshasa and other parts of Congo. The process involves a revaluing among communities of traditional moral values and the importance of kin and residence groups. Devisch, Lapika Dimomfu, Le Roy and Crossman argue that this reawakened sense of communitarianism among poor and marginalized communities, including the study communities, creates a 'revitalized social capital' and 'new moral fabric' that prepare them to reject the 'paternalistic and bureaucratic way in which health is handed down' and become less dependent on government agendas and external agencies. It is also a precursor for community action.

In other chapters, the revaluation of traditional or local knowledge turns on the post-modernist assertion of multiple realities (Guba and Lincoln 1989; Lincoln and Guba 1985), and recognition is given to the notion that health behaviour is often predicated on a logic or explanatory model that may not be compatible with biomedical understandings of illness. Such is the case, for example, in Chapters 8 and 10 by Willms and Vélez and their respective colleagues. The social scientist members of Vélez's research team occupied themselves with the question of why Zenú parents do not take their children to hospital when they become sick with visceral leishmaniasis. Emphasis is placed on understanding indigenous knowledge as it relates to disease aetiology in order to explain health-seeking behaviour. Similarly, Willms and his co-authors use ethnographic research methods to uncover Zimbabwean traditional healers' understandings of HIV/AIDS. In both chapters, local knowledge is respected as rational, although sometimes dysfunctional in terms of giving rise to behaviour that is deemed by outsiders not to be in the best health interests of the study population or community. Chapter 8 presents an elegant attempt to merge indigenous and biomedical understandings of HIV/AIDS to create what the authors refer to as 'culturally compelling' health interventions.

From culturally appropriate to culturally compelling interventions

Discovering how to reach individuals and communities in a meaningful way so that they adopt health-promoting behaviours has been an evolving role of health social science research and intervention. Early on, the focus was on the design and implementation of *culturally appropriate* health interventions that are sensitive to the language, idioms, expressions and nuances of meaning of the targeted socio-cultural group (Nichter and Nichter 1996; Were 1992). A broader definition of culturally appropriate, however, emerges in the current work. Culturally appropriate interventions are those that are both tailored to people's perceptual and situational realities, and embrace the importance of social, economic and political factors in determining health behaviour.

In Chapter 8 by Willms, Johnson, Chingono and Wellington the medium by which the message is delivered is as important as the message itself. Thus the structure of workshops with traditional healers followed that of a traditional healing ceremony, and materials and items used in the practice of traditional healing were brought to the workshops to invoke the atmosphere of the *matare* and make the role-play exercises more authentic. The importance of the ancestral spirits in the healing process was also recognized and respected. Each morning of the workshop, the local spiritual leaders led the group in a private prayer asking the spirits to open the way for them to learn. The enactment of other ceremonial practices, including songs, beating of drums and dancing, was actively encouraged. Moreover, 'the traditional healers' unequal relationship with Western medical practitioners, and their political struggle for power in relationship to this group, were carefully considered'.

Similarly, Groth-Marnat and his co-authors in Chapter 5 underscore the important place of traditional ritual practices, such as the kava ceremony, alongside Fijian cultural values and health beliefs in reinforcing the community's decision to stop smoking. Gogna and Ramos in Chapter 9 argue for culturally appropriate interventions that are 'comprehensive' in that they take into account both lay notions of health and illness and 'cultural scenarios of gender and sexuality and interpersonal relations ... that shape and guide men's and women's perceptions, choices, decisions and actions regarding the prevention and treatment of STDs'.

As Willms and his colleagues note in Chapter 8, 'individuals and communities may respond favourably to [such culturally appropriate interventions]: the messages communicated may be appreciated, understood, and, at very least, not offend culturally'. Yet people may not necessarily feel vulnerable or at risk and therefore compelled to change their behaviour. The challenge now confronting health social scientists is to create interventions that are *culturally compelling* – that is, 'interventions that are not only culturally appropriate in language, idiom, and expression, but persuasive in their ability to make persons feel vulnerable, alter the nature of their assumptive world, and compelled, thereby, not only to think, but feel and act differently'. It is the gap between what people *know* and what people *do* that remains to be bridged.

The knowledge–behaviour gap   The knowledge–behaviour gap has frustrated health social scientists, public health practitioners and policy-makers alike. It is the crux of many of the health problems addressed by the case study chapters. Gogna and Ramos, for example, ask in Chapter 9 why, despite the relatively high degree of risk awareness among the men and women they studied, individuals are resistant to adopting recognized STD prevention and treatment strategies. Similarly, Higginbotham, Freeman, Heading and Saul ask in Chapter 3 why certain segments of the study community, although aware of the relationship between lifestyle and risk for heart disease, do not undertake to change their health behaviour.

Much of the current health social science discourse around developing health educational interventions rests on two assumptions: a) change what people know and they will change their behaviour; and b) what people know is often muddled, incomplete, biased or downright incorrect. In fact, local knowledge is sometimes in danger of being prized merely as a source of appropriate metaphor or analogy to be mined in the construction of customized health messages. Faith in these assumptions is buoyed by current good-evidence-makes-for-good-decision-making thinking in clinical practice, health policy and programme management. The next leap forward for health social science is to challenge the idea of 'seamless translation' of evidence into action or knowledge into practice and seek new conceptual frameworks or models that explicitly address the knowledge–behaviour gap.

Chapter 9, in particular, presents exciting theoretical insights into the complex and dynamic relationship between knowledge and practice. It draws attention to the social construction of knowledge (Guba and Lincoln 1989; Lincoln and Guba 1985) and the powerful role of interpersonal relationships in influencing health behaviour. Women's inability or reluctance to negotiate condom use with spouses or permanent partners is an example noted by the authors as well as by other health social science researchers interested in the behavioural dimensions of the HIV/AIDS pandemic (Malow et al. 2000; Soler et al. 2000; Spittal 1995). In addition, the chapter acknowledges that people's actions are guided as often by emotions such as anger, embarrassment, fear, shame, love, lust and joy and values such as courtesy, trust, honesty, respect, fidelity and loyalty as they are by 'rationality'.

A number of health education interventions have exploited the power of emotions, in particular fear, to elicit behaviour change (e.g., 'scare 'em straight' anti-drug campaigns), conferring on them the status of 'motivators'. Yet emotions and values have not been accorded a place in predominantly knowledge-based models of health behaviour.

Gogna and Ramos' conclusion that 'people's attitudes towards STD prevention and treatment are the product of several and sometimes conflicting logics (e.g., not hurting one's partner or potential partner, avoiding emotional conflicts, and protecting oneself and/or one's partner from what are perceived as dangerous situations)' holds an obvious, common sense truth that has been largely ignored by some attitude theories such as the Health Belief Model (Becker and Maiman 1983; Mechanic 1978;

Rosenstock and Becker 1974; Rosenstock and Kirscht 1974). These theories parse health behaviour into readily measured determinants or 'variables' and privilege the logics of cost-benefit and actuarial reasoning. That we think about and approach the world using a variety of sometimes competing and sometimes complementary logics or ways of reasoning – including aesthetic (Good 1994), moral (Murray 1993), value-based (Weber 1993), protection motivation (Plotnikoff and Higginbotham 1998; Rogers and Prentice-Dunn 1999) and lay epidemiologic (Davison et al. 1992) reasoning – is gaining recognition within the health social sciences. Such new understandings of health knowledge are likely to lead to innovative strategies for health intervention.

Knowledge construction In highlighting the need for intervention strategies aimed at producing behavioural change by encouraging reflection on internalized images and norms and values, Chapter 9 takes a step in the direction of addressing, on an intervention level, the knowledge–behaviour gap. The proposed approach, which derives from De Koning and Martin's (1996) assertion that knowledge construction is based on the development of a critical awareness of the circumstances influencing one's life, engages men and women from the study community in a same-sex group process of individual self-reflection. Such a strategy seems more likely to result in sustained health behaviour change than the didactic approach of communicating messages, composed even in the most appropriate of cultural terms.

Chapter 8 offers a second example of a health intervention approach that aims not only to 'customize' but, to borrow Tom Peters' (1992) phraseology, 'customerize' the resulting intervention strategy. The authors describe how the workshops were tailored to the complex social, cultural, economic and political reality of traditional healing practice and how they engaged healers in a participatory learning process. As the health intervention's 'customers', the traditional healers were involved in defining the problem, searching for solutions, and applying them in their everyday practice. In short, knowledge was constructed rather than transferred.

Assessment tools as tools for intervention Participatory learning processes are also the focus of health interventions documented in Chapters 4 and 7. In one of the action-research projects Prawitasari Hadiyono describes in Chapter 4, focus group discussions were used to assess prescribers' and consumers' beliefs and practices regarding injection drug use in districts of Indonesia. A second series of discussion groups, referred to as Interactional Group Discussions (IGDs), brought patients and prescribers together to learn from each other as well as from members of the project team who acted as facilitators.

In this study, qualitative research techniques, in particular group interviewing techniques, functioned both as an assessment or investigative tool and as an intervention tool. This allowed for a research-action design, entailing an iterative process of data collection–analysis–intervention–data collection–analysis. The intervention component in such a study design also functions as a member-checking exercise (Lincoln and Guba 1985; Patton 1990), in which the results of the preliminary analysis are fed back to the research participants or to a new group of participants recruited for the intervention phase.

Similarly, Sewankambo and his co-authors in Chapter 7 argue that genograms can be put to use as both an assessment (data collection) tool and an intervention tool. This idea embraces, rather than attempts to control for, the fact that all research impacts to some degree on those who are researched. Genograms may therefore also be used as a participatory learning tool, provoking discussion and action in the community.

Diagramming and visual sharing of information are popular and proven methods used in participatory rural appraisal (PRA). As Chambers (1997: 134–5) observes:

> With a questionnaire survey, information is transferred from the words of the person interviewed to the paper of the questionnaire schedule. The learning is one-off. The information becomes personal and private, unverified and processed and appropriated by the interviewer. In contrast with visual sharing of a map, model, diagram, or units (stones, seeds, small fruits, etc.) or lengths (sticks, etc.) used for counting, estimating, ranking, scoring, and comparing, it is open to all who are present to participate. Different people add details, crosscheck and correct each other. The learning is progressive. The information is visible, semi-permanent, and public to the group, and can be checked, verified, amended, added to, and owned, by the participants.

While the drawing of genograms may not be suitable for use in a group process, by virtue of the information they contain about sexual liaisons, they present a potentially powerful tool for participatory learning, and, at the sametime, complement traditional verbal qualitative data collection techniques.

Collective action in communities The value of collective action by community members in the research endeavour is a theme that cross-cuts all the chapters. Cornwall's (1996) categories of community participation – co-option and compliance, consultation, cooperation, co-learning and collective action – are represented alone or in various combinations. A co-option and compliance model is demonstrated in Chapters 2, 10 and 11, where community involvement is limited to dutiful participation as research subjects. Community members answer the researchers' questions and, in the case of the Zenú indians, provide blood samples and comply with other diagnostic procedures. As Briceño-León points out, the housing programme intervention described in his chapter 'was implemented on a community-wide basis and took advantage of intra-community tensions, cooperation and power struggles, but was not centred on collective action'.

Many of the chapters – specifically Chapters 4, 6, 7, 8 and 9 – involve a combination of co-option and co-learning. A co-option model dominates the research component. Using ethnographic or survey methods, the researchers seek to uncover indigenous or lay understandings of illness or health-seeking behaviour. The community is not invited to present 'the people's perspective' on the health problem and hence help to define the problem, as it is in a consultation model of participation. Instead, the researchers formulate the health problem and community members respond to queries about their health knowledge and behaviour. In contrast, the intervention component of these studies embraces co-learning. The community members acquire new knowledge and skills through dialogue and interaction both with one another and with the action-research team. They become partners in formulating and implementing solutions to the health problem defined and described by the researchers. The action-research project described by Willms and his colleagues in Chapter 8 also incorporates a dimension of cooperation models of participation, in that a traditional healer was involved in the planning and execution of the research as a member of the project team.

Although initially conceptualized along the lines of a 'community activation' intervention programme, involving collective action, the Coalfields Healthy Heartbeat (CHHB) programme described by Higginbotham and colleagues in Chapter 3 eventually adopted a hybrid cooperation/consultation model of community participation. Rather than evolve as a self-sustaining community action group responsible for initiating heart health activities, as hoped at the project's outset, the CHHB involved consultation with the community to define and endorse a list of issues and strategies. Subsequently, the steering committee initiated awareness-raising activities that were then carried out by the community worker.

Last but not least, Chapter 5 describes collective action on the part of the community and the medical team to address high rates of smoking within the village. The decision to quit smoking was initiated by the community itself and formalized with a public pledge and a ceremony in which a taboo was placed on smoking. The medical team acted as a catalyst for change and assisted in evaluating and documenting the initiative's success.

The chapters offer several lessons about community participation. Chapter 5, for example, reveals the sometimes serendipitous nature of successful intervention to change health behaviour. A community's or individual's readiness for change may, in part, rest on a kind of historical confluence of situational, social and cognitive factors. So too might the individual and social energy available for change rest on such a confluence. The chapter also gives insight into what can be achieved given commitment, a long-term relationship within a community, patience, and not a lot of money. These striven-for ideals of community action (minimum financial resources excepted) are seldom enjoyed by most health social scientists interested in affecting change in communities.

The need to 'know' the community – its cultural, economic, political and social context – is fundamental to working with communities to effect change. Prolonged engagement with the community; involvement of community members in a project's design, development, implementation and evaluation; and prior ethnographic research are strategies described in the various chapters for getting to know the community. Otherwise, as Higginbotham et al. point out, 'the conflicting and sometimes naive expectations of the researchers and the community can derail community action'.

That communities are not homogeneous entities is another lesson offered by the chapters. Various individuals and groups in a community may have different interests, goals and attitudes. Communities are often defined in geographical terms – as groups of people living in the same place – in part, perhaps, because of the ease with which such definitions allow members to be enumerated. It is easier to count households than it is to count people by, for example, sexual orientation or even occupation. Enthusiasm to understand 'local' knowledge better can sometimes overlook important differences between persons residing in the same place.

Finally, Chapter 11 points out that not all 'community-based' programmes need entail collective action. 'When the end product is one for collective consumption, such as a school, strategies for collective action should be set up,' Briceño-León argues, 'but with goods for family consumption such as housing they are not necessary.' This is not say, however, that community participation in the design, development and implementation of health interventions is not desirable, but merely that the community does not necessarily need to work together as such to achieve programme goals.

One of the challenges facing health social scientists is to foster greater collaboration with communities on the research side of action-research endeavours. As many of the case studies illustrate, a co-option model still dominates. Another challenge is to understand communities sufficiently –

often requiring in-depth knowledge of historical, socio-economic and political processes – so that the potential 'triggers' for precipitating social action towards local change can be identified. It is clear that there are means of releasing 'latent' social energy within a community group. Often, as health social scientist researchers, we are mere witnesses to 'indigenous mobilizations of change', such as the taboo put in place against smoking in the Fijian village and the spontaneous formation of the citizens' group opposing the aluminium smelter (as detrimental to residents' health) in the Australian Coalfields.

Transdisciplinary approaches to health problems Most of the chapters describe research carried out by a team of investigators from different disciplines, although they are focused on the contribution of the social science members. The case studies therefore do not offer much of a perspective on the interface between the social science members and other members of the teams. Yet it would appear that the nature of the collaboration between team members was either multidisciplinary or interdisciplinary. Chapter 10 provides an example of a multidisciplinary team approach in which the various team members worked consecutively or concurrently from a specific disciplinary perspective to address a common problem (Rosenfield 1992). The social scientist members of the team worked independently to address the human behavioural aspects of disease acquisition, while other members focused on the eco-epidemiology of visceral leishmaniasis. A second aspect of their role within the team was to act as 'cultural ambassadors', paving the way for the rest of the research team in the study community. This is a likely and powerful role for social science team members, who are often chosen not only for their skills in establishing rapport and building trust with community members, but also for their facility in speaking the local language. It is also a tremendous and often stressful responsibility to bear on behalf of the team.

An interdisciplinary team approach, in which 'different disciplines address inter-connected aspects of a specifically defined health problem, mainly bringing to bear their own theories and conceptual frameworks' (Albrecht et al. 1998: 59), is evidenced in the chapter by Sewankambo and his colleagues. When family medicine perspectives and tools were combined with those from anthropology, a means of visually representing the impact of HIV/AIDS on people and communities and initiating a participatory learning process was imagined. Similarly, the Australian Coalfields heart disease researchers applied interdisciplinary collaboration in the early stages of the intervention. The specific focus was a 'silent epidemic' of coronary heart disease, which was analysed jointly by epidemiologists, biostatisticians, health promoters and social anthropologists using concepts of risk factors, risk reduction and risk imposition. It was only after assembling and juxta-posing multiple explanations of the Coalfields epidemic and its context that recurring patterns were identified and made understandable using complexity theory.

Chapter 4 is unique in the insight it offers into the evolving relationship among the members of the team over several projects. The team's on-going working relationship, Prawitasari Hadiyono notes, resulted in a collaboration that adopted a 'multidisciplinary approach in the beginning, an interdis-ciplinary approach in the process, and ... a transdisciplinary approach in the long run'. Within this transdisciplinary approach team members arrived at a shared conceptual framework that drew together disciplinary-specific theories, concepts and approaches to address the problem (Rosenfield 1992). Within this conceptual framework, disciplinary boundaries are, as Albrecht et al. (1998: 60) describe, 'blurred' or 'transcended' and 'a new trans-disciplinary way of explaining a problem is created'.

Fundamental to transdisciplinary thinking is the realization that problems exist beyond the boundaries of disciplines, in the realm of 'transdisciplinary space' (Albrecht 1990: 5). Such thinking rests on ideas encountered earlier in this chapter – chiefly, that context counts and that reality is socially constructed and continually in flux. Transdisciplinary thinking embraces the post-modernist assumption of multiple realities and is sensitive to the local and diverse social, cultural, economic and political contexts in which health problems manifest themselves and to the ways in which people understand and explain their world. It eschews mechanistic models of how the world is structured and seeks dynamic, process-oriented explanations of health problems. In short, transdisciplinary thinking takes the view that health realities are, in Chambers' (1997) words, 'local, com-plex, diverse, dynamic, and unpredictable'.

The promotion of transdisciplinary thinking in health research, however, faces significant challenges. Albrecht et al. (2001) list four key barriers to developing transdisciplinary explanations of health problems. The first is *reductionism*: the attempt to reduce a complex whole into its constituent parts. For example, clinical pharmacologists may reduce antibiotic resist-ance to the problem of an inadequate course of a specific class of drugs or even further to the cellular-level properties of harmful bacteria. Not considered are the social, economic and cultural contexts influencing how patients and their families use self-medication during episodes of illness. A second barrier Albrecht et al. note is *macro-reductionism*. This arises when the problem explanation is given exclusively in terms of its broadest possible context, as when investigators inappropriately use macro–level data (e.g., occupation profile of inner-city residents) to interpret small-scale phenomena (e.g., a gay couple's decision about practising safe sex). A third barrier identified is *discipline rigidity* and super-specialization. Disciplines gain their positions of authority within social institutions by controlling knowledge and developing professional bodies that accredit the practice and use of such knowledge. Cooperation and sharing knowledge across boundaries is sacrificed to fulfil the desire for greater and greater specialization. The *complex and unpredictable* nature of health outcomes is the fourth barrier to transdisciplinary teamwork. Because of such complexity, health problems can emerge that could not be predicted, or readily understood, using causal models suggested by reductionism (micro or macro) (Albrecht et al. 2001, ch. 4). The attempt by Velez and his colleagues to control visceral leishmaniasis (VL) in Colombia (Chapter 10) demonstrates how problem complexity can create difficulties in team formation. Dimensions of complexity require expertise across many fields: diagnosis, case finding, prevalence and epidemiology of VL; identification of the insect vector and its habits; ecology of the parasite's animal hosts; cultural constructions of VL symptoms within indigenous knowledge about natural and supernatural disease causation; rural health service delivery, and so forth.

A further challenge to widespread application of transdisciplinary thinking in health is the difficulty researchers face in creating 'common conceptual frameworks' through which collaborating disciplines can combine perspectives towards fuller explanations of health problems. Such frameworks need to be usable by any discipline to achieve novel insights about the problem and devise innovative strategies for their resolution (Albrecht et al. 1998: 59). Rosenfield (1992) recorded success in building such a framework in a Brazilian malaria project when the transdisciplinary team formed a common understanding of the problem as one of jungle migrants coping with a new disease. Kunitz (1994: 297–325) invoked the twin concepts of domination and adaptation (cultural and biological) to explain patterns of disease-led devastation of indigenous people in the face of colonization. Elsewhere, Treloar et al. (1996) discovered that 'mindlessness' was a unifying concept for their team of HIV physicians, infection control educators and health psychologists in understanding and reducing hospital staff exposure to infectious diseases through needlestick injuries. However, Albrecht and Higginbotham (2001) have recently encouraged health social scientists to adopt complexity theory, an emerging 'metatheory' across the sciences, as a powerful common conceptual framework for transdisciplinary health research. In the final section of this chapter, this argument is elaborated along with a range of other future directions for health social science.

Future Directions for Health Social Science Research

Complexity theory   In this final part of the chapter, we identify several new research directions and methods that are likely to occupy the attention of health social scientists in the years ahead. The first of these is complexity theory. As discussed throughout this text, applied health social science bridges the gap between fields of study emphasizing contextual processes and those focused on the health status of people and populations. One of the great advantages of complexity theory, introduced in Chapter 3, is that it can fully occupy 'transdisciplinary space': enabling biomedical insights to be combined with those from ethnographic fieldwork, and epidemiological data to be combined with critical analyses from political-economy. Complexity theory is a radical approach to health social science that analyses health problems as emergent properties of open, dynamic systems. Complexity principles explain the evolution of interlinkages between apparently separate systems, including those of the physical world, biology, ecology, psychology, society and politics. Importantly, complexity concepts suggest how dynamic patterns emerging from the interactions among these systems affect people's health. For example, the concept of a 'dissipative structure' explains health problems in terms of energy flows between systems. In Higginbotham and colleagues' case study of CHD in the Coalfields (Chapter 3), the larrikin sub-culture was defined as a dissipative structure that achieved coherence and self-organization at the group level by exporting waste (disorder) into the surrounding society and promoting a lifestyle that, in the long run, is harmful to the group's biological system.

In terms of themes raised by the case studies, complexity theory can help show 'situational realities' and demonstrate how such realities produce various forms of local or indigenous knowledge. For example, complexity analysis of the high rates of heart disease in the Coalfields showed how this 'silent epidemic' emerged through the historical interplay between industrial conditions, beliefs about the importance of 'risk factors' and 'risk imposition', gender relations, health promotion campaigns, and community mobilization in response to perceived health threats in this locality.

In essence, the value of complexity theory for the development of health social science is its ability to incorporate multi-level analyses, ranging from the biological, to the institutional and ecological. It is thus an ideal way to investigate the 'knowledge–behaviour gap' from all relevant perspectives. By incorporating a range of 'logics or ways of reasoning', including lay beliefs and rationales, complexity theory enables health social science researchers to understand dialectical relationships emerging from interactions between themselves and the study community and informing subsequent research directions. Because of this, we anticipate transdisciplinary scientists will turn to complexity principles in order to build common conceptual frameworks that allow them to synthesize their methods and findings about a shared health problem.

Translational research

Bridging the knowledge–action gap   A critical impediment to improving human health is the gap between knowledge and practice or evidence and action, which can diminish the successful implementation of health research. Dennis Willms and colleagues have recently sought to bridge this gap through the promotion of 'translational research'. Translational research entails translating scientific and experiential evidence into culturally compelling health interventions at the local level. Willms (2000) characterizes this style of research as a 'participatory, transdisciplinary and transcontextual process of structured reflection and action'. It is problem-driven and reconciles a variety of evidence sets through dialogue and negotiation of multiple stakeholders, including patients, practitioners, policy-makers and programme planners. Evidence sets may be derived from academic research (such as epidemiology or anthropology), from lived experience ('lay epidemiology'), or from the practice of indigenous or traditional medicine. They encompass a variety of logics or ways of knowing (for example, cerebral or expert, intuitive, physical, experiential and contextual, emotive and spiritual). In brief, translational research, akin to transdisciplinary thinking, aims to merge evidence derived from diverse forms of knowledge into a unifying framework for understanding and seeking solutions to a health problem.

Narratives as the currency of translational research   Translational thinking requires creatively imagining what it would be like to think differently, to empathize across sectors and disciplines, and to devise new ways of talking about health problems. It involves eliciting and building on experiential stories or narratives from a full cross-section of stakeholders as a first step in designing, disseminating, sustaining and evaluating action to improve health. Willms (2000) notes that experiential evidence is the currency traded through illness narrative and narratives of what does or does not work in health or health programmes. For example, through the narratives of sufferers of chronic illnesses, translational researchers gain insight about the processes by which those sufferers absorb and synthesize into their own health understandings evidence drawn from such diverse sources as biomedical diagnoses and treatments, different forms of alternative or folk medicine, embodied experience, advice from friends and relatives, health advice from the media or the internet, and their own health understandings.

Knowledge translation At the core of translational research is the distinction between 'knowledge transfer' and 'knowledge translation'. Currently, most efforts to promote the transition from evidence to action involve knowledge transfer. This approach is based on the premise that researchers, policy-makers and research subjects share fundamental assumptions (epistemological frameworks) about the nature of evidence, which allow a 'seamless transition' from evidence transfer to action. However, this linear perspective 'ignores the complex dynamics of evidence transmutation, cross-sectorial and cross-cultural reasoning and participatory processes' (Willms 2000).

Rather than assuming a linear relationship between access to information and changed perceptions and practices, translational research explores how participants synthesize and transform (that is, transmutate) a variety of evidences. Translational research holds that the translation or construction of knowledge involves participatory learning in which stakeholders take ownership of the problem and its solution. Knowledge translation occurs through 'conceptual events': organized gatherings for shared learning through which individuals, health professionals and other stakeholders engaged in a particular health problem reflect on the full range of its determinants, and create new understandings and appropriate languages to frame their concerns about the problem. Conceptual events ideally lead to the negotiation of equitable and collaborative problem solutions. These participatory opportunities give equal time and voice to dissonant perspectives and involve iterative processes of dialogue, reflection and action. Willms observes (2000) that conceptual events 'have the potential to form the basis for design, dissemination, and evaluation of health interventions that are equitable, sustainable, culturally-appropriate, and psychologically-compelling'. The workshops with traditional healers, described by Willms and colleagues in Chapter 8, are conceptual events in that they successfully reconciled two different ways of understanding the risks associated with HIV/AIDS – that derive from the traditional healers' (*n'gangas*) experience in diagnosing and treating patients with AIDS on the one hand, and biomedical explanations of HIV/AIDS transmission on the other. The events allowed a safe negotiation of contrasting experiential and scientific world views whereby the healer's concept of 'dirt' (a substance that is responsible for a category of illnesses associated with sexual activity) was able to merge with the medical notion of the HIV virus.

Transconceptual evidence and transcontextual experiences As an alternative to the linear assumptions of evidence transfer outlined above, translational research strives to understand 'transconceptual evidence' and 'transcontextual experiences' that occur at the intersection of diverse knowledge systems and ways of knowing. An example of transconceptual evidence is the connection between experiential evidence from the practice of homoeopathic medicine and research findings by chemists from the California Institute of Technology (Cal Tech). Cal Tech scientists found that water, and other fluids occurring in nature, have a 'memory' of their previous composition, a memory beyond the known laws of chemistry. Homoeopathy, involving medicine taken in greatly diluted form, is claimed to work even when no trace of the active ingredient can be detected in the solution consumed by the patient (Juan 2000: 6). In effect, the notion of 'fluid memory' is a common conceptual framework linking the diverse epistemologies of biotechnologists and homoeopathic practitioners and patients. Similarly, transcontextual experiences occur when the same understanding or practice emerge simultaneously in multiple and culturally diverse contexts. An Australian example is the belief held by both traditional Aborigines and National Park scientists that burning selected forest areas preserves the ecological health of the environment.

Cybermedicine and health social science   A fascinating new research direction opening up for health social scientists is 'cybermedicine'. Cybermedicine is a sub-area of 'medical informatics', a 'field that concerns itself with the cognitive, information processing, and communication tasks of medical practice, education, and research' (Greenes and Shortcliffe 1990). Cybermedicine applies internet and other global networking technologies to preventive medicine and public health. Unlike 'telemedicine', which is concerned with the exchange of mainly confidential, clinical information between health providers and patients, cybermedicine involves an open exchange of information about general health issues. It also provides health care consumers with access to personal health information such as laboratory results, assessments of their risk factors for particular diseases, and information about drugs which they have been prescribed (Eysenbach et al. 1999). Information may be shared between individual health care consumers, health professionals, and various other stakeholders interested in equity of access to health-related information. Eysenbach, a leading cybermedicine theorist, identifies one of its greatest potentials as the ability to act as the medium by which health care consumers 'attain a healthy balance between self-reliance and seeking professional help' (2000: 1714).

Cybermedicine can also assist health professionals to improve health outcomes by providing targeted information to those at risk of, or suffering from, a particular disease. For example, an individual's health record can be linked to relevant general health information to provide tailored messages aimed at assisting that person to self-manage a particular condition, or to change their health-related behaviour and attitudes. Computer-based decision aids can also assist clinicians to incorporate a patient's preferences or stated values with clinical data on their condition, and juxtapose a patient's medical history with geographical, ecological or structural constraints that affect health outcomes (Barry 1999). This is a valuable step towards a more participatory process of diagnosing and treatment, although the dialogue between patient and doctor remains fairly limited.

Initially, most computer-based decision support systems were developed to assist clinicians to provide advice about diagnosing and managing disease. More recently, these systems have been adapted to the specific needs of health care consumers. For example, 'HouseCall' generates a diagnosis based on an individual user's symptoms and medical history and offers easy-to-read information on a variety of topics. This information permits people to decide if they should see a doctor or alerts patients to potentially harmful drug interactions or other health risks (Eysenbach 2000: 1714).

Health social science research directions within cybermedicine Dugdale (2000) has recently observed that cybermedicine opens up a number of research avenues for health social scientists, such as further developing electronic decision-support tools for consumer health education and patient self-support; evaluating the impact of electronic exchanges of information on traditional face-to-face doctor–patient relationships; investigating inequalities in access to medical knowledge derived from the new technology and the way in which inequality affects social, economic and power relationships; and research into the way in which information gained from electronic means is absorbed and translated into terms that are meaningful within the everyday health understandings of health care consumers.

Cybermedicine and complexity theory Health informatics research currently emphasizes the evaluation of the quality of information being disseminated to health providers and consumers (Dugdale 2000). However, we should not assume a linear relationship between access to information and changed perceptions and practices. How health consumers synthesize and transform new knowledge gained from cybermedicine with their present understandings about health and health care derived from 'lay epidemiology'[1] (Davison 1993) is an important research area for health social scientists. A benefit of complexity theory is that it provides a framework for investigating the non-linear processes by which people and their environments adapt and self-organize in response to the new electronic information, and the ensuing evolution of the new information-age health systems.

Cybermedicine and translational research Another future direction is the potential to combine the principles of 'translational research' with cybermedicine. Translational research aims to bridge the gaps between the 'epistemological frameworks' of various stakeholders interested in combating diseases, such as the fight against AIDS in developing countries (see Chapter 8). Cybermedicine offers the opportunity to apply translational research activities to bring together the meaning systems of epidemiological and biomedical researchers with those of lay populations who have access to electronic health information. To date, commendable efforts have been made to provide 'plain language' versions of complex medical information. For example, the *United States Pharmacopoeia Dispensing Information* (Vol. 2) provides electronic advice specifically tailored for patients about contra-indications, side-effects and interactions with other medications. Also, the *Annals of Internal Medicine* provides two versions of its latest research papers, one for scientists and the other for 'public access'. This latter version gives an opportunity to translate complex concepts and definitions, such as those relating to 'risk', into forms that are understandable in everyday language. This process could reduce misunderstandings that occur when research findings reach the public through the distorting lens of the popular media. Nevertheless, this language translation is a one-way process, involving no dialogue between the health information provider and consumer.

Willms (2000) envisions translational research as providing the concepts and methods health social scientists can use to explore how various 'evidence sets', including the 'experiential evidence' of sufferers with a particular health problem, can be reconciled though dialogue and negotiation via electronic information-sharing. The aim is to produce a negotiated framework for solving particular health problems or managing specific conditions. For example, during a health promotion campaign aimed at diabetes awareness, an open teleconference or teleforum could be advertised and arranged for all interested stakeholders to discuss their 'evidence', whether 'medical, epidemiological, contextual or experiential' (Willms 2000). The aim is to provide the context for sharing knowledge in a way that promotes the emergence of a new framework for understanding and managing that disease.

Cybermethods and health social science The new information and communication technologies described above promise to transform health social science methods themselves. The internet has given rise to numerous 'communities' of individuals who share a common interest, concern or vocation. As a result, it holds out new possibilities in terms of how social scientists relate and gain access to those communities.

Some researchers are currently experimenting with synchronous or 'real-time' computer-mediated communication (CMC), using audio- and videoconferencing software and hardware to conduct on-line interviews and focus groups. Other forms of real-time interaction between researchers and study participants are less costly and, for the moment, less technologically restricted. These include moderated on-line focus groups using Internet Relay Chat or the adaptation of standard World Wide Web browsing software to conduct on-line interviews (Chen and Hinton 1999).

Most ventures into cybermethodology to date, however, have employed e-mail as the lowest common denominator for CMC and have combined on-line data collection techniques with traditional, face-to-face methods. For example, Peter Murray (1997) has explored the use of virtual focus groups (VFGs) via closed e-mail-based discussions. Fox and Roberts (1999) joined the *gp-uk* electronic discussion group as 'participant-observers' to examine the impact of CMC on the social and professional relationships of British general medical practitioners who subscribe to the list. In a recent study, Risdon et al. (2000) employed an e-mail listserv to explore the considerable challenges gay and lesbian physicians face in their training as they become professionalized. In addition to face-to-face interviews and focus groups, data were also collected via the internet by posting messages on relevant study themes to a gay, lesbian and bisexual listserv for three months. Content analysis of archived discussion group or bulletin board messages can inform research proposal development and the creation of guides for on- or off-line interviews or focus groups. Researcher-created websites have been used to elicit illness narratives from site visitors (Fleitas 1998).

Cybermethods allow researchers to collect data that they might not be able to collect as successfully through other methods. Risdon et al. (2000) were able to explore sensitive issues in a context that permitted study participants a high degree of 'safety' by virtue of the medium's anonymity. In addition, the researchers were able to 'identify' and recruit study participants from an otherwise difficult to enumerate population.

By enabling researchers to interact with geographically dispersed groups of individuals, on-line methods bring a new scope to participation in qualitative research – indeed, making such research translocal (Ito 1996). On-line methods also promise to improve the efficiency and reduce the costs of traditional research. All data are in the form of electronic text, obviating the need for transcription and facilitating data management using the latest software for such purpose.

On the down side, the nonverbal cues available to the researcher in face-to-face interactions are missing. The communities that emerge around the new information and communication technologies are composed of the technologically empowered (Ebo 1998), who tend to be more affluent and more educated than the general population. The possibilities afforded by cybermethods are greatly circumscribed in many developing world countries, where even the most basic access to CMC is greatly limited. Data for 1998 indicate, for example, that one-quarter of the world's countries have a teledensity of one telephone for every 100 people (compare to Sweden, for example, with a teledensity of 70/100) (UNDP 1999). There are great disparities between North and South in terms of access to CMC. An estimated 88 per cent of internet users live in industrialized countries (UNDP 1999).

Internet-inspired methodologies also present new twists on old ethical considerations around informed consent, participant confidentiality and data security. With the transient nature of much electronic discussion group participation, how does the cybermethodologist negotiate informed consent? Is archived information that is publicly *accessible* open to public *dissemination* (Fox and Roberts 1999)? How do researchers ensure that information imparted by study participants is inaccessible by unauthorized persons?

The use of cybermethods also reignites discussion within the field around the 'presence' and 'absence' of the researcher in the research setting (Rutter and Smith 1999). A greater temptation may exist for researchers, intentionally or unintentionally, to engage in covert research or, at minimum, to 'lurk' more than participate in the research setting. Researchers also need to be cautious of the anonymity of CMC and the potential for identity-bending on the part of study participants. Despite these pitfalls, the internet represents an exciting new tool for health social scientists.

On a final note, health social scientists themselves represent a widely geographically dispersed community of professional interest. The internet can facilitate intra- and inter-regional collaboration and discussion around best practices in research and teaching. In this respect, other disciplines – in particular, the health disciplines – are leading the way (Goh et al. 1998).

Applying Health Social Science: Current Context and Challenges

Health social scientists in developing and developed countries face a variety of contextual challenges as they seek to adopt 'best practice' in applying social science methods and theory to existing and emerging problems of human health. The context of the new information technology, for example, challenges us to adopt the benefits of this technology while recognizing the 'digital divide' that potentially increases old inequities in power and knowledge generation, or creates new ones.

A second contextual challenge arises from uneven advances in research knowledge for developing and evaluating health interventions across different disease areas. While a considerable depth of knowledge has accrued in recent years in the prevention and control of HIV/AIDS, heart disease, and some vector-borne diseases, relatively little is understood about improving interventions for halting the spread of oncocercosis or dengue, or reducing domestic violence. Our challenge here is to create effective means for transferring or extrapolating knowledge from rapidly developing (usually well-funded) research areas to other, poorly understood or newly emerging problems. For example, Margaret Chesney and colleagues' (2000) extensive investigations into strategies for enhancing adherence to complex regimens of AIDS medication are being mined to identify techniques to help diabetics follow equally complicated care programmes (M. Chesney, personal communication). Similarly, what has been learned in the past two decades about controlling vector-borne diseases in Latin America (Barta and Briceno-Leon 2000) should be examined for strategies to reduce the impact of chronic lifestyle diseases on the rise in Latin America (Briceño-León et al. 2000) Southeast Asia (Higginbotham et al. 1998), and elsewhere (Murray and Lopez 1997).

A third and alarming contextual reality is increasing disparities in health status between and within countries. The last century has witnessed great strides forward in improving health in developing and developed countries. For example, overall life expectancy of the population worldwide has improved. In 1997, 84 countries enjoyed a life expectancy at birth of more than 70 years, up from 55 countries in 1990. Within this group of countries, the number of developing countries has risen from 22 to 49 (UNDP 1999). Yet disparities in health status persist or are increasing. Ironically, many improvements in health, gained through recent advances in knowledge and technology, have been won at the health expense of vast numbers of individuals, primarily in developing countries (Farmer 1998). Within countries, those living in absolute poverty, compared with those who are not poor, are estimated to have a five times higher probability of death between birth and five years, and a 2.5 times higher probability of death between the ages of 15 and 59 years (WHO 1999). Over one-third of the world population, primarily in the developing world, still lack access to essential drugs; one-quarter are without access to safe water (WHO 1998). In 1995, an estimated ten million children in the developing world died from avoidable conditions such as malnutrition, diarrhoea, acute respiratory infection, malaria, measles or complications of childbirth (WHO 1998). Almost all DALYS (Disability Adjusted Life Years) from these conditions occur in developing countries. Only 1 per cent is registered in high-income countries (WHO 1999). Most notably, the health gap between countries is widening in countries ravaged by war and prolonged internal conflicts as well as those African countries suffering most severely from the AIDS epidemic. The incidence of socio-behavioural illnesses is climbing dramatically in Eastern and Central European countries where infrastructures have collapsed (Neufeld 2001).

The problem is much deeper and more complex than a simple equation between economic prosperity and good health. As Nobel laureate Amartya Sen (1999) observes, African-Americans have higher incomes than people in some developing countries such as Sri Lanka, yet their health status is worse. Social and health conditions prevent people from using their personal, family and community capabilities to realize opportunities for wellbeing. The health and development research context is thus one that is cognizant of inequalities in distribution of wealth, social organization, culture and values, as well as investments in health research.

Tremendous inequities exist not only in health status, but also in regard to funding for health research. Less than 10 per cent of the approximately US$70.5 billion per year (1998 estimate[2]) of public and private sector funds spent on health research is directed at those diseases and conditions that account for nearly 90 per cent of the global burden of illness (Global Forum for Health Research 1999). A substantial proportion (43.3 per cent or US$30.5 billion) of global expenditure on health research is made by the pharmaceutical industry (including biotechnology companies) (Michaud et al. 2000). The amount spent on behavioural and social science research globally, and in the developing world specifically, is difficult to ascertain. A recent study conducted for the Council on Health Research for Development (COHRED) in three Southeast Asian countries (Malaysia, the Philippines and Thailand), however, suggests that only a small fragment is spent on social science research. Of the total investments in health research and development (R&D) in 1997 and 1998, a large proportion (94 per cent, 80 per cent, and 62 per cent for Malaysia, the Philippines and Thailand respectively) was spent on medical sciences research. The Philippines and Thailand spent only 14 per cent and 29 per cent respectively of their total investments on health R&D on health economics and social sciences research combined (De Francisco and Alano 2000).

The International Conference on Health Research for Development held in Bangkok, Thailand in October 2000 challenged health researchers 'to generate new knowledge which addresses the problems of the world's disadvantaged, and increases the use of high quality, relevant evidence in decision-making' (Bangkok Declaration 2000). Within the realities of this health and development context, health social scientists need to continue to advocate strongly for the essential role that social and behavioural science research plays in understanding health problems and designing, implementing and evaluating interventions that are locally relevant, culturally compelling and inclusive of all stakeholders. They must also work together with other health researchers at global, national and local levels to forge consensus on directions, priorities and values for pursuing health research. What is more, health social scientists need to inject themselves and their research into the policy process in order to translate research into action for improving the health of specific populations. Of course, for this to occur effectively, capacity development of indigenous health social scientists must be strongly promoted nationally, as shown, for example, by the Philippine Health Social Science Association. Donors and external 'experts' enhance this process by acknowledging and encouraging leadership roles for local health social scientists.

Finally, Amartya Sen (1999) provides a critical challenge to health social scientists when he states that: 'Development ... has to be primarily concerned with enhancing the lives we lead and the freedom that we enjoy. And, among the most important freedoms that we can have is the freedom from avoidable ill-health and from escapable mortality' (p. 620). Sen argues that health constitutes a precondition for national development; disease decreases the ability of people to attain the freedom 'to live long and to live well' (p. 619).

The best-practice case studies presented in this book demonstrate how micro-scale and grassroots or indigenous experiences can be generalized and applied to health development, not only for the developing world, but also for disadvantaged and marginalized groups within industrialized countries. The cases show how it is possible with restricted resources, but using traditional knowledge, collective action and transdisciplinary approaches, to achieve health gains. In conclusion, and in response to Sen's perspective, we argue that health social science is the science of development. It strives to improve human health, enabling people to reach their full potential and control their own destiny.

Notes

1. One of the social mechanisms associated with the process of understanding risk and its operation is 'lay epidemiology'. Illness and deaths that occur in personal networks are discussed and noticed as part of normal social life. The 'data' accumulated on illness and its apparent causes and distributions are then used to support or challenge aetiological hypotheses (Davison et al. 1992).

2. Public and private sectors worldwide are conservatively estimated to have spent about US$70.5 billion in 1998 (or about 2.6 per cent of total global health expenditures) on health research (Michaud et al. 2000)

References

Albrecht, G. (1990) 'Philosophical thoughts on a transdisciplinary model of human health', in N. Higginbotham and G. Albrecht (eds), *Transdisciplinary Thinking in Health Social Science Research: Definition, Rationale and Procedures*, Newcastle: Centre for Clinical Epidemiology and Biostatistics, University of Newcastle.

Albrecht, G., S. Freeman and N. Higginbotham (1998) 'Complexity and human health: The case for a transdisciplinary paradigm', *Culture, Medicine, and Psychiatry* 22: 55–92.

Albrecht, G. and N. Higginbotham (2001) 'Complexity and human health: across the health hierarchies', in N. Higginbotham, G. Albrecht and L. Connor, *Health Social Science and Complexity in Transdisciplinary Perspective*, Sydney: Oxford University Press.

Albrecht, G., N. Higginbotham and S. Freeman (2001) 'Transdisciplinary thinking in health social science', in N. Higginbotham, G. Albrecht and L. Connor (eds), *Health Social Science in Transdisciplinary Perspective*, Melbourne: Oxford University Press.

Bangkok Declaration (2000) International Conference on Health Research for Development, 10–13 October 2000, Bangkok, Thailand (available at http://www. conference 2000.ch/pdf/declaration/pdf)

Barry, M. J. (1999) 'Involving patients in medical decisions: how can physicians do better?', *JAMA* 282: 2356–7.

Barta, R. B., R. Briceño-León (2000) *Domenças Endêmicas: Abordagens Sociais, Culturais e Comportamentais*, Brazil: Oswaldo Cruz Foundation.

Becker, M. and L. Maiman (1983) 'Models of health-related behavior', in D. Mechanic (ed.), *Handbook of Health, Health Care and the Health Professions*, New York: The Free Press.

Briceño-León, R., C. Minayo and C. E. A. Coimbra Jr. (2000) *Salud y Equidad: Una Mirada desde las Ciencias Sociales*, Brazil: Oswaldo Cruz Foundation.

Chambers, R. (1997) *Whose Reality Counts? Putting the First Last*, London: Intermediate Technology Publications.

Chen, P. and S. M. Hinton (1999) 'Realtime interviewing using the world wide web', *Sociological Research Online* 4(3).

Chesney, M. A. (personal communication) 'Diabetes in America: the current epidemic', paper presented at Workshop on Maintenance of Behaviour Change and Adherence to Treatment Regimens, 15 November 2000, Sixth International Congress of Behavioural Medicine, Brisbane, Australia.

Chesney, M. A., M. Morin and L. Sherr (2000) 'Adherence to HIV combination therapy', *Social Science & Medicine* 50(11): 1599–605.

Cornwall, A. (1996) 'Towards participatory practice: participatory rural appraisal (PRA) and the participatory process', in K. de Koning and M. Martin (eds), *Participatory Research in Health. Issues and Experiences*, London: Zed Books.

Davison, C. (1993) 'Health and culture in the South Wales valleys', in S. Parsons (ed.), *Changing Primary Health Care: A Collection of Papers from the Teamcare Valleys Conference*, pp. 44–51.

Davison, C., S. Frankel and G. Smith (1992) 'The limits of lifestyle: re-assessing "fatalisms" in the popular culture of illness prevention', *Social Science & Medicine* 34(6): 675–85.

De Francisco, A. and B. Alano (2000) 'Resource flows in developing countries: selected county studies and practical examples', paper presented at the International Conference on Health Research for Development, Bangkok, Thailand, October 2000.

De Koning, K. and M. Martin (1996) 'Participatory research in health: setting the context', in K. de Koning and M. Martin (eds), *Participatory Research in Health: Issues and Experiences*, London: Zed Books.

Dugdale, A. (2000) Unpublished grant proposal.

Ebo, B. (1998) *Cyberghetto or Cybertopia?: Race, Class, and Gender on the Internet*. Westport, CT: Praeger Publishers/Greenwood Publishing.

Eysenbach, G. (2000) 'Recent advances: consumer health infomatics', *British Medical Journal* 320 (24 June): 1713–16.

Eysenbach, G., E. R. Sa and T. L. Diepgen (1999) 'Shopping around the internet today and tomorrow: towards the millennium of cybermedicine', *British Medical Journal* 319: 1294, <http://www.bmj.com/cgi/content/full/319/7220/1294>

Farmer, P. (1998) *Infections and Inequalities: The Modern Plagues*, Berkeley: University of California Press.

Fleitas, J. (1998) 'Spinning tales from the world wide web: qualitative research in an electronic environment', *Qualitative Health Research* 8(2): 283–92.

Fox, N. and C. Roberts (1999) 'GPs in cyberspace: the sociology of a "virtual community"', *Sociological Review* 47(4): 643–71.

Global Forum for Health Research (1999) *The 10/90 Report on Health Research 1999*, Geneva.

Goh, L. G., S. T. Liaw and K. C. Lun (1998) 'Collaboration over the Internet – the Melbourne–Singapore way', *Medinfo* 9(2): 764–7.

Good, B. L. (1994) *Medicine, Rationality, and Experience. An Anthroplogical Perspective*, Cambridge: Cambridge University Press.

Greenes, R. A. and E. H. Shortcliffe (1990) 'Medical informatics: an emerging academic discipline and institutional priority', *JAMA* 263: 1114–20.

Guba, E. G. and Y. S. Lincoln (1989) *Fourth Generation Evaluation*, London: Sage.

Higginbotham, N., G. Albrecht and L. Connor (2001) *Health Social Science: A Transdisciplinary and Complexity Perspective*, Melbourne: Oxford University Press.

Higginbotham, N., A. Saul and and P. Heller (1998) 'Lifestyle diseases in Southeast Asia: potential lessons from health social science research on community understandings of risk and vulnerability', *Indonesian Journal of Clinical Epidemiology and Biostatistics* 5(2): 1–5.

Ito, M. (1996) 'Theory, method and design in anthropologies of the internet', *Social Science Computer Review* 14(1): 24–6.

Juan, S. (2000) 'Crystal clear memory', *Sun Herald*, 30 July, p. 6.

Kunitz, S. J. (1996) 'Disease and the destruction of indigenous population', in T. Ingold (ed.), *Companion Encyclopedia of Anthropology: Humanity, Culture and Social Life*, London: Routledge, pp. 297–325.

Lincoln, Y. S. and E. G. Guba (1985) *Naturalistic Inquiry*, Newbury Park, CA: Sage.

Malow, R. M., T. Cassagnol, R. McMahon, T. E. Jennings and V. G. Roatta (2000) 'Relationship of psychosocial factors to HIV risk among Haitian women', *AIDS Education and Prevention* 12(1): 79–92.

Mechanic, D. (1978) *Medical Sociology: A Comprehensive Text*, New York, NY: The Free Press.

Michaud, C., A. de Francisco and A. Young (2000) 'Global resource flows into health research in 1998 and trends during the nineties: first results', paper presented at the International Conference on Health Research for Development, Bangkok, Thailand, October 2000.

Murray, C. J. L. and A. D. Lopez (1997) 'Global mortality, disability and the contribution of risk factors', *The Lancet* 349(17) May: 1436–42.

Murray, P. (1997) 'Using virtual focus groups in qualitative research', *Qualitative Health Research* 7(4): 542–9.

Murray, T. (1993) 'Moral reasoning in social context. Part of a Symposium on New Medical Technologies', *Journal of Social Issues* 49: 185–200.

Neufeld, V. (2001) 'Health research for development: realities and challenges', in V. Neufeld and N. Johnson (eds), *Forging Links for Health Research. Perspectives from the Council on Health Research for Development*, Ottawa: IDRC Books.

Nichter, M. and M. Nichter (1996) 'Education by appropriate analogy', in M. Nichter and M. Nichter (eds), *Anthropology and International Health*, Amsterdam: Gordon and Breach, pp. 287–305.

Patton, M. Q. (1990) *Qualitative Evaluation and Research Methods*, 2nd edn, Newbury Park, CA: Sage.

Peters, T. (1992) *Liberation Management: Necessary Disorganization for the Nanosecond Nineties*, New York: Alfred Knopf; London: Macmillan.

Plotnikoff, R. and N. Higginbotham (1998) 'Protection motivation theory and the prediction of exercise and low-fat diet behaviours among Australian cardiac patients', *Psychology and Health* 13: 411–29.

Risdon, C., D. Cook and D. Willms (2000) 'Gay and lesbian physicians in training: a qualitative study', *Canadian Medical Association Journal* 162(3): 331–4.

Rogers, R. W., S. Prentice-Dunn (1999) 'Protection motivation theory', in D. Gochman (ed.), *Handbook of Health Behavior Research: Vol 1. Determinants of Health Behavior: Personal and Social*, New York: Plenum.

Rosenfield, P. (1992) 'The potential of transdisciplinary research for sustaining and extending linkages between the health and social sciences', *Social Science & Medicine* 35(11): 1342–57.

Rosenstock, I. M. and M. H. Becker (1974) 'Social learning theory and the health belief model', *Health Education Quarterly* 15: 175–83.

Rosenstock, I. M. and J. P. Kirscht (1974) 'The health belief model and personal health behavior', *Health Education Monographs*, 2: 470–3.

Rutter, J. and G. Smith (1999) <*professional-stranger@ethno.org*>: 'Presence and absence in virtual ethnography', American Sociological Association paper.

Sen, A. (1999) 'Health in Development', *Bulletin of the World Health Organization* 77(8): 619–23.

Soler, H., D. Quadagno, D. F. Sly, K. S. Riehman, I. W. Eberstein and D. F. Harrison (2000) 'Relationship dynamics, ethnicity and condom use among low-income women', *Family Planning Perspectives* 32(2): 82–8, 101.

Spittal, P. (1995) 'Deadly choices: women's risk for HIV infection in a truck stop-trading centre in rural south-western Uganda', PhD dissertation, Hamilton, Ontario: Department of Anthropology, McMaster University.

Treloar, C. J., N. Higginbotham, J. A. Malcolm, D. C. Sutherland and S. Berenger (1996) 'An academic detailing education program aimed at decreasing exposure to HIV infection among health care workers', *Journal of Health Psychology* 1(40): 455–68.

UNDP (United Nations Development Programme) (1999) *Human Development Report 1999*, New York, NY: Oxford University Press.

Weber, J. (1993) 'Exploring the relationship between personal values and moral reasoning', *Human Relations*. 46: 435–63.

Were, M. K. (1992) 'The community as focus of development in Africa', in *Proceedings of the First International Conference of the Social Science and Medicine Africa Network*, Nairobi: 6–16.

WHO (World Health Organization) (1998) *World Health Report 1998: Life in the 21st Century. A Vision for All*, Geneva: WHO.

— (1999) *World Health Report 1999: Making a Difference*, Geneva: WHO.

Willms, D. (2000) 'Cultivating partnerships to design equitable health interventions: a translational research agenda', unpublished draft.

About the Contributors

Sonia del Pilar Agudelo is a bacteriologist, PhD and a graduate of the Universidad de Antioquia-Colombia and Universidad de Barcelona-España. She is currently a research associate at the Programa de Estudio y Control de Enfermedades Tropicales (PECET) and professor in the Department of Microbiology and Parasitology at the Universidad de Antioquia in Medellín, Colombia.

Roberto Briceño-León is professor of sociology in the Faculty of Social Sciences and of Parasitology, Faculty of Medicine and Health Sciences, at the Central University of Venezuela. He is also the director of the Laboratorio de Ciencias Sociales in Caracas, Venezuela and secretary of the International Forum for Social Sciences in Health. He has over fifteen years' experience carrying out research on vector-borne diseases and applying social and behavioural science approaches to improving health conditions in Latin America. On behalf of the WHO/TDR programme he created and, for six years, coordinated the Latin American Small Grants programme for support of social and economic research and intervention in the region. He is a member of the WHO advisory committees on trypanosomiasis and health promotion. Roberto Briceño-Leon has authored a book on housing, social behaviour and transmissible disease (*La casa enferma* [*The Ill House*], 1990) and edited several books: *Las enfermedades tropicales en la sociedad contemporánea* (1993), *Las Ciencias Sociales y la Salud en América Latina: Un Balance* (1999), *Salud y Equidad: Una Mirada desde las Ciencias Sociales* (2000), and *Domenças Endêmicas: Abordagens Sociais, Culturais e Comportamentais* (2000). He has published widely on the issues of community participation, health education, social behaviour changes and health sector reform.

Alfred Chingono is a lecturer in the Department of Psychiatry at the University of Zimbabwe School of Medicine. He is a founding member of the National AIDS Coordinating Programme, where he held the portfolio of national counselling coordinator with responsibilities for training health workers and other paraprofessionals in HIV/AIDS counselling. He has been a training consultant within the African region for the Global Programme on AIDS (WHO) and an HIV/AIDS programme development and evaluation consultant to the Ministry of Health. Since 1993, when he joined the International Clinical Epidemiology Network, he has been interested in strengthening the social science perspective in health-related research, interventions and programme evaluation.

Peter Crossman is a research assistant with the Africa Research Centre, Department of Anthropology at the University of Leuven, Belgium. He has previously held posts with international development project and policy organizations in Africa and Europe. Following research on endogenization of curricula at African universities, he is currently involved in research on the Shembe church in KwaZulu-Natal (South Africa) with respect to 'The Civilizing Missionaries, the Ancestor Cult and Post-Missionary Christianity as a Cornerstone of an African Alternative Modernity'.

René Devisch, PhD, is professor of anthropology in the Department of Anthropology at the University of Leuven, where he is the coordinator of the Africa Research Centre and director of the master's degree in 'Cultures and Development Studies'. Alongside his involvement in anthropological collaboration with family physicians in Antwerp and Brussels from 1980 to 1986, his own research in the field of medical anthropology has extended to Tunis and S. Ethiopia. Supervisory visits of doctoral research have taken him to Cairo, W. Congo-Kinshasa, N. Ghana, S. Nigeria, N.W. Tanzania, N.W. Namibia, S.W. Kenya, and Druze communities in N. Israel.

Layi Erinosho is professor of sociology and formerly foundation dean of social sciences at Ogun State University, Ago-Iwoye, Nigeria. He holds the following degrees: BSc (Ibadan) 1968; MA, PhD (Toronto) 1971 and 1975 respectively. Professor Erinosho is a former president of the Social Science Council of Nigeria and has previously served as a consultant to WHO, UNDP and USAID. Currently, he is the executive secretary of the Social Science Academy of Nigeria. He is the author of eight scholarly publications in the field of psychiatric and health sociology.

Sonia Freeman is a social science researcher at the Centre for Clinical Epidemiology and Biostatistics and the Clinical Unit in Ethics and Health Law at the University of Newcastle. She has worked on a number of transdisciplinary research projects, including the Oceanpoint Community Health Study and the Coalfields Heart Disease study. Sonia co-authored several chapters in Higginbotham, Albrecht and Connor (2001) *Health Social Science: A Transdisciplinary and Complexity Perspective*, as well as the landmark article, 'Complexity and human health: the case for a transdisciplinary paradigm' (1998), in *Culture Medicine and Psychiatry*.

Jorge Gallego is a biologist who graduated from the Universidad de Antioquia-Colombia. He is currently a research associate at the Programa de Estudio y Control de Enfermedades Tropicales (PECET) and professor in the School of Medical Veterinary, Medellín, Colombia.

Mónica Gogna is a sociologist and senior researcher at CEDES (Center for Study of State and Society) and member of CONICET (National Council for Scientific and Technical Research). She has carried out research in the fields of women's studies and reproductive health. Since 1993, Mónica has co-coordinated the Regional Program on Social Research, Training and Technical Assistance in Reproductive Health and Sexuality, based at CEDES. She is a professor and convenor of regional and local workshops on qualitative methodology applied to the field of reproductive health and sexuality.

Gary Groth-Marnat received his PhD from the California School of Professional Psychology in 1977. He is currently senior lecturer in the clinical health PhD/M Psych programme at Curtin University in Perth, Australia. Areas of interest include psychological assessment, clinical neuropsychology, hypnosis and cross-cultural health psychology. He has published three editions of the *Handbook of Psychological Assessment, Clinical Neuropsychology in Clinical Practice*, and over one hundred journal articles and chapters in books.

Gaynor Heading, PhD, lectured in qualitative and quantitative research methods at the University of Newcastle, Australia, prior to becoming involved in medical general practice policy, research and evaluation. She is currently the New South Wales (NSW) state coordinator for rural divisions of general practice, working for the NSW Rural Doctors Network, the rural workforce agency. Gaynor has a background in the sociology of health and cultural studies. Her current research interests include community sustainability and health partnerships, general practice, the body and food.

Nick Higginbotham is associate professor and head of the Discipline of Community Medicine and Clinical Epidemiology, Centre for Clinical Epidemiology and Biostatistics, School of Population Health Sciences, Faculty of Medicine and Health Sciences, University of Newcastle, Australia. He has over twenty years of experience applying social and behavioural science approaches to improving health and mental health in Asia and the Pacific. In 1986, he founded the health social science graduate programme at the University of Newcastle, while at the same time initiating the social science component of the Rockefeller Foundation's International Clinical Epidemiology Network (INCLEN). Subsequently, Nick helped form a global organization for strengthening social science contributions to improving human health, the International Forum for Social Science and Health, and its regional division, the Asia Pacific Network. Nick has authored three textbooks covering the fields of culture and mental health, psychotherapy and behaviour change, and transdisciplinary health social science. He has published numerous research reports addressing such health issues as heart disease prevention, asthma locus of control, pharmaceutical use, complexity theory, hospital infection control, dietary and exercise change, and prevention of disability in the elderly.

Susana Jaramillo is an anthropologist who graduated from the Universidad de Antioquia. She is a specialist in environmental administration. She works with Interconexión Eléctrica SA – ISA, Medellín, Colombia.

Nancy A. Johnson is a health social scientist with over twelve years of ethnographic/qualitative field research experience. Based in Hamilton, Ontario, Canada, she consults on qualitative research design, data collection and analysis as well as the development of health and social science-related manuscripts. Previous research projects span a broad range of areas including the design of culturally appropriate AIDS educational interventions in Zimbabwe; community-based maternal/child health programmes for Latin American immigrants in Hamilton, Canada; patient-centred breast cancer treatment decision-making; and decisions to withdraw life support in intensive care settings. Ms Johnson is a co-editor of *Forging Links for Health Research: Perspectives from the Council on Health Research for Development* (IDRC Books, 2001) and *Nurtured by Knowledge: Learning to Do Participatory Action-Research* (Apex Press, 1997).

Lapika Dimomfu, PhD, is professor of medical anthropology at the University of Kinshasa and director of CERDAS (the UNESCO-funded Center for the Co-ordination of Social Science Research and Documentation for Africa South of the Sahara). As a consultant to the World Health Organization he has assessed multiple projects aimed at the promotion and improvement of plural health care in West and Central Africa.

Jaak Le Roy, MD, is a psychiatrist, psychoanalyst and group analyst at the Regional Community Mental Health Centre (RIAGG) in Maastricht, the Netherlands. He is a consultant to organizations as well as a teacher and supervisor in several post-doctoral training programmes on psychotherapy, group dynamics, counselling and organizational development. As a researcher, he is involved in joint research projects in the field of public health and community-based mental health care in developing countries. He was president of the European Association of Transcultural Group Analysis (1990–98) and of the Belgian School of Psychoanalysis (1994–

97). He has prepared a doctoral dissertation in medicine on the research in Kinshasa reported on in the case study.

Simon Leslie is the Australian president of the Surfers' Medical Association and is in private practice in Woolongong, Australia. He has a strong love for the Fijians and their traditional community style of living, seeing it as a model for all society on a planet that desperately needs solutions to the problems of energy consumption, consumerism, violence and environmental degradation.

Maerewai Molileuu is a member of the Nabila Village Health Committee.

Gloria Palma, MD, PhD, is currently head of the National Program for Science and Technology in Health in COLCIENCIAS, a government agency that promotes research in Colombia. She is also a research associate at the Corporación CIDEIM (Centro Internacional de Entrenamiento e Investigaciones Médicas) and professor in the Department of Microbiology at the Universidad del Valle in Cali, Colombia. Additionally, she is president (2000–03) of the Colombian Society of Parasitology and Tropical Medicine.

Johana E. Prawitasari Hadiyono graduated in clinical psychology from the University of Arizona, Tucson, Arizona, USA in 1985. She is a faculty member and chair, Department of Clinical Psychology, Faculty of Psychology, Gadjah Mada University (GMU), Yogyakarta, Indonesia. She is also an active member at the GMU Centre for Clinical Pharmacology and Drug Policy Studies and Department of Public Health, Faculty of Medicine. Her main interests include studies in non-verbal communication of emotions; rational use of drugs; clinical psychology professional training; modifying psychological assessment and intervention to health issues; and community development. She has been an active member of INRUD (International Network for Rational Use of Drugs) since 1990 and APNET (Asia Pacific Network of the International Forum for Social Sciences in Health) since 1994, a regular member of the ICP (International Council of Psychologists) since 1991 and and international affiliate member of the APA (American Psychological Association) since 1986.

Silvina Ramos is a sociologist whose fields of specialization include social research and training in medical sociology, qualitative methods and reproductive health. Currently, she is a senior researcher in the Health, Economy and Society Department at CEDES (Center for Study of State and Society) and academic coordinator of the master's degree in social sciences and health (FLACSO/CEDES). Since 1993, Silvina has co-coordinated the Regional Program on Social Research, Training and Technical Assistance in Reproductive Health and Sexuality (Argentina, Chile, Colombia and Peru).

Pilar Ramos-Jimenez is associate professor of the Behavioral Sciences Department at De La Salle University in Manila. She is a university fellow and holder of the Concepcion Garcia's Chair for Women's Studies. She is also De La Salle University's coordinator of the Health Social Science Graduate Program, a research fellow of its Social Development Research Center, and president of the Pi Gamma Mu Honor Society in Social Science Philippines Beta Chapter. Dr Ramos-Jimenez was the secretary of the Asia-Pacific Network of the International Forum for Social Sciences in Health from 1997 to 1999 and president of the Philippine Health Social Science Association in 1996. She was the convenor of the 1994 Asia-Pacific Social Science and Medicine Conference and the 1996 Conference on Gender, Sexuality and Reproductive Health and the Teaching of Health Social Science, held in the Philippines. Her recent publications are on reproductive health, gender and sexuality, urban health and immunization.

Mark Renneker is assistant clinical professor in the Department of Family and Community Medicine at the University of California, San Francisco and a founding member of the Surfers' Medical Association.

Ann Saul is a doctoral candidate in the Department of Sociology and Anthropology at the University of Newcastle, Australia. Her PhD research is a qualitative study of midwifery and childbirth options in New South Wales. Ann studied at Girton College Cambridge, where she completed her social science degree in 1974. She has been involved in research and consumer activism in maternity issues in Britain and Australia for many years. Since 1992 she has taught social science to health science students and professionals at the University of Newcastle.

Nelson K. Sewankambo is dean of Uganda's Makerere University Medical School and a Trustee of the International Clinical Epidemiology Network (INCLEN). He teaches and conducts research in internal medicine, clinical epidemiology and medical anthropology. An HIV/AIDS clinical specialist, Nelson is engaged in several HIV intervention studies in southwestern Uganda, as well as in behavioural research.

Patricia A. Spittal is a research scientist with the British Columbia Centre for Excellence in HIV/AIDS and assistant clinical professor in the Department of Epidemiology at the University of British Columbia, Canada. She has conducted extensive doctoral and post-doctoral field studies in aboriginal communities in Canada and in high-conflict situations in Uganda. Her areas of expertise include women and development, gender and health, and the cultural impact of conflict on women and HIV infection in rural traditional communities.

Bruno Travi is a DVM who graduated from the Universidad de Buenos Aires, Argentina. He was named Investigador de Carrera (National Council for Research and Technology, Argentina) and did his post-graduate training in Parasitology at the Tulane University Primate Research Center, Louisiana, USA. He then joined the Centro Internacional de Entrenamiento e Investigaciones Médicas (CIDEIM) based in Cali, Colombia, where he currently acts as deputy director. He also coordinates the Unit of Biology and Ecology of Transmission, in which a variety of nationally and internationally supported projects on animal models and field studies of vector-transmitted diseases are carried out.

Hector Wing-hong Tsang is assistant professor in the Department of Rehabilitation Sciences, Hong Kong Polytechnic University. Before joining the university, he worked for ten years as an occupational therapist in several clinical settings, providing clinical services and supervising students on placement. In recent years, his interest has been in the field of psychiatric rehabilitation, especially implementing vocational and social skills training programmes for people with severe mental illness. Dr Tsang's teaching and research are concerned with psycho-social rehabilitation. He teaches courses in research methodology, psycho-social rehabilitation and behavioural management for people with developmental disabilities. At present, Dr Tsang is involved in research projects related to predicting rehabilitation outcome in Hong Kong psychiatric hospitals and cross-cultural issues of skills training in collaboration with UCLA and the University of Chicago Center for Psychiatric Rehabilitation in the USA.

Iván D. Vélez holds an MD, an MSc and a PhD from the Universidad de Antioquia-Colombia, Universidad de Montpellier-Francia, and the Universidad de Granada-España, respectively. He is currently the director of the Programa de Estudio y Control de Enfermedades Tropicales (PECET) and professor in the Medical School at the Universidad de Antioquia in Medellín, Colombia.

Sunia Vuniyayawa is a member of the Nabila Village Health Committee.

Maureen Wellington is assistant director of health services for the City of Harare Health Department and an epidemiologist and coordinator of activities in primary health clinics. She is also an honorary lecturer in the Department of Community Medicine at the University of Zimbabwe and a faculty member of the Clinical Epidemiology Unit at the University of Zimbabwe Medical School. She holds an MSc degree from McMaster University in Hamilton, Canada, an MBChB from the University of Zimbabwe and a BSc from the University of Rhodesia, Zimbabwe. Her research interests include communicable diseases, especially STI/HIV/

AIDS, and diarrhoeal diseases. She is an active member of the Zimbabwean National Drugs and Therapeutic Committee, Mental Health Board for Harare and Parirenyatwa Psychiatric Units and the International Clinical Epidemiology Network.

Dennis G. Willms is associate professor in the Department of Anthropology, Faculty of Social Sciences, McMaster University (Hamilton, Ontario, Canada) and a recipient of an OHTN Career Scientist Award (Ontario HIV Treatment Network). He received his PhD from the University of British Columbia in 1984. With a focus on the behavioural risks associated with HIV transmission, most of his ethnographic and collaborative research is being conducted in Canada, Kenya, Uganda and Zimbabwe. At present, he is examining the processes associated with translating varieties of evidence into culturally compelling interventions. He is also the founding director of the Salama SHIELD Foundation, a registered charity in support of health and development initiatives in sub-Saharan Africa. Dennis lives in Kitchener, Ontario with his wife Rita and their two sons Luke and Mark.

Index

Selected Titles on Health from Zed Books

Zed Books publishes widely on international health policy issues. Here is a selection of our more recent titles.

Inger Agger, *The Blue Room: Trauma and Testimony among Refugee Women*

Inger Agger and Soren Buus Jensen, *Trauma and Health under State Terrorism*

Sara Bennett, Barbara McPake and Anne Mills (eds), *Private Health Providers in Developing Countries: Serving the Public Interest?*

British Medical Association, *Medicine Betrayed: The Participation of Doctors in Human Rights Abuses*

Zafrullah Chowdhury, *The Politics of Essential Drugs: The Makings of a Successful Health Strategy*

Korrie de Koning and Marion Martin (eds), *Participatory Research in Health: Issues and Experiences*

Anita Hardon and Elizabeth Hayes (eds), *Reproductive Rights in Practice: A Feminist Report on the Quality of Care*

Anita Hardon, Ann Mutua, Sandra Kabir and Elly Engelkes, *Monitoring Family Planning and Reproductive Rights: A Manual for Empowerment*

Najmi Kanji et al., *Drugs Policy in Developing Countries*

Meri Koivusalo and Eeva Ollila, *Making a Healthy World: Agencies, Actors and Policies in International Health*

Axel Kroeger et al., *The Use of Epidemiology in Local Health Planning: A Training Manual*

Anika Rahman and Nahid Toubia (eds), *Female Genital Mutilation: A Guide to Laws and Policies Worldwide*

Judith Richter, *Vaccination Against Pregnancy: Miracle or Menace?*

Ilkka Taipale (Physicians for Social Responsibility) (ed.), *War or Health? A Reader*

Meredeth Turshen, *The Politics of Public Health*

Gill Walt, *Health Policy: An Introduction to Process and Power*

For full details of this list and Zed's other subject and general catalogues, please write to: The Marketing Department, Zed Books, 7 Cynthia Street, London N1 9JF, UK or email: sales@zedbooks.demon.co.uk

Visit our website at: http://www.zedbooks.demon.co.uk